Cordula Rabe

Camino de Santiago

The Way of St. James from the Pyrenees to Santiago de Compostela and beyond to Finisterre and Muxía

All stages – with alternatives and height profiles

seit 1920

ROTHER • MUNICH

ROTHER Walking Guides

ALGARVE
ROTHER WALKING GUIDE

Andalucía South
ROTHER WALKING GUIDE

Azores
ROTHER WALKING GUIDE

Camino de Santiago
ROTHER WALKING GUIDE

Corsica
ROTHER WALKING GUIDE

Costa Blanca
ROTHER WALKING GUIDE

Costa Brava
ROTHER WALKING GUIDE

CÔTE D'AZUR
ROTHER WALKING GUIDE

CRETE
ROTHER WALKING GUIDE

Cyprus · South & North
ROTHER WALKING GUIDE

La Gomera
ROTHER WALKING GUIDE

GTA Grande Traversata delle Alpi
ROTHER WALKING GUIDE

Iceland
ROTHER WALKING GUIDE

La Palma
ROTHER WALKING GUIDE

Madeira
ROTHER WALKING GUIDE

Mallorca
ROTHER WALKING GUIDE

Mont Blanc
ROTHER WALKING GUIDE

Norway · South
ROTHER WALKING GUIDE

Provence
ROTHER WALKING GUIDE

PYRENEES 1
ROTHER WALKING GUIDE

PYRENEES 2
ROTHER WALKING GUIDE

PYRENEES 3
ROTHER WALKING GUIDE

Sardinia
ROTHER WALKING GUIDE

Tenerife
ROTHER WALKING GUIDE

Norway · South
ROTHER WALKING GUIDE

TUSCANY NORTH
ROTHER WALKING GUIDE

Valais · East
ROTHER WALKING GUIDE

VALAIS
ROTHER WALKING GUIDE

VANOISE
ROTHER WALKING GUIDE

Vienna · Vienna Woods
ROTHER WALKING GUIDE

ZUGSPITZE
ROTHER WALKING GUIDE

Foreword

The Way of St. James enjoys universal popularity. With just under 190,000 pilgrims registered in Santiago de Compostela, the Holy Year of 2010 – last one until 2021 – was a record year. In 2012 there were 192,488 pilgrims recorded, by far the majority of them following the classic route of the Camino Francès.

The sheer numbers speak for the popularity of the pilgrim path, but they can also have an adverse effect – although they shouldn't. It's true that the Camino is altogether busier than a few years ago, but the statistics are somewhat inflated by the pilgrims who walk the route during the high season around Easter and in summer, as well as all those who just complete the last 100km on foot, or the last 200km by bike. Those pilgrims who start the walk outside of these busy times, i.e. in the spring or autumn, or even in winter, and also avoid the classic starts and destinations of each stage, are still able to experience that very special atmosphere which constitutes the Way of St James. Perhaps it is the mixture of fascinating landscapes and wonderful historic and cultural locations which make it unlike any other long distance walk. But, above all, the Camino is defined by that particular spirit amongst the pilgrims who come from all over the world, each one having quite different reasons for making the pilgrimage and yet pursuing a common aim: to experience the Way of St James with all its highs and lows, its daily surprises and fascinating encounters.

This walking guide provides a lot of practical information including the description of the route, its local services and the most important sights along the way. It is also intended to be a travel companion to the areas of Spain you are walking through. Since not every St. James pilgrim is coincidentally an authority on Spain, notes on festivals, traditions and gastronomic specialities have been included to whet the appetite and to help a better understanding of the culture. Of course, the information does not claim to be complete, since that would go beyond the framework of this guide.

The Way of St. James is not a totally fixed phenomenon. Quite often there are changes in the route due to the building of new roads or the improvement of the line of the route and pilgrim hostels are always opening and closing. During the Holy year of 2010 there were many new hostels – and the number is still rising – but time will tell how many of these will continue to exist. Please inform the publishers if you notice any changes. At this point I would really like to thank those readers who have already submitted useful tips and suggestions.

It only remains for me to wish you a thoroughly enjoyable walk – ¡Buen Camino!

Altea, Spain, spring 2013   Cordula Rabe

Contents

Tourist tips

The use of this guide

The most important information is introduced in a kind of fact-file before the description of each stage. Then follows the description of the route. The sights and cultural peculiarities are interspersed in the text and are highlighted in yellow. The small map showing the line of the route contains important symbols for local services and waypoints (see p. 8 GPS) as well as the height profiles of each stage. Tips for alternative overnight accommodation (symbol for hotels/B&Bs) can be found in the height profile, but only in places without hostels (for places with hostels see the subheadings for 'local services'). From the diagrams with the height profiles you can pick out the gradients as well as the time details and distances between important places along the way. To help with your own planning, one section from the previous stage and one section from the following stage have been included in the profile. The walking maps also give the distances between hostels (small blue box with yellow writing).

Pilgrim hostels

A note is made in the description as to whether the hostels are run by the town, the church, societies or private institutions. Hostels with a Christian background often offer voluntary worship and prayers. The classification of one ◉ to three ◉◉◉ St. James shells is to help you grade the hostels. The allocation of shells is dependant on the equipment (e.g. kitchen, washing machine), the ratio between price and performance or the condition of the sanitation facilities. A plus point is usually the presence of a kitchen (equipped with the essentials) as it helps pilgrims keep the costs down. The assessment relates in no way to the attention given by the *hospitaleros* as these change quite frequently in most of the hostels. The prices and other details shown were correct in spring 2012, and may therefore change. Unless mentioned otherwise, the hostels are to be found directly en route. When there are several hostels in one place, they are named, if at all possible, in the order in which you come across them. In many places, B&Bs, hotels, *hostales* (basic and cheap hotels) or even private rooms offer beds at favourable prices for pilgrims. It's best to wait until you reach a place before getting up-to-date information. (See also the section on pilgrim hostels on p. 18.)

Somewhat austere and modern: the municipal pilgrim hostel in Muxía.

Explanations of symbols and abbreviations

Symbol	Meaning	Symbol	Meaning
♠	pilgrim hostel	✚	health centre, hospital
⌂	hotel/bed & breakfast	⊠	post office
◭	campsite	i	tourist information
✗	restaurant	🚌	bus connection
▣	Bar (kind of snackbar)	🚃	train connection
🛒	supermarket/shop	✈	airport
@	internet access (often also with WiFi)	▙	mass
⛏	well (blue point on map)	‡	church, chapel, monastery
€	bank (cash dispenser)	)(	pass, col
A	chemist	⌐ ⌐	turn-off to the left/right
		☀	viewpoint

Abbreviations

Alb.	*albergue* = pilgrim hostel
CH	pilgrim hostels run by church institutions
MH	municipal pilgrim hostels
PH	private (also tourist) hostels, often also for non-pilgrims
RH	pilgrim hostels often run by volunteers with religios background; often with opportunity for common worship/mass
SH	pilgrim hostels run by (St. James) societies
XH	hostels of the Galician government (*Xunta de Galicia*)
YH	youth hostel (*albergue juvenil*)

B = number of beds in hostel; M = number of mattresses in hostel
SR = single room; DR = double room

C/	*Calle* (road/street)
s/n	no house number (*sin número*)

Roads: BU-703 = country roads; N-121 = national highway; A-15= motorway

Local services

For every village or town along the way there are symbols to show the available local services that might be of interest to pilgrims (see above for the explanation of symbols). There is often only one bus service a day in small places and as for the shop, it is frequently only a small corner shop. The addresses for medical care refer to the Centros de Salud, medical centres of the national health service (usually: Mon.–Fri. 8.00–15.00, in larger places there's sometimes a 24 hour service), but in towns, mostly hospitals. A doctor comes once or twice a week to small villages. Ask locally for information regarding private doctors.

Gastronomy and fiestas

Special mention is made in the guidebook of any regional or local gastronomic specialities and fiestas. Each town or village has at least one large celebration every year that is held in honour of its patron saint and there are also local and national events. They offer a fantastic opportunity to become acquainted with Spanish traditions and way of life. The Spanish processions in Holy Week (Semana Santa in Spanish) are especially moving and begin on Palm Sunday (Domingo de Ramos) depending on the region.

Walking times

The times given in this guide are based on a rate of 3.5–4.5km an hour (depending on the terrain); the individual times in the walk descriptions always refer back to the preceding place. The times can vary enormously depending on your personal fitness, the state of the paths and weather conditions.

Bad weather or even snow can increase the walking times considerably as here, near Roncesvalles, in the middle of April.

GPS data

The GPS data for this guide is available in a free download from the Rother website (www.rother.de) for which you will need the following password: wfCasgb0388qvt (username: gast).

All the GPS routes were recorded on the ground by the author. The tracks and the waypoints have been checked by the author and the publishers to the best of their knowledge. Nevertheless mistakes and variations cannot be ruled out. It is also possible that some details might have changed in the meantime. GPS data is, without doubt, an excellent planning and navigational tool, but careful preparation, good route-finding ability as well as experience in judging the conditions at the time are essential. One should never totally rely on the GPS device and its data for following a route.

Walking the Way of St. James

One of the greatest characteristics of the Way of St. James is that of uniting people of quite different generations, nationalities and motives. Besides a spiritual and religious motivation there can be a great many other reasons for walking the path which is over 1,000 years old: thanks to excellent local services with well marked paths and a dense network of overnight accommodation on offer, the Way of St. James is the ideal long distance walk for anyone who would like to experience for the first time the adventure of a long journey on foot. Its architectural and cultural monuments make it a unique passage through the history of Spain. Connoisseurs of Spain as well as newcomers can gain insights into another unfamiliar area of Spain that has absolutely nothing in common with the clichés of flamenco, bull fighting, paella and beaches. The path offers you some interesting encounters with nature whether in the mountain region of the Pyrenees, along the endless barren wastes of the Castillian plateau, or in green Galicia right up to the bleak Atlantic coast. Not to be forgotten are the meetings and exchanges with fellow hikers who all have the same goal, but quite different reasons for achieving it.

Best time to go

The majority of pilgrim hostels open from Easter to the middle/end of October, somewhat fewer are also at your disposal in winter. Most pilgrims set off in May and September/October. The temperatures at this time of year are pleasant and the days sufficiently long. However, the hostels are often crowded at these

The virtually shadeless and deserted meseta is almost always a challenge, whether in the heat, cold, wind or rain (Stage 14, just before Boadilla del Camino).

times. Many Spanish people traditionally use the week from Palm Sunday to Easter Sunday (Semana Santa in Spanish) for walking the Way of St. James. Although the choice of hostels has increased in the meantime, there can often be a shortage at these major walking times so you may have to fall back on alternative types of accommodation. There are less people in March/April and June. Also there's heat is intense in July and August and although this is the traditional holiday period for the Spanish, the crowds along the path keep within reasonable limits, except for in Galicia.

Be prepared for it to rain in Galicia at any time of year. Snow can fall in the mountains well into April. This refers especially to the Somport pass (1st stage of the Camino Aragonés), the crossing of the Pyrenees from Saint-Jean-Pied-de-Port to Roncesvalles (1st stage of the Camino Francés), the Montes de Léon (stages 22 and 23) as well as the O Cebreiro pass (stages 25 and 26).

Way of St. James in winter

From November at the latest into April the weather and smaller choice of hostels make the journey more difficult. However, many connoisseurs appreciate the quiet atmosphere on the path and in the hostels during this period. For a winter walk especially you should plan more time. The cold, rain, snow, fog and the short days force you into making the stages shorter and there might also be issues with diversions on account of inaccessible paths, and with heavier winter clothing. Also, the possibility of getting lost in snow or poor visibility at high altitudes or in remote areas should not be underestimated. You are particularly advised against undertaking the Route Napoleon from Saint-Jean-Pied-de-Port in bad weather and to choose the alternative near to the road instead.

Many hostels are closed from October to Easter or at least between Christmas and the New Year or 6th January. Make sure that you get up-to-date information about what accommodation is available before starting out on each stage.

Montes de Léon, end of April between Foncebadón and El Acebo (Stage 23).

Fitness levels

In principle, the Way of St. James is also achievable for inexperienced walkers. The grades are easy except for a few exceptions and there are hardly any extreme variations in height to be overcome. Nevertheless there are always some pilgrims (also younger people) who have to give up or take longer breaks because they are ill-prepared or have underestimated the special demands of a long distance walk. Especially the unac-

Walking along the Santiago Way is both a natural and a cultural experience (Stage 5, just before Cirauqui).

customed high temperatures in Spain present something of a complication. If you overdo the allotted daily quota and/or drink too little, this can cause heart and circulation problems. Greater loss of fluid and swollen feet due to the heat will also increase the chance of blisters or even inflammation of the tendons.

To train for walking long distances every day, it is recommended that you undertake lengthy walks or hikes of several hours once to twice a week. If you are unsure about your fitness, you should consult your doctor before you go.

Planning your time and choice of route

Roncesvalles or Somport? There are two possible starting points for the Spanish Way of St. James. The 'classic' start is in Roncesvalles, Navarra, or a stage before that with a crossing of the Pyrenees from the French Saint-Jean-Pied-de-Port (772/797km to Santiago). The second alternative starts at the Pyrenean pass of Somport in the Aragón region (886km to Santiago). Both paths meet up in Obanos or Puente la Reina.

The first deciding factor will be your personal time limits. For the roughly 65km long Camino Navarro from Roncesvalles to Obanos you should plan 3 days, or even a day longer if you start in Saint-Jean-Pied-de-Port. For the 165km long Aragonian path (Camino Aragonés) you should reckon on about 6 to 7 days, or a day more for a possible detour to the monastery of San Juan de la Peña.

The Camino Navarro has been, since the Middle Ages, the main route across the Pyrenees since three of the four big Ways of St. James through France meet up in Saint-Jean-Pied-de-Port. These days the Camino Navarro, amongst others, is very popular due to the short distance to Puente la Reina and the good local services – and therefore rather overcrowded over the Easter period and in the main seasons. If you start in France, you should give some thought to the crossing of the pass. The Camino Aragonés is quieter, even at peak

The monastery of Roncesvalles is one of the classic starting points.

times. In the Middle Ages it brought together those pilgrims coming from southern France, Switzerland and Italy, but was never as popular as the Camino Navarro which is characterised to this day by somewhat of a crush in the hostels and relatively long stages. If you prefer quieter walks you will, nevertheless, like the scenically varied alternative since it goes primarily through small, remote villages. It is also offers an alternative for those who would like to avoid the San Fermines in Pamplona from the 6th to 14th July.

From Saint-Jean-Pied-de-Port or Roncesvalles you should plan, if at all possible, at least four full walking weeks. The path can actually be completed in about 25 days, but it's better to have some room to play with. From Somport it takes two to three days longer.

The Way of St. James by bike

It is becoming more and more popular to cycle the Way of St. James. In 2012 about 14 % of the pilgrims who registered in the pilgrim office in Santiago had arrived by bike. One advantage is the shorter time: if you are able to travel 50-60km a day, the section from the Pyrenees to Santiago can be completed in about two weeks. There isn't usually a problem taking your bike on the plane if you notify the airline when you book your flight. Cycling pilgrims are allowed to stay overnight in the pilgrim hostels if they have a pilgrim passport, although those on foot normally take preference. More and more hostels are setting themselves up especially for cyclists offering reservations as well as parking areas for the bike. They display, for example, the red and yellow 'Bike-Line' logo on the front door. Information about accommodation, transport within Spain and cycle hire can be found on www.bicigrino.com, www.bicicamino.com or www.caminodesantiagoenbici.es.

Cycling pilgrims should take care when cycling past those on foot. Your enjoyment of the walk can be really spoilt if, on narrower paths, you are frequently having to jump out of the way of cyclists coming up from the rear. There also tends to be more disturbance in the pilgrim hostels from sport-orientated cyclists or those travelling in groups than from rather tired pilgrims who are on foot and looking for the spiritual experience, or at least some quiet after a long day's hike.

A good alternative for cyclists, and also value for money, is campsite accommodation, either in your own small tent (price per person 4–6 €, per tent 4–6 €) or bungalows which are often available. More and more campsites are offering special rates for pilgrims.

The Way of St. James with children

Children are not often seen on the Way of St. James. One reason might be the considerable exertion (walking every day, heat, rain, cold etc.) for the children as well as the parents who have to carry part of their child's luggage as well as their own. The choice of a bike with child's seat or trailer might be an alternative, but this requires a high degree of fitness in the mountains. With the appropriate preparation and planning of the stages suitable to the stamina of the child, there is basically nothing against making the pilgrimage with children. However, it is sensible to choose your stages with a high density of accommodation so that, if necessary, you can abandon the route at any time and proceed with the project in more moderate temperatures in spring or autumn. Spain is a very child-friendly country and children are always welcome in the hostels, as long as they are considerate to other pilgrims and obey the hostel rules.

Taking your dog on the Way of St. James

Here too you should carefully consider whether your dog is able to cope with the constant stress. Moreover, most places of accommodation do not allow dogs for hygenic reasons (nor restaurants or bars). On the following (Spanish) webpage you will find a list of hostels from Terradillos onwards (stage 17) that accept dogs: www.caminodesanti-agoconperro.com. Campsites are a good alternative (so as not to disturb those pilgrims possibly less enthusiatic about dogs) provided the accommodation is in tents and not bungalows.

Which way do we go?

Costs

For a four week walk along the Spanish Way of St. James you should calculate at least 900 € for accommodation (in pilgrim hostels) and food (not including travel there and back). You will probably need 25-30 € a day, but if you cook for yourself or with other pilgrims, the costs will be lower.

Equipment

Footwear, clothing and rucksack should be carefully chosen and prepared. After all, you will be carrying everything about your person for about 770km or more, i.e. about 190 hours or in other words, eight full days!

Take advice from a specialist shop when buying your footwear and be sure not to set off with hiking boots that have not yet been walked in. If, when wearing them in, you already experience some problems, consider buying new boots or if the pain persists, even making a visit to an orthopaedic doctor. Boots that are too old are to be avoided as well as they will probably no longer withstand the strain. Special trekking socks are a good idea for keeping your feet dry. Clothing should not be new either, to avoid rubbing. Specialist light walking gear that can breathe is ideal. Special hiking trousers with legs that can be zipped off are practical and weight saving. Choosing a rucksack in consultation with a specialist is also worthwhile. Size and shape should be determined by your objective. When packing, consider carefully what you really need and what you don't. A weight between nine and eleven kilos is ideal.

If you have no previous experience of hiking lengthy distances with a rucksack, you should try out the weight of the packed rucksack and its effects on the shoulders, ankles and feet by going on a trial hike.

Opinions are divided as to whether Nordic walking poles are a good idea. If you can't do without them, you should put rubber stoppers on the metal ends out of regard for fellow pilgrims to avoid making a noise on tarmac.

Getting there

Somport: from Spain by rail to Jaca or Canfranc Estación (www.renfe.es, also in English), then bus (www.jacetania.es, link *Portal del ciudadano – Información Autobuses*) to Somport, journey time from Jaca about 40 mins. (2,70 €), several a day from the bus station in Jaca, last bus stop about 22.00. From France by train (www.sncf.com) via Pau to Oloron (35 mins., four times a day), bus to Somport from Oloron (about 60 mins.).

Saint-Jean-Pied-de-Port: from France by train from Bayonne. Journey time about 75 mins. (www.sncf.com), price about 9.20 € (from Biarritz about 3 hrs./from 10.90 €). Only from mid June-mid Sept. is there a direct bus from Pamplona/bus station which departs 14.00, arrives around 16.00, price 15 € www.alsa.es).

Roncesvalles: by bus from Pamplona/bus station Mon.–Fri. 18.00, Sat. 16.00 (1st July-31st Aug.; Mon-Fri. 10.00 and 18.00, Sat. 10.00 and 16.00), NB: no service on Sundays or Bank Holidays! Journey time 1.30 hr., price 6 €, bicycle 6 €, tel: Autobuses Artieda 948 300 287, www.autocaresartieda.com, tickets at

Equipment lists

What you should take with you

- pilgrim passport (see page 21)
- a pilgrim shell
- walking poles if you use them
- needle and thread
- pocket knife
- head torch (better than a normal torch because it keeps the hands free)
- lightweight sleeping bag as there is usually no bed linen in the hostels; in winter a warmer sleeping bag – heating in the hostels is often insufficient
- sleeping mat, in case you have to sleep on the floor
- sunglasses, something to cover your head, high factor suncream
- small travel first aid kit (see below)
- light rain gear (protection for your rucksack too)
- protective shoe cream (optional)
- hand wash
- light, comfortable shoes for sight-seeing
- light slippers for the wash rooms
- water bottle(s), at least 1½ litre capacity
- swimming gear (optional)
- a length of string for a washing line
- ear plugs (for a good night's sleep in the dormitories)
- cloth bag, e.g. for dirty washing (no noisy crinkly plastic bags, please! Other walkers wanting peace and quiet will thank you for it)
- hard-wearing clothing appropriate for the season and suitable for hand washing
- if necessary, a stone (see Cruz de Ferro page 161)
- possibly a small tent (cyclists/pilgrims with dogs; campsites are, however, usually closed in winter)

Tips for your first aid kit

- personal medication in plentiful supply, especially if you suffer from allergies, since antihistamine tablets are only available on prescription in Spain.
- pain killers
- magnesium tablets for muscles
- plasters, roll of sticky tape, special blister pads (with details from the chemist of how to apply)
- antiseptic (current product in Spain: Betadine)
- healing ointment
- anti-insect spray/cream
- foot cream

Important documents

- identity card or passport
- pilgrims from Great Britain or Ireland need a European Health Insurance Certificate in case of illness. For travellers from non-EU countries (e. g. USA, Australia, Canada) a private health and/ or travel insurance is recommended
- regarding chronic illnesses or allergies, it might be sensible, in case of an emergency, to put information regarding necessary medicines, together with medical terms that are internationally understood, with your identity documents

the bus station (from April to Sept. if possible 1½–2 hrs. before departure) or from www.autobusesdenavarra.com (no returns or change of date of travel possible). Tickets for bikes can only be bought at the kiosk (not online). A ticket bought online does not guarantee a place for the bike, so it is recommended that you arrive early at the bus station.

Arrival by taxi: Information about taxis from Pamplona to Roncesvalles or Saint-Jean-Pied-de-Port: Teletaxi San Fermín, tel: 948 351 335 or 948 232 300 (sometimes need to keep trying), www.taxipamplona.com (under 'compartir *taxi*' you can reserve a seat in a communal taxi). 2012 taxi prices Pamplona–oncesvalles 57 € (Sat./Sun./public holiday/night 70 €), Pamplona–Saint-Jean-Pied-de-Port about 96 € (Sat./Sun./public holiday/night 120 €), Roncesvalles–Saint-Jean-Pied-de-Port about 50 €. Airport–Roncesvalles 60 € (SatSun./public holiday/night 75 €), airport–Saint-Jean-Pied-de-Port 100 € (Sat./Sun./public holiday/night 125 €).

Route finding

The path from Spain is marked throughout and at short intervals with yellow arrows (Spanish flecha amarilla) and/or St. James shells (also red and white waymarkers on the Camino Aragonés and in France – 'GR 65 Camino de Santiago'), also cairns in places. It's unlikely that you will go wrong. The guide points out any places where the route is unclear. Local people will gladly point you in the right direction if you simply ask for the 'Camino de Santiago?'.

Unfortunately there are more and more inaccurate arrows appearing which direct the walker away from the route and to bars and restaurants instead without making this clear – a real nuisance forcing you to make an unplanned detour.

Blisters

Blisters can make the nicest walk into a torturous one. Even if you are not immune to blisters, it is possible to reduce the risk. You should avoid rubbing at all costs and keep your feet dry. It is very hot in summer in Spain and as a result, your feet can swell up badly and sweat more than usual. Re-tying your shoe laces several times a day helps to avoid rubbing.

Usually reliable: the yellow arrow and the St James/pilgrim shell.

It's worth investing in special hiking socks that, with their mixture of fibres, keep the feet dry. 100 % cotton or pure new wool socks have proved unsuccessful. Wearing clean socks every day is the best thing for your feet.

A quick footbath in a cool stream might seem appealing, but be careful – softened skin tends to form blisters faster than dry skin. It's more healthy and effective to take your boots off as often as you can during the day to give your feet a breather and dry your socks. Carrying loads that are too heavy, taking too few breaks and not drinking enough fluids are often the causes for blisters and also inflammation of the tendons.

It can prove very effective at the first sign of an abrasion to put several layers of sticking plaster, or a blister pad and sticking plaster, onto the abrasion point in order to avoid further rubbing.

If blisters have formed, burst them only if they are bothering you. Make two small insertions with a needle or a pair of fine nail scissors (sterilise both to avoid infection) to drain out the fluid. Do not remove the skin from the blister! Cover over with several layers of plaster or with a special plaster and sticking plaster. If the blister is already open go to a doctor for treatment if in doubt. In less severe cases keep the wound com-

Airing your boots overnight to dry them out will help prevent blisters.

pletely clean to avoid the risk of a serious infection. Special blister pads are ideal for treating blisters. Thanks to their special compound, they can assist the healing process and reduce the rubbing if applied correctly. To stop a blister pad from coming off, cover it over with sticking plaster. Never take the plaster off before the blister has healed (see directions for use) unless the blister is sore under the plaster. Normally you can the leave the plaster on for a maximum of 3 days and then, if necessary, keep covering it with sticking plaster.

Food

As a general rule, drink plenty of fluids, even after the walk. Keep your water bottles filled – the fact-file section under the heading of 'Local services' indicates places where there are springs. On hot days and for long sections of the walk you should have at least 1½ litres of water with you. Always take more with you than you need as the next spring may not be in use.

In some areas there are neither villages nor springs for drinking water for many kilometres. Make sure, therefore, that you have adequate provisions, especially water (see Remarks in the information section for each stage). It is also sensible to have something to eat with you at all times (a muesli bar, fruit, bread) in case one stage turns out to be longer than expected. Dissolvable magnesium tablets to suck help prevent muscle cramps and tendonitis.

The three course pilgrim menu served everywhere (*Menú del Peregrino*) is a bit of a gamble. For around 10 € it can sometimes be quite sufficient, at other times not so good. Be careful with alcohol. Combined with the unaccustomed exertion and heat it can have a disastrous affect on the circulation.

The daily quota and planning of stages

Choose short stages wherever possible at the beginning until your body has adapted to the regular exertion and found its own rhythm. If your legs feel heavy some days, don't give up: the next day they will normally feel better again.

The stages described in the walking guide are simply suggestions. Every hiker should plan a day's walking according to his/her physical condition and the mood of the moment. If there are a lot of pilgrims on the Camino you can often avoid the crush by staying overnight in a place just before or after the more classic stage destinations. It is better to schedule more rather than less days in the planning of the walk and, from experience, it is not worth determining beforehand your daily quota of walking. Physical discomforts, unaccustomed heat, bad weather, or even a spontaneous lengthy stop for sightseeing, can bring the timetable into disarray. The slowest member of a walking party always determines the speed of the group.

Pilgrim hostels

The network of pilgrim hostels (in Spanish *albergue/refugio/hospital de peregrinos*) is becoming more and more dense. Together with hostels run by religious institutions or societies, and some community run ones, there's an increasing number of private hostels describing themselves as tourist hostels (Spanish *Albergue Turístico*) which, especially outside the pilgrim season, also accept non-pilgrims. On offer is a range of basic sleeping hostels to classy hostels with a comprehensive range of equipment (washing machine, drier, internet, kitchen etc.). Amongst those people running the hostels you will find

San Juan de Ortega pilgrim hostel.

many former pilgrims to whom the care of pilgrims is a matter of the heart, but also normal business people who have a rather more commercial focus. Therefore many new and modern hostels have emerged which leave nothing to be desired as regards the furnishings, space (more and more often with double and single rooms at hotel prices too) and cleanliness, but which unfortunately lack something in atmosphere. In other words: you can be very comfortable even in a basic hostel provided there is the opportunity to enjoy the harmonious company of other pilgrims with mutual tolerance and respect.

The prices for an overnight stay in 2012 were between 5 and 15 €. Some hostels are financed by voluntary contributions (*donativos*) which should reflect the usual prices for accommodation. In Navarra and Castilla y Léon the grading of pilgrim huts (eg. the number of beds – mostly bunk beds, in Spanish *litera* – space per pilgrim) and the prices are now regulated by law.

In Castilla y Léon insignia with one to three shells denote the following catagories: non-profit making hostels (*sin ánimo de lucro*) with a basic standard have one shell and are not allowed to charge more than 5 € (rather misleading description by the legislator as *donativo* – donations). Hostels with a higher standard (for example, a bit more space per person) have two or three shells and can set their prices correspondingly higher.

Particularly municipal and religious hostels allow only one overnight accommodation unless there are health problems. Private (tourist) hostels are often not so strict and more than one night is possible, for example, in Santiago de Compostela and Finisterre. As a rule, larger groups of travellers or pilgrims with accompanying transport are not accepted, especially at peak times, and pilgrims on foot are not always happy to welcome these 'cheats'. Many private hostels offer reservations which can be particularly useful on the last 100km.

A short beak can often relax the body and the mind.

Large animals may sometimes bar your way, but otherwise they are not dangerous.

Most of the hostels open in the afternoon (possible change to opening times), and there should be no noise after 22/23.00.
Should you want to get up early in the morning, so as not to disturb the other pilgrims, pack your bags as far possible in advance and put them in a convenient place so that you will be able to leave the dormitory quickly and quietly.
Pilgrim hostels are generally safe, nevertheless you are advised never to leave any valuables lying about (mobile phones, cameras, personal documents) and on the whole to carry only the necessary cash with you. Places with banks and cash dispensers are indicated in this guide.

Bed bugs
Unfortunately bedbugs (in Spanish *chinches*) is the topic of conversation all the way along the Way of St James . Although the hygienic conditions in the hostels are strictly regulated and controlled and the carers/*hospitaleros* are required to regularly disinfect the accommodation and carry out pest control, outbreaks are occurring time and again. In order to reduce the risk, try not to put your rucksack on the ground (which is not always easy to do when stopping for a break out in the open). Nor should you put your sack on the bed or against the wall which will help to prevent the creatures from getting into the mattresses or other places. And most importantly – if you have seen bedbugs on yourself or your luggage, let the hostel carer know immediately. There is no shame in this and then he/she can take the necessary steps without delay. If you are susceptible to bites it might be wise to carry anti-histamine pills with you.

General: all opening times and prices given are based on those in 2012. Depending on the season, numbers of pilgrims or the *hospitalero*, there may be changes in the opening times expecially of the hostels.

Chemists (*Farmácia*): they are mostly open from 9.30–13.30 and 16.30–20.00 in larger towns and sometimes round the clock. Notices about emergency services are on the door and published in the newspaper.

Bank: usually open Mon.–Fri. 8.00–14.00 or 15.00.

Public holidays/fiestas: 1st January, 6th January (*Día de los Reyes Magos*, 3 Kings), Good Friday, 1st May, 15th August (*Asunción de la Virgen María*, Assumption Day), 12th October (*Día de la Hispanidad*), 1st November (*Todos los Santos*, All Saints), 6th December (*Día de la Constitución*, Day of the Constitution), 8th December (*Inmaculada Concepción*, the Immaculate Conception), 25th December.

Internet: you will usually find internet cafés in larger places. Many hostels have PCs with internet and/or Wi-Fi, also bars.

Shop opening times: usually Mon.–Sat. 9.30–13.30 and 16.30–20.00. Large department stores open all day Mon.–Sat. 10.00–21.00 or 22.00.

Emergency: the emergency number is 112 (English, German and French).

Pilgrim passport and certificate: the pilgrim passport (in Spanish *credencial*) dates back to the covering letter in the Middle Ages or the reference that pilgrims took with them as personal identification. Today it grants you an overnight stay in a pilgrim hostel and is the necessary proof for obtaining the certificate of pilgrimage (*compostela*). The compostela is available only to those who can prove, with the stamps (*sellos*) in the pilgrim passport, that they have completed at least the last 100km to Santiago de Compostela on foot and declares the pilgrimage to be on religious grounds. If they name any other motive or at least the last 200km were by bike or on horseback, they will receive a welcome letter. The passport needs to be stamped as evidence once a day in your place of accommodation, in churches, monasteries, at the police station or tourist offices and presented at the end of the walk in the pilgrim office in Santiago (Rúa do Vilar, 1, open daily 9.00–21.00). Theoretically two stamps a day are necessary, but in fact this is only insisted upon for the last 100km (ie. from Sarria). If you continue to Finisterre, you will receive the Fisterrana as proof when you get there, in Muxía the Muxiana.

The pilgrim office accepts only the official *credencial* (14-sided folded document with a brown pilgrim staff and pumpkin on the envelope) and the one issued by societies of the Way of St. James abroad as long as they are authorised by the diocese of Santiago (information at www.peregrinossantiago.es). The pilgrim passport is best obtained beforehand (preferably not at the last minute). Those walking a long distance require at least 2 copies). It is obtainable (mostly online and for a small contribution) from the following places:

- **Great Britain:** Confraternity of St. James, Marion Marples, Secretary, 27 Blackfriars Road, London SE1 8NY, United Kingdom, tel: 00 44 (0) 20 7928 9988, fax 00 44 (0) 20 7929 2844, homepage: www.csj.org.uk.
- **Ireland**: Irish Society of the Friends of St. James. The Secretary, 36, Upper Baggot Street, Dublin 4, Ireland (postal address only!). You can order the pilgrim passport by telephone: 00 (353) (0) 85 781 9088, e-mail: stjamesirl@gmail.com, or by using the order form on the homepage: www.stjamesirl.com.
- **USA:** pilgrims from the USA will find an order form on the homepage www.americanpilgrims.com. E-mail: info@americanpilgrims.com.
- **Canada:** *In French*: Du Québec à Compostelle, Association québecoise des pèlerins et amis du Chemin de Saint-Jaques, postal address: 650, rue Girouard Est, Saint-Hyacinthe, (Québec), J2S 2Y2, Canada. There's an application form on: www.duquebecacompostelle.org. *In English*: Little Company of Pilgrims, Canadian Company of Pilgrims. There's an order form on the homepage (please allow three to four weeks for turnaround time): www.santiago.ca. *Credencials* are available to members only (only one membership is required per household). E-mail: austin@santiago.ca.
- **Australia**: Australian Friends of the Camino, P.O. Box 601, Stirling, South Australia 5051, Australia, homepage: http://afotc.org. Further information can be found on the homepage of the website of the Confraternity of Saint James, www.csj.org.uk/Other English-language Asssociations.
- **Spain:** you can get your pilgrim passport issued when you arrive e.g. in hostels like Roncesvalles, Pamplona, Puente la Reina (hostels of the Padres Reparadores), Logroño, Burgos, León, Ponferrada or O Cebreiro, from the St. James societies (in France: St-Jean-Pied-de-Port in the *Acceuil*/pilgrim office) or from parish offices (Jaca, Iglesia de Santiago, information in the hostel.

Police: there are three kinds of police: the *Policía Local* (local police, in small villages mostly in the town hall), the *Guardia Civil* and the *Policía Nacional* (national police). In an emergency you can turn to any of these three places.
Post office/stamps: opening times Mon.–Fri. 8.30–14.30 (in larger towns also from 8.30–20.30), Sat. 9.30–13.00. Stamps (*sellos*) can also be bought from tobacco shops (*tabacos/estanco*). Parcels abroad from Spain are expensive (2kg about 27 €). It's cheaper to send small parcels poste restante (*lista de correos*) to a Spanish post office at your destination although they will only keep them there for 14 days. The central post office (*oficina principal*) of Santiago is situated in Rúa do Franco, 4 (near cathedral).
Telephone: Spanish telephone numbers are always nine digits. If the first number is a 9, it's a landline, a 6 is a mobile, 900/901 or other numbers are service numbers, free or liable to a charge. The international code for Spain is 00 34. Coins or telephone cards (*tarjeta telefónica prepagada*, available from tobacconists) can be used in telephone boxes.

Beginnings

There had already been a period of brisk comings and goings on the Iberian peninsula by the time of the discovery of the apostle's tomb. One after the other, Greeks, Carthaginians and Romans had settled in the country that was inhabited by Iberian and Celtic descendents and rich in mineral resources. Visigoth rulers founded the first Christian kingdoms from the 5th century onwards. In 711 Arabian armies crossed over to Gibraltar and very quickly conquered wide areas of present day Spain and Portugal. In 1722 with the first victory over the Moors by the Christians in Covadonga began the more than 700 year long 'Reconquista', the reconquest of the Christian realms from the hands of the Islamic invaders.

According to legend it was a star that led the hermit, Pelagius. Since the 6th century there had been references to the fact that James, brother of John the Apostle, had gone on a mission to Spain after the death of Christ. After returning to Palestine he was beheaded on the orders of King Herod (41–44 AD). The body of the Christian martyr was miraculously carried on a boat steered by angels to Galicia from Palestine and was washed ashore at Iria Flavia (today Padrón). After a few difficulties James' disciples eventually had the body buried at the place where it was eventually discovered.

Bishop Theodomir of Iria Flavia declared the relics to be genuine. Alfonso II, king of Asturia and León, had a church built in honour of James (in Spanish *Santiago*) at the place where the body was found, the 'star field' (*Campus stellae*; current explanation for *compostela*). The foundation stone for Santiago de Compostela was laid, the third largest destination for pilgrimages in Christendom next to Rome and Jerusalem. Fame of the apostle's tomb and the deeds of James quickly spread through the Christian world. Known as '*Matamoros*' (the Moor-slayer) and riding on a white stead, he is said to have

become involved in the Reconquista in the battle of Clavijo (La Rioja) – which in fact never took place.

Santiago developed very quickly into an important destination for pilgrimages, also because the journey to Jerusalem had become too unsafe on account of the crusades. Myths and legends abounded along the way. By the foundation of new towns and the revival of reconquered villages, the kingdoms in the 9th/10th centuries also protected

The Pórtico de la Gloria in the cathedral of Santiago de Compostela. Statues of the apostles Peter, Paul, James and John.

the countryside traversed by the Way of St. James. Places like Puente la Reina, Logroño, Santo Domingo de la Calzada, Burgos, Sahagún, León and Astorga grew in size and flourished thanks to the lucrative business for inns, workshops, shops and hospitals. Today's pilgrim route along the Camino francés established itself at the same time and was named after the many pilgrims who came from and via France. Orders of Knights like the Knights Templar and the Santiago Knights attended to the safety along the Camino.

Heyday of pilgrimages

The Way of St. James enjoyed prosperity from the 11th century to the beginning of the 13th century. Christians from all over Europe came in their droves to Santiago and up to 1,000 pilgrims came daily to the apostle's tomb. There are contemporary depictions of the typical costume worn by a St. James pilgrim: a broad-brimmed hat turned up at the front, a loose-fitting coat, a pilgrim staff, a gourd for a water container, a bag for important pilgrim documents and the St. James shell, to begin with an insignia of the pilgrim association, but later a recognisable symbol of Santiago pilgrims. The beautifully shaped St. James shell (in Spanish vieira, also a gastronomic delicacy) has been a common symbol for pilgrimages since the 4th century until it was given its own St. James' legend: a Portuguese knight had fallen into the sea at Iria Flavia after the shining figure of St. James had caused his horse to stumble and was completely covered in St. James shells as he was rescued from the water.

The cathedral of Santiago was built between 1078 and 1211. It was the golden age of Romanesque architecture and sculpture which reaches its high point in the skillfully worked Pórtico de la Gloria (1166–1188) in Santiago cathedral. Pope Calixt II declared 1122 to be a Holy Year which has since then been celebrated if the 25th July (St. James' day) falls on a Sunday (cycle: 11-6-5-6 years). The next Holy Year will not be until 2021.

The first travel guide for Spain

The five books of the Codex Calixtinus or Liber Sancti Jacobi published in 12th century were attributed to Pope Calixt II. The real author is, however, the French monk, Aimeric Picaud. The Codex is considered to be the first travel guide to Spain. In the first four books Picaud primarily gives details about the relics to visit along the way (an important part of medieval pilgrimages) and reveals myths, legends, reports of miracles and liturgical texts. In the fifth book Picaud describes the routes, regions, country and people and gives practical advice. He gives detailed warnings about evil tax collectors, cut-throat innkeepers, fraudulent traders and poisonous rivers. He tells of the 'ungodly Basques', of the people of Navarre who eat like dogs and pigs, of the 'evil and corrupt' people of Castilla. He only makes mild criticisms of Galicians. Although 'quick-tempered and quarrelsome', they most closely resemble the French.

Decline of the pilgrim movement

After the marriage of Isabella I of Castilla and Fernando II of Aragón, the 'Reyes Católicos' in the year 1469, and with it the merging of the two most

Pilgrims have walked along the path across the Castilian plain to the tomb of St. James for hundreds of years. (On the way to Hornillos del Camino, Stage 13).

powerful Spanish kingdoms, and after the end of the Reconquista with the conquest of Granada in 1492, plagues, the split of Christendom by the reformation and religious wars in the late Middle Ages lead to the easing-off of the pilgrim movement. From the 15th century robbers, and mock pilgrims seeking adventure, terrorised the now less frequented and protected route. In 1589 the relics of the apostle were hidden from the English seafarer and pirate Francis Drake – and forgotten. The pilgrim movement, which was already in decline, came almost completely to a standstill in the following centuries. In the 18th century pilgrim journeys were disapproved of because they were associated with pagan superstition. At the start of the 19th century the Spanish church experienced a severe set-back on account of the dissolution of the monasteries for the replenishment of the national coffers.

In the Holy Year of 1867 just 40 pilgrims turned up for the celebrated mass on 25th July in Santiago. In order to revive the St. James cult, a search began for the relic. In 1879 it was found between the walls of the apse. A papal bull from Pope Leo XIII declared it to be genuine in order to silence sceptics.

The Way of St. James under Franco

Vague attempts at a revival of pilgrimages came to an abrupt end at the latest in the Spanish Civil War (1936–1939). Nevertheless dictator Franco monopolized St. James for his own purposes. He claimed that one of the battles had been won by the Nationalists thanks to St. James. Santiago was again proclaimed the patron saint of Spain by decree of Franco's dictatorship. At

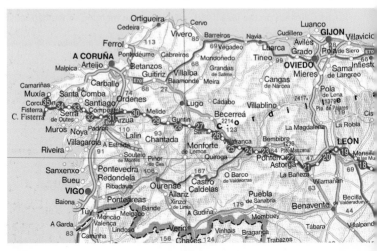

first it was mainly art historians who were interested in the treasures along the Way of St. James. Not until the tentative opening of Spain to the rest of Europe in the 60s did religiously motivated pilgrims return, especially from France.

The modern pilgrim movement

After the death of Franco (1975) and the adoption of the democratic constitution (1978) the apostle's tomb and the Way of St. James came to international notice again. Pope John Paul II visited the apostle's town in 1982, the first Holy Year in democratic Spain, as well as in 1989. In 1987 the Camino de Santiago was declared a European cultural path and included by UNESCO in its list of world heritage sites. The yellow arrow has been adopted as the waymarker since the 80s and the network of pilgrim hostels is still expanding to this day. The Holy years of 1993, and even more so 1999, were also successfully marketed for the first time internationally. The Holy Year of 2004 mobilised hundreds of thousands of pilgrims once again from within Spain and abroad. The pilgrim's office in Santiago issued in 2004 about 180,000 pilgrim certificates – more than ever before. In the following years it was roughly 100,000 and in the Holy Year of 2010 the number of pilgrims was about 190,000. In 2012 just under 192,488 pilgrims registered in the pilgrim office of Santiago de Compostela (pilgrims who weren't issued with a certificate were not counted in the statistics). Most pilgrims come from Spain, Germany, Italy, Portugal and France.

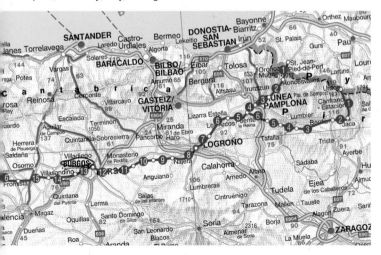

The Camino Aragonés – from the Somport pass to Obanos

The autonomous region of Aragón comprises 1.3 million inhabitants and stretches across a surface area of 47,720km^2; its capital is Zaragoza. Aragón is divided into three provinces – Huesca, Teruel and Zaragoza.

The history of Aragón is closely connected with the foundation of the Spanish state. In the 11th century Ramiro I founded the kingdom of Aragón with Jaca as its capital and San Juan de la Peña as its religious centre. Aragón gained importance during the Reconquista, the recapture of the areas of Spain occupied by the Moors (711–1492). The marriage of Fernando II of Aragón with Isabella I of Castilla in the year 1469 and the unification of the two kingdoms finally laid the foundation for the overall state of Spain. At the start of the 18th century, Aragón lost its status as an independent kingdom and fell under the jurisdiction of Castilla. In the Spanish civil war 1936–1939 the front between the Republicans and the Nationalist troops of Franco ran right through the middle of Aragón and for a long time the province of Teruel was hotly contested.

Together with the cultivation of olives, sunflowers and soya for the production of edible oils and the growing of cereal, Aragón today is gaining more and more importance as an industrial region. Near Zaragoza, situated in the centre of the Ebro valley, one of the most modern industrial parks in Europe is now being established.

The Camino Aragonés (the Aragon Way) runs for about 100km through Aragón. It starts on the 1640m high Pyrenean pass of Somport. Accompanied by the Río Aragón it leaves the mountains and at Jaca swings westwards into the Canal de Berdún, the wide valley of the Aragón. It follows this valley as far as the Yesa reservoir and after Undués de Lerda reaches the region of Navarra. Continuing still as the Camino Aragonés, after another 70km in Obanos, it meets the Camino Francés coming from Roncesvalles.

The Camino Aragonés is above all a natural experience. The Pyrenees, whose peaks are sometimes still covered in snow right up until June, have an extremely rich flora and fauna. The cornfields in the broad and fertile valley of the Río Aragón look like a sea of green in spring while, later in the year, they take on the appearance of a yellow and brown patchwork quilt. Further west the Sierra de Leyre, up to 1300m high, forms an impressive contrast to the tourquoise-green Yesa reservoir.

Pilgrims come through only two largish towns on this route, namely Jaca (pop. 12,300) and Sangüesa (pop. 5,000). Only small or tiny settlements and completely abandoned villages lie inbetween as Ruesta, for example. The historical highpoints are Jaca and San Juan de la Peña. There are relatively few places to stay along the Aragón Way so that the length of each daily stage is determined by the local services available and can therefore sometimes be quite long.

Starting point: Somport on the Spanish-French border (1,640 m).

Hostels: Somport, PH, ⊕⊕, 55 B/13 € (6 € breakfast). Alb. Aysa, tel: 974 373 023. Ski hostel, restaurant, telephone, rather basic hostel. All day, Oct./Nov. closed. **Candanchú** (1537m, pop. 110), PH, ⊕⊕⊕, 48 B/12,75 €. Refugio Pepe Garcés, tel: 974 372 378/664 012 867. Ski hostel, on the right in the village. Wi-Fi, washing machine/drier. All day, all year. **Canfranc Est.** (1,192m, pop. 550), PH, ⊕⊕, 40 B/18 € (cheaper for pilgrims). Alb. Pepito Grillo, tel: 974 373 123. Bar, nice atmosphere, all day, all year. **Canfranc Pueblo** (1,059m, pop. 100), PH, ⊕⊕, 74 B/May–Sept. 10,50 €, rest of the time 13,50 €. Alb. Refugio de Canfranc, tel: 974 372 010. Touristic hostel, mainly for organised groups, best to phone ahead or reserve at www.sargantana.info. Bar, Wi-Fi. 16.00–22.00, May–Nov. **Villanúa** (950m, pop. 450), PH, ⊕⊕⊕, 70 B/from 13 €. Alb. Tritón, tel: 974 378 181. In the village, reception Hostal Alto Aragón. Restaurant, washing machine. All day, all year (best to enquire beforehand in winter). **Jaca** (815m, pop. 12,300) **(1)** PH, ⊕⊕⊕, 11 B/14 € (with breakfast), SR 25 €/DR 20 €. Casa Mamré, c/ del Arco, 1. Tel: 974 363 271. On the way to the MH, tourist hostel. **(2)** MH, ⊕⊕⊕, 32 B/10 €. In the centre, shells in the ground show the way; kitchen, internet, information material. Reception: winter 17.00–20.00, summer 16.00–22.00, ask about evening closing times when there. Closed mid December to March.

Grade and route: well marked (yellow arrows and red and white waymarkers, GR 65.3 long distance path). To Villanúa sometimes stony and steep descents. After that predominantly level earth and gravel paths.

Height difference: 100m in ascent, 910m in descent.

Critical points: (1) As you leave Canfranc Estación read the description carefully. **(2)** The left alternative from Villanúa is waymarked (GR 65.3.1).

Scenery: the path to Villanúa goes through a delightful Pyrenean landscape with beautiful mixed deciduous woods. Many electricity pylons and the nearby N-330 road can be off-putting.

Local services: Somport ⚔ 🚌; Candanchú 🖃 ⚔ 🏠 🚌 € @; Canfranc Est. 🖃 ✉ ⚔ 🏠 🚌 € ⚔ i 🏥 ➕ @ Avd. Arañones, 14, tel: 974 373 013; Canfranc Pueblo 🖃 🏠 🚌; Villanúa ⚔ 🏠 € 🚌 @; about 5km after Villanúa 🏠 www.lorache-casarural.es, reduction for pilgrims; Castiello de Jaca (913m, pop. 260) ⚔ 🖃 🚌 🏠; Jaca 🖃 🖃 ⚔ ✉ @ 🅰 ✉ 🚌 i 🏥 Iglesia de Santiago Mon.–Fri. 19.30, Sat./Sun. 19.00, summer 20.00 ➕ Paseo de la Constitución, tel: 974 362 586.

Remarks: many pilgrims stay overnight in Jaca and travel with the first bus (8.25, arrival about 9.00) onto the pass.

Along beautiful paths from the mountains into the valley.

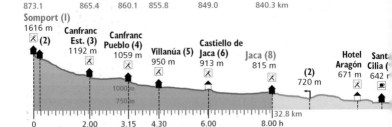

873.1   865.4   860.1   855.8   849.0   840.3 km

Somport (I)
1616 m   Canfranc
⚑ (2)   Est. (3)   Canfranc
         1192 m   Pueblo (4)   Castiello de
              ⚑   1059 m   Villanúa (5)   Jaca (6)   Jaca (8)   Hotel   Sant
                    ⚑   950 m   913 m   815 m   Aragón   Cilia (
                          ⚑   ⚑   ⚑   (2)   671 m   642 r
                                              720 m   ⚑   ▣
1000 m
750 m
                                              32.8 km

0   2.00   3.15   4.30   6.00   8.00 h

A few steps from the **Aysa hostel (1)** in **Somport** you will find the first sign-post for the Way of St. James. After ¼ hr. via some steps and a beaten path you come to the ruins of the former **Santa Cristina** pilgrim hospital **(2)** at the eastern edge of **Candanchú**. With its history of over 80 years, it is the oldest, if not the homeliest, winter sports resort in the Aragonian Pyrenees.

> ⓘ *The 1640m high **Somport pass**, the 'Summus Portus', the highest pass, was already in use by the Romans and Arabs. In the Middle Ages, pilgrims coming from eastern France and Italy crossed over the pass while the three other great French pilgrim routes joined in the French Saint-Jean-Pied-de-Port further west.*
> *The **Santa Cristina pilgrim hospital** was founded in 1104. According to the medieval pilgrim guide, the Codex Calixtinus, together with the Hospital Mont-Joux in the Alps and the Hospital of Jerusalem, in its time it was one of the three pillars of Christian charity 'created by God'. However it never reached the popularity of Roncesvalles and was abandoned in the 17th century.*

Ascend some steps on the left, cross over a road and a little later on the N-330. Then follow the asphalt path and the beaten path shortly afterwards going left which goes downhill and is very stony in places. After passing a solitary house on the meadow the path continues straight ahead, not sharp right (waymarker). The path winds its way downhill through a mixed decidu-ous wood. At the sign 'Camping Canfranc' go through the narrow wooden gate. After the second gate keep left. Warning signs (peligro variadas brus-cas de agua) alert you to the danger of suddenly rising water levels near to the banks of the stream.

After a good 2 hrs. you pass the **hostel (3)** and soon afterwards reach the former international station of **Canfranc Estación**. Walk through the elongat-ed village and at the end follow the road which runs on the right of the stream and small reservoir, then continue through the tunnel (sign Túnel IP 79m). Im-mediately afterwards some steps lead down left into the river valley. The path turns sharp right at the bottom and after a few steps look out for the small set of steps on the left. A good 1 hr. later you arrive in **Canfranc Pueblo (4)**.

*At the opening in 1928 the 241m long, neoclassic **railway station** (estación) of **Canfranc** was the biggest in Spain and the second biggest in Europe. In 1970 rail traffic to France was discontinued and today only the regional train stops in the winter sports resort. The building is due to be refurbished with a part of it converted into a hotel, but there's not enough money at present. A tower can be seen before Canfranc on the **Coll de Ladrones** (16th century; meaning 'hill of the robbers') from which they kept a lookout for smugglers. The defensive tower of **Torre de Fusileros** (15th century, restored in the 19th century) at the right hand exit from the village had the same purpose. Beyond Canfranc Pueblo a well-preserved medieval **pilgrim bridge** spans the Aragón.*

From Canfranc Pueblo continue along a lovely path above the river into **Villanúa** 1¼ hrs. away. The path to Castiello de Jaca goes off right at the entrance to the village. For the Villanúa **hostel (5)** follow the alternative route (GR 65.3.1) on the left into the village.

Alternative east (7.5km/1¾ hrs., GR 65.3.1, red and white waymarkers and others, scenically delightful):
At the small village square with the spring (after the Alto Aragón hostel) go left past the church to the edge of the village. Turn right here into the small road which you now follow straight ahead. Shortly after the cemetery (*cementerio*) ignore the sign onto the path on the right and after just under 30 minutes there's a well on the right below and a little later the asphalt finishes and the gravel starts. After roughly another 30 minutes follow the GR 65.3.1 as it turns sharp right downhill. You reach the Río Aragón, ascend slightly up to a roundabout and on the other side of the N-330 take the little road uphill on the left that is lined with street lamps. After a total of 1¾ hrs. the upper village of **Castiello de Jaca (6)** is reached.
Before the church go right to a little road with a spring (left). The two alternatives join here.

Typical medieval bridge over the Río Aragón.

Alternative west (7 km/1¾ hrs., GR 65.3; flatter, yellow arrows; goes past Villanúa. Disadvantage: follows the N-330 for about 3km):

The path curves round to the right next to the N-330. After ¾ hr. leave the N-330 to the right and meet it again briefly nearly half an hour later at the turn-off to San Adrián, Aratorés and Borau (Villa Juanita) and half an hour after that reach the upper village of **Castiello de Jaca (6)**.

After the junction of the two alternatives, carry straight on to reach the lower village, cross over the N-330 and leave the village following the yellow arrows. A good half an hour later the Camino goes under the N-330 to the right. Continue along a broad gravel path beside the N-330 to reach, ½ hr. after the underpass of the N-330, the **Ermita de San Cristóbal (7)** and then with a short steep ascent, **Jaca**, lying on a high plateau. On the left hand side of the road go as far as the cathedral and from there follow the brass shells in the ground as they read left along c/ de Bellido to the **municipal hostel (8**; just under half an hour).

---

i *The beginnings of the small cathedral town of **Jaca** (province of Huesca) date back to an Iberian settlement. In the 3rd century BC the town was seized by the Romans. In 758 the earldom was one of the first Spanish towns to repulse Moorish power after a duration of only 44 years. This event is still remembered every year with the fiestas of the Moros y Cristianos (Moors and Christians). In the 11th century Jaca becomes, under King Sancho I Ramírez, the first capital of the newly founded kingdom of Aragón. Jaca plays no further role in the course of history. Today this lively little town lives chiefly from (ski) tourism.*

*The **cathedral** (in Spanish 'catedral'; 11th century; open 11.30–13.30 and 16.00–20.00) is the oldest significant Romanesque building in Spain. Worthy of attention are the main portal with the monogram of Christ in the arch, the first chrismon of this kind on a Spanish church, the south portal, the Romanesque capital as well as the checkerboard-like border decoration inside the church. The bones of Santa Orosia, the patron saint of Jaca, have been buried below the high altar.*

*The **citadel** (ciudadela), a fortress built in 15th century as protection against the French, serves today as the barracks for a branch of mountain hunters (guided tours only: all year round Tue.–Sun. 11.00–14.00 afternoons depending on the season 16/17.00–19/20.00, 10 € citadel and museum, www.ciudadeladejaca.es). There's also a herd of deer living In the moats.*

*Civic buildings worth mentioning are the town hall (**ayuntamiento**, 16th century) and the **Torre de Reloj** (clock tower, 15th century), an apartment house with beautiful Gothic windows.*

***Public holidays:** 1st Friday in May: Moros y Cristianos, processions with spectacular costumes and stylised re-enactments of the battles between the Moors and Christians. 25th June: fiesta in honour of the patron saint, Santa Orosia.*

***Gastronomy:** jaqueses (cream-filled pastry coated with honey and almonds), corazones de Jaca (puff pastry hearts with cream filling).*

Hostels: Santa Cilia (642m, pop. 200), MH, ●●●, 18 B/10 €. Tel: 646 880 279. In the village straight on from square with spring, right at the bar (with small shop). Kitchen, evening meals, washing machine. Separate bathrooms and dormitories for men and women. All day, all year. **Arrés** (694m, pop. 30), SH, ●●●, 22 B+M+space for sleeping mat in chapel just outside/donations; kitchen, communal meal in the evening. March–Sept., rest of time key from Marí Luz (bar-rest. El Granero), renovated old building, all day.

Grade and route: the direct route to Santa Cilia is easy, well marked, for the most part unsurfaced paths next to a busy road (N-240) to Santa Cilia, but to Arrés predominantly next to N-240, otherwise woodland paths; moderately difficult ascents and descents. The alternative via San Juan de la Peña is longer with a greater height difference.

Height difference: 190m in ascent, 310m in descent.

Critical points: none.

Scenery: scenically beautiful except for the closeness of the road on the direct route; lovely views from higher points across the Canal de Berdún to the Pyrenees.

Local services: 11,7km/2¼ hrs. after Jaca ⚔ ⌂ Hotel/Rest. Aragón; Santa Cilia ⚔ ⌂ ▣ @ ⌾ (July/Aug. with bar); ⚔ ▲ ¾ hr. after Santa Cilia; Puente la Reina de Jaca (605m, pop. 80) ⚔ ⇌ ▣ ⌂ (detour before Arrés); San Juan de la Peña/Monasterio Nuevo ⚔ ⌂; Santa Cruz de la Serós (788m, pop. 150) ⚔ ▲ ⌂; Arrés ⚔ ⌂.

Remarks: (1) Jaca is the last good opportunity for shopping and banks until you reach Sangüesa (80km). **(2)** shops and bar-restaurant in Santa Cilia not always open. **(3)** At Puente la Reina de Jaca (not to be confused with the place with almost the same name in Navarra) the route branches off northwards from the Yesa reservoir. However, this route is not recommended as it runs for the most part next to the main road and there are hardly any hostels. Although the medieval village of Berdún and the monastery of Leyre are well worth seeing, they are not worth the long diversion. The southern route has therefore become more and more popular, which is why there are are also more hostels. **(4)** There's a detour from Sangüesa to the 2.5km long gorge of Foz de Lumbier.

The yellow arrows and brass shells in the ground lead from **Jaca (1)** past the Torre de Reloj and the Iglesia de Santiago to the edge of town, then through an area of housing. At the end of the development turn right, then left and continue next to the N-240. At the cemetery cross over the road to the right onto a lovely hiking path. After a total of 1¼ hrs. at a factory for building materials (*Fábrica de Pretensados*) you reach the left hand **turn-off (2)** to San Juan de la Peña (for description, see below).

Direct alternative: the path to Santa Cilia goes across the road on the right to a picnic area. There it follows the row of poplars and passes an abandoned military base. A little later on the path turns left over the N-240 and continues as a nice woodland path above the road. Shortly afterwards you come to a stream with a footbridge. After the stream follow the woodland road right for about 100m to the signpost for the 'GR 65.3 Santa Cilia'.

An unsurfaced woodland path now leads uphill. From the top there are lovely views across the Canal de Berdún to the Pyrenees. After ½ hr. (from the start of the ascent) the path goes downhill again to the **Hotel Aragón** (1½ hrs. after the turn-off to San Juan de la Peña). Here, too, is a turn-off to San Juan de la Peña via Santa Cruz de la Serós; see below for the description. It's now ¾ hr. on the left of the N-240 to reach **Santa Cilia (9)**.

The little village of Arrés.

Next to the N-240 and past the holiday centre, *Centro de vacaciones Pirineos*, you come to the **bridge (10)** that leads on the right to **Puente la Reina de Jaca** (¾ hr. from Santa Cilia). Continue straight ahead along the little road in the direction of Arrés. After just under ¼ hr. the direct path to Arrés turns off left. It ascends gently and then leads along a high path at the foot of the 866m hill of Brasanés. After a good ¾ hrs. you arrive in **Arrés (11)**. If, on the other hand, you stay on the little road, you can walk below Arrés directly to Artieda.

Detour to San Juan de la Peña monastery

There are several possibilities for this detour:

Alternative 1: from Jaca by taxi to the monastery (30 €), from there on foot via Santa Cruz de la Serós to Santa Cilia (10.6km/2¾ hrs.).

Alternative 2: from Jaca to Hotel/Restaurant Aragón (11.7km/2¾ hrs.). You can ask to leave your rucksack there, then follow the road left to Santa Cruz de la Serós (3.5km/¾ hr.) and ascend from there to San Juan de la Peña (3.9km/1½ hrs., 330 vertical metres). Or take the rucksack with you to Santa Cruz, and leave it there if necessary, and on the return to Santa Cilia take the route described in alternative 4 via Binacua (1½ hrs.).

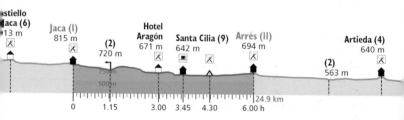

840.3   835.1   828.4 825.0 821.4   815.4 km

| stiello Jaca (6) ▪13 m | Jaca (I) 815 m | (2) 720 m | Hotel Aragón 671 m | Santa Cilia (9) 642 m | Arrés (II) 694 m | (2) 563 m | Artieda (4) 640 m |

750m
500m

0   1.15   3.00 3.45   4.30   6.00 h   24.9 km

Capital on a pillar in San Juan de la Peña.

Alternative 3: ascent from Santa Cilia (then possibly 2 nights in the hostel). Depending on the route about 12km/4–4½ hrs. 330m of ascent, via Binacua 480m of ascent.

Alternative 4: (30.1km/8¾ hrs.; 900m in ascent, 1060m in descent; height profile p. 41). GR 65.3.2, Jaca – Atarés – San Juan de la Peña – Santa Cruz de la Serós – Santa Cilia; scenically very beautiful and remote, but quite long and strenuous; possibly unclear waymarkers in places. Only recommended to experienced walkers as a first or second stage. An overnight stop in Santa Cruz de la Serós, e.g. in Hostal Santa Cruz (tel: 974 361 975, www.santacruzdelaseros.com) shortens this stretch by 24.4km/7¼ hrs.:

From **Jaca (1)** follow the Way of St. James left to the factory for **building materials (2**; 1¼ hrs.). Take the path there to the left uphill. (sign 'GR 65.3.2

Atarés/San Juan'; look out for the red and white waymarkers.) Ascend the gravel path uphill to a sharp left hand bend. Cairns, yellow arrows and red and white waymarkers indicate the small path that leads uphill below the power line. At the fork in a small clearing keep right and ascend a stony, steep path.

After a good hour (from N-240) you finally reach a first **hill (3)** at 1,020m. Follow the red and white marked path left to an agricultural track. Turn right onto this track at first, but after only a few steps a small path turns off left again which is stony at the start and winds its way steeply downhill, and then leads more gently in a good ¾ hr. to **Atarés (4)**. Turn left into the village, walk down across the Pl. Mayor (fountain) and ascend the gravel road on the far side of the village.

Go right at the next turn-off after 20 mins. and a few minutes later go left onto the small path. After 1½ hrs. steep ascent you are standing on a **pass (5)** festooned with cairns (1,148m). Shortly afterwards the path joins the country road further below which you follow to the right. It climbs just under 1,200m in altitude and leads in about an hour to the new monastery (*monasterio nuevo*). (About half an hour along the way the alternative route, waymarked in red and white, turns off right across the Praderías de San Indalecio. This is roughly 1.5km longer and leads round a wide bend directly to San Juan de la Peña.) Past the new monastery (hotel/restaurant) you come through the wood to the old monastery of **San Juan de la Peña (6; ¼ hr.).**

> ℹ️ *The monastery of **San Juan de la Peña** (monasterio viejo) was founded in the 9th century. In the 11th century it was the religious centre of the new kingdom of Aragón. Legend has it that the alleged Holy Grail (which is now in Valencia) had been kept here until the 14th century. After several fires the monastery was abandoned in the 17th century. The parts that are still preserved (chapter house, the Mozarabic crypt and the upper church, tombs of the kings of Aragón) date back to the 10th–12th century. The cloister built underneath the rock overhang (peña) is quite distinctive with its masterly worked capitals on the top of columns from the 11th and 12th centuries. (Opening times: March–May 10.00–14.00 and 15.30–19.00, June–14th July 10.00–14.00 and 15.00–20.00. 15th July–Aug. 10.00-20.00. Sept.–15th*

View from Arrés across the, in summer, green Canal de Bérdun.

Oct. 10.00–14.00 and 15.30–19.00. 16th Oct.–Feb. 10–15.30 (16th Oct.–Dec. Sat. 10–16.30); changes possible. Guided tours in several languages, 45 mins. Pilgrims: 4 € (with visit to the church in Santa Cruz de la Serós). Internet: www.monasteriosanjuan.com (also in English). The new monastery (**monasterio nuevo**, with hotel, restaurant and museum) dates back to the 17th–18th century. During the war of independence (start of the 19th century) the building was almost completely abandoned. There's a pilgrimage to the monastery on the last Sunday in May.

The **Sierra de San Juan de la Peña** nature reserve has been under environmental protection since 1920. Here you can see, amongst other things, species of vultures such as the Buitre Leonado (griffon vulture), the Alimoche (Egyptian vulture) or, with a wing span of up to 2.8m, the Quebrantahuesos (lammergeyer, literally translated as 'bone breaker'), but also wild boar and fallow deer. The flora is very rich too.

The descent to Santa Cruz de la Serós begins below the old monastery on the left of the ticket office (signpost. Ignore the turn-off right after a few minutes to the Monasterio Nuevo). The broad footpath descends gently at first, then once more ascends, after a sharp right hand bend, to a crossroads with signs. Keep left here (the alternative described above joins diagonally from the right at this point). The path downhill is now more clearly marked, but it is steep and stony. After a good hour you arrive in **Santa Cruz de la Serós (7)**.

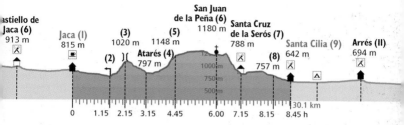

840.3 835.1 833.0 830.1 826.0   820.4 817.0 812.6 810.2 km

astiello de
Jaca (6)
913 m

Jaca (I)
815 m

(3)
1020 m

(5)
1148 m

San Juan
de la Peña (6)
1180 m

Santa Cruz
de la Serós (7)
788 m

Santa Cilia (9)
642 m

Arrés (II)
694 m

(2))(
Atarés (4)
797 m

(8)
757 m

1000 m
750 m
500 m

30.1 km

0   1.15 2.15 3.15 4.45   6.00 7.15 8.15 8.45 h

ℹ️ **Santa Cruz de la Serós** has two interesting churches: the Romanesque *Iglesia de Santa María* (end of the 11th century), exceptionally well preserved building of the at one time oldest convent in Aragón (abandoned in 17th century), as well as the Romanesque **chapel of San Caprasio** (beginning of 11th century, Lombard style of architecture). Typical of the region are the conical chimney constructions that have been preserved in the village which are topped with '**espantabrujas**' (witch-scarers) where family life used to take place in winter.

Leave the village along the main road and at the spring take the farm track up to the left (waymarked red and white). When you arrive at the top walk in a constant up and down along small paths to reach **Binacua (8)** in 1 hr. N.B. ignore the farm track that leads down to the left before the village. Go straight on and keep left past the village. After that descend with a view across the Canal de Berdún, then the path swings round to the left and you arrive in **Santa Cilia (9**; ½ hr.).

An autumn afternoon at Arrés. If the hostel is full pilgrims can roll out their sleeping mats in the small chapel.

Hostels: Artieda (640m, pop. 110), PH, ⊜⊜⌂, 20 B/8 €. Tel: 948 439 316. In the centre of the village, tourist hostel. Telephone, internet (in the village; ask in the hostel), small restaurant; beautiful view into the valley from terrace. From about 11.30, all year.
Ruesta (547m, pop. 4), PH, ⊜⊜, 62 B/12 € (half board 24 €, B&B 15 €), tel: 948 398 082. Proprietor: CGT union, tourist hostel, two re-novated old buildings in an otherwise dilapidated village, lovely situation. Wi-Fi. Sale of fruit and snacks, restaurant; reservations possible. All day, all year.
Grade and route: easy and well marked; lots of quite easy up and down to Artieda, predominantly on farm tracks and dirt paths; 4km/1¼ hrs on little used country road, the A-1601 between Artie-da and Ruesta.

Height difference: 340m in ascent, 420m in descent.
Critical points: none.
Scenery: scenically quite attractive route through cornfields in the Aragón valley; from Artieda lovely views of the reservoir of Yesa and the Sierra de Leyre lying to the north; before Ruesta just under 4km long path through a very beautiful forest and bush, but depending on the time of year swarming with tiresome flies.
Local services: Artieda ⌂ ▪ @ ⊣; Ruesta ✕ @, in summer △ below the village.
Remarks: take plenty of water and provisions with you (possibly even for the following days) as no opportunities to buy food for 18km.

In **Arrés (1)** walk a few paces down the main road in the direction of the Aragón valley. A path turns left at the information board. Follow this path to the gravel road steeply downhill, turn left there and take the turn-off going immediately down to the right. Stay on this farm track until it joins the farm track running parallel to the river. Go left here and keep straight ahead. At the two fords with bridges (**2** and **3**) after roughly 2½ hrs. the path comes past a quite

Yesa reservoir in spring.

bizarre moon landscape of grey, cylindrical eroded mounds of earth. After another 1¾ hrs. the nice little village of **Artieda (4)** is reached situated on a rounded mountain top. Go left into the village steeply up the path. If you do not want to go into Artieda, follow the waymarkers on the right.

From Artieda go back to the information board at the edge of the village and turn right there down the main road. At the bottom turn left onto the Camino. The gravel road joins the A-1601 country road. Follow this road for long stretches without shade for a good hour.

Ruesta: the hostel in the foreground.
Right: a September morning on the way to Artieda.

Then a path turns off to the left uphill. Shortly afterwards it crosses the A-1601 and brings you to the very beautiful woodland path above the reservoir, the Embalse de Yesa. At the ruin of **San Juan Bautista chapel** (5; a good ¾ hr.; only remains of the monastery of San Juan de Maltray) the path swings to the left and ascends a short incline to the half derelict village of **Ruesta** (6; ¼ hr.).

> *i* The **Embalse de Yesa** (Yesa reservoir) had already been planned in the 1920s as a water depot for dry areas like Las Bardenas between Pamplona and Zaragoza. Construction began in 1936. On completion in 1959, 2,400 hectares of land had been flooded (almost half of it, arable land). The Roman thermal baths at Tiermas also disappeared. Robbed of their livelihood, the people emigrated and left behind ghost villages like **Ruesta**, **Escó** and **Tiermas**.
>
> The reservoir also destroyed the original route of the Way of St. James which went from Ruesta to Tiermas and from there to the monastery of Leyre. It is only doable at low tide (if necessary ask in the Ruesta hostel).
>
> There have long been plans to dam up the lake even further and triple its capacity. Work has begun in the meantime, inspite attempts by environmentalists such as the Río Aragón Anti-development Organisation (slogan: ¡Yesa no!) to bring a court order to stop the work. Instead they are demanding a modernisation of the agricultural watering system and a more sparing use of water. Parts of the Way of St. James between Artieda and Ruesta are also threatened by the development.
>
> **Ruesta** lies on a hilltop like a ship. The ruins of the castle rise up to the west (of Arab origin, end of the 10th century) into the sky, while the remains of the Iglesia Santa María (16th century) can be seen to the east. In the Middle Ages Ruesta housed Aragón's oldest Jewish quarter. Ruesta has been abandoned since 1959 and the reconstruction has failed through lack of money. Entry into the ruins is forbidden due to the risk of buildings collapsing.

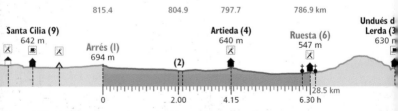

Hostels: Undués de Lerda (630m, pop. 70), YH, ⬤⬤◠, 56 B/from 8 €. Tel: 948 888 105 and 976 714 797. Palace from the 16th entury, near to the church in the centre of the village. Meals, laundry. Reception Mon.–Fri. 9.30–17.00, Sat./Sun. 10.30–20.00), all year. **Sangüesa** (401m, pop. 5,000), **(1)** MH, ⬤⬤, 14 B/5 €. Run by ASPACE (society for the mentally handicapped. C/Enrique Labri (turns off from the roundabout as a paved one-way street); kitchen, dining room, basic, but clean and tidy. Reception 12.00–18.00, you can register after that by calling 659 068 769. Pilgrims receive a key. From about mid Feb.–Nov. **(2)** Cantolagua campsite, ⬤⬤, 20 B/10 €. Tel: 948 430 449. Restaurant, laundry, internet, swimming pool. All day, all year.

Grade and route: moderate to easy. From Ruesta uphill for 7km/2 hrs. Easy from Undués de Lerda to Sangüesa. The waymarkers generally from Navarra onwards (new yellow arrows).

Height difference: 400m in ascent, 570m in descent.

Critical points: none.

Scenery: you walk along beautiful woodland paths from Ruesta onwards through a mixed deciduous wood. At higher altitudes lovely views of the reservoir and the Sierra de Leyre. Shortly after Undués de Lerda to Sangüesa, broad gravel roads without any shade.

Local services: ⬛⬛ (camping in summer) just after Ruesta; Undués de Lerda ⬛⬛⬛; Sangüesa ⬛⬛€@⬛⬛⬛⬛ ⬛⬛⬛⬛ Iglesia de Santiago Mon.–Sat. 20.30, Sun./public holidays 12.00 and 20.00 ⬛ Paseo Cantolagua, tel: 948 871 443.

Remarks: (1) Remember to take food and water with you. **(2)** During fiestas in Sangüesa (Sept), check notices in hostels regarding the running of the bulls. During this period the hostels can sometimes be booked up quickly.

A paved path goes downhill from **Ruesta (1)**. After about 500m there's a spring and after the playground/camping area (summer) there's another one. Shortly afterwards the path goes past the Romanesque chapel, **Ermita de Santiago (2**; 11th century).

Then you walk uphill through the wood, at first along a beaten path, later on an unmade forest road. After a good 2 hrs. you come onto the plateau (856m) before Undués de Lerda. The prominent silhouette of the village soon emerges on the horizon. Numerous wind farms in the distance belong to the autonomous region of Navarra. At times very stony paths run for 1¼ hrs. across a hilly landscape to **Undués de Lerda (3)**. About ¾ hr. after the village a

A constant companion on the Way of St. James – the yellow arrow.

sign marks the border with **Navarra** (in Basque, Nafarroa). From here the path is well marked. About 1¾ hrs. along broad gravel roads bring you to **Sangüesa (4)**.

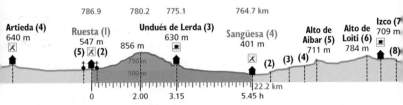

| Artieda (4) 640 m 🏠 | 786.9 | Ruesta (l) 547 m (5) 🏠 (2) | 856 m | 780.2 | Undués de Lerda (3) 630 m 🏠 | 775.1 | Sangüesa (4) 401 m 🏠 | 764.7 km (2) (3) (4) | Alto de Aibar (5) 711 m | Alto de Loiti (6) 784 m | Izco (7 709 m (8) |

750 m
500 m

0   2.00   3.15   5.45 h   22.2 km

ℹ️ *Sangüesa* (in Basque, *Zangoza*) is the first largish town in Navarra on the Aragon Way. In the 12th century under Alfonso I, king of Navarra and Aragón, the original, northwestern settlement of **Rocaforte** was replaced by the then fortress-like new town on the Río Aragón and the bridge was built over the river to facilitate commerce.

The medieval pilgrim movement brought the town prestige and wealth. Many noblemen's palaces are proof of this today. The Gothic **Palacio del Príncipe** de Viana is of particular interest (13th century, former king's residence, today a library) and the Baroque **Palacio de Vallesantoro** (18th century, today the cultural centre – Casa de Cultura) with a richly decorated, wood carved canopy. A most important religious building is the **Iglesia de Santa María la Real**, (12th/13th century). The south portal decorated with 300 sculptures (in places very weathered, unfortunately) is one of the masterpieces of the Romanesque period. Worth seeing inside the church are, for example, the gold-trimmed high altar (16th century) and the Gothic Eucharist (15th century; every half hour before mass, mass: Mon.–Fri. 19.30, Sun. 10.00 and 13.00, 1.95 € for a guided tour, information from the tourist office, www.sanguesa.es).

Further afield: Iglesia de Santiago (12/13th century) with painted figure of St. James (16th century) at the entrance (open Tue.–Sat. 10–13.30 and 17–21.00, Mon. 17–21.00, Sun. 10–12.30 and every 30 mins. before mass). **Iglesia de Salvador** (14th century, restoration planned). **Convento de San Francisco** which Francis of Assisi is said to have founded after his (not documented historically) pilgrimage to Santiago in 1212 as the first Franciscan monastery in Spain (open every 30 mins. before mass; mass: Mon.–Fri. 9.00 and 11.30, Sun. 11.00 and 19.00, Sat. 20.00).

Public holidays: 11th–17th Sept.: festival in honour of the patron saint of San Sebastián, including bull running (together with Pamplona, Tafalla and Tudela, the only place where bulls are used instead of young cows).

Gastronomy: pochas de sangüesa (hearty bean stew), cordero al chilindrón (lamb with paprika).

Hostels: Izco (709m, pop. 50), MH, ⬤⬤⬤, 8 B+M/8 €. Tel: 948 362 210. In community centre. Well-equipped kitchen, small shop, washing machine. Spacious, clean. All day, 1st May–15th Oct., for the rest of the time ask in the village or telephone. **Monreal** (540m, pop. 500), MH, ⬤⬤⬤, 21 B/7 €, tel: 636 412 952. Centre of the village, below the church. Small kitchen in the common room, washing machine, relatively spacious dormitory, someone comes to stamp passports and take money in the afternoon. All day, all year.

Grade and route: easy to moderate. Well marked throughout. Predominantly farm tracks and well beaten paths. Continual up and down can be tiring. More level ground from Izco onwards.

Height difference: 500m in ascent, 360m in descent.
Critical points: none.
Scenery: delightful scenery, uninhabited, in places wooded undualting landscape, reminiscent of the central German uplands. Beautiful views.
Local services: Rocaforte (464m, pop. 40) 🛏 on the left, in the recreation area high up in the village; Izco 🍴🛏🚌; Abínzano (701m, pop. 15) 🛏🚌; Salinas de Ibargoiti (556m, pop. 120) 🛏🚌; Monreal 🛏 🍴€🏧🗙🚌Ⓐ@ (summer, in information centre next to hostel).
Remarks: on the 20km long stretch from Sangüesa to Izco only one spring, no places for refreshments, take food and water with you.

Go left out of the **municipal hostel (1)** as far as the end of the street, go left past the Iglesia de Santa María la Real and then after the Río Aragón, turn right. A little further on turn left and then immediately right (straight on: Lumbier and Foz de Lumbier) to **Rocaforte (2;** ¾ hr.). Ignore the yellow mountain bike signs (BTT) to the right and, as you near the village, past the barbecue site at Fuente de San Francisco, walk uphill onto the wide plateau. Two taps (**3** and **4;** water not drinkable) on the path to **Alto de Aibar (5;** 1¾ hr.). The path is only noticeably steep just before the pass and straight afterwards it winds its way down a beaten path to the left and meets an ascending forest road again.

Ascend a moderate incline to reach the top of the **Alto de Loiti (6;** 1¾ hrs). Take the wooded path from here downhill to quickly reach **Izco (7;** ½ hr.). Walk up to the right at the small square in the centre of the village to reach the hostel.

With a bit of luck you can see griffon vultures along the way – griffon vultures watch pilgrims rather less often.

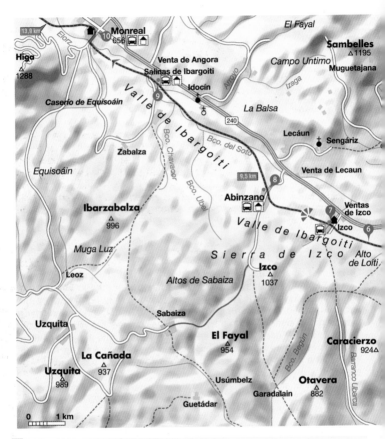

The map shows the following labels:

- **Monreal** 656
- 13,9 km
- **Higa** △ 1288
- El Fayal
- **Sambelles** △ 1195
- Venta de Angora
- Campo Untimo
- Muguetajana
- Salinas de Ibargoiti
- Idocín
- Valle de Ibargoiti
- La Balsa
- Izaga
- Caserío de Equisoáin
- Arroyo
- 240
- Bco. del Soto
- Lecáun
- Sengáriz
- Zabalza
- Bco. Chavador
- Equisoáin
- Bco. Uber
- 9,5 km
- Venta de Lecaun
- **Abinzano**
- **Ibarzabalza** △ 996
- Valle de Ibargoiti
- Ventas de Izco
- Izco
- Muga Luz
- Sierra de Izco
- Alto de Loiti
- Leoz
- Altos de Sabaiza
- **Izco** △ 1037
- **Uzquita**
- Sabaiza
- **El Fayal** △ 954
- Bco. Begun
- **Caracierzo** 924△
- **La Cañada** △ 937
- **Uzquita** △ 989
- Usúmbelz
- **Otavera** 882
- Barranco Ubarca
- Garadalain
- Guetádar
- 0   1 km

The stretch from Sangüesa leads, without any cultural highlights worth mentioning, for many kilometres through an extensively unpopulated area. From Monreal
you become aware of the catchment area of Pamplona and the network of roads
that goes with it. The abundance of **songbirds** and **birds of prey** will delight bird
fanciers. With a little bit of luck experienced birdwatchers will also see vultures
(buitres) as the gorges of **Foz de Lumbier** and **Foz de Arbayún** only a few kilometres away are home to the most significant colonies of **griffon vultures** (buitre
leonado) in Spain. **Egyptian vultures** (alimoche) and **lammergeyer** (quebrantahuesos) are also resident there.

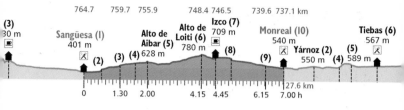

From Izco it's a really pleasant walk along broad gravel paths and farm tracks. The striking cone of the 1,288m high Monte Higa can be seen in the distance and Monreal lies at its base. After ½ hr. you arrive in **Abínzano (8)** and from here it's 1 hr. to **Salinas de Ibargoiti (9)**. Shortly before reaching the village follow an asphalt road for a short way to the right, but then leave it again to the left and come to the village centre this way. The arrows lead you immediately from here to the left. A lovely shady woodland path soon leads to **Monreal (10;** ¾ hrs.).

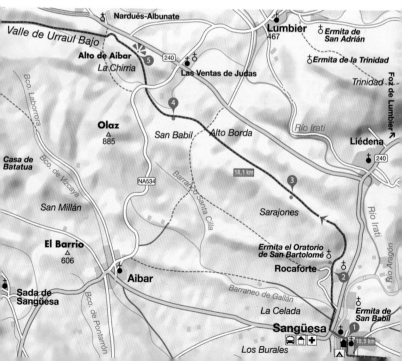

Hostels: Tiebas (567m, pop. 440), **(1)** MH, ◐◐◐, 14 B/8 €. C/ Mayor, 18, tel: 600 941 916. Washing machine, kitchen, meals, internet. 11–22.00, all year. **(2)** PH, ◐◐◐, 6 B/10 € (3 DR 40 €). Tourist hostel El Rincón de los Sabios, c/ Mayor, 35, tel: 600 648 227. Washing machine/drier, kitchen, meals, internet. 10–22.00, all year. **Obanos** (418m, pop. 920), PH, ◐◐◐, 36 B/7 €. Alb. Usda, tel: 676 560 927. Microwave, comfortable renovated old building. 13.30–22.00, April–around mid Oct.

Grade and route: easy. Well marked. Long stretches through undulating countryside. On small paths and farm tracks to Tiebas at the foot of Monte Higa (1288m). Then more open and flatter landscape.

Height difference: 250m in ascent, 370m in descent.

Critical points: none.

Scenery: rather unspectacular scenery. A dense network of country roads, national roads and motorways alert you to the area of Greater Pamplona. Shortly after Monreal the nearby motorway is somewhat disturbing. Olive trees and vineyards soon characterise the countryside towards Tiebas.

Local services: Guerendiáin (589m, pop. 25) ⊡; Tiebas ⊠ ⊡ @ ⊟; Olcoz (585m, pop. 40) ⊟ ⊡; Enériz (426m, pop. 350) ⊠ ⊡ ⊟ ⊡; Santa María de Eunate ⊡; Obanos ⊠ ⊡ ⊟ ⊡ ⊟ Ⓐ ⊟ @ € ⊡ 19.00 (summer).

Remarks: no refreshments between Monreal and Tiebas (shops closed if fiesta, such as in Sangüesa).

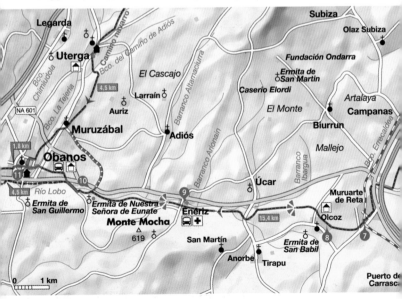

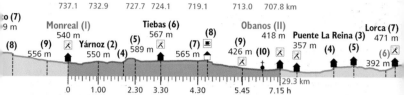

o (7)   Monreal (I)   Tiebas (6)   Obanos (II)   Lorca (7)
9 m   540 m   567 m   418 m   Puente La Reina (3)   471 m
(8)   (9)   [X] Yárnoz (2)   (5)   (7) (8) (9)   357 m   (4)   (5)   (6)[X]
        556 m   550 m 589 m (4) 565 m 426 m (10)[X] [X] [X]   392 m

0   1.00   2.30   3.30   4.30   5.45   7.15 h   29.3 km

Walk straight on from the **hostel (1)** to the main road and follow this left uphill out of **Monreal**. After just under 2km take the path on the right which con-
tours round Monte Higa. The noise from the motorway soon dissipates. The
small villages of **Yarnoz (2**; 1 hr.), **Otano (3**; ½ hr.) and **Ezperun (4**; ½ hr.)
follow on from each other on the right of the path. After Ezperun you can see
Pamplona to the north in the distance. You pass by **Guerendiáin (5)** ½ hr.
later.

After another hour reach **Tiebas (6)**. The remoteness enjoyed along the
Aragón path ends temporarily from Tiebas onwards. Walk straight on
through the village, go left at the fork, shortly afterwards left again and past
the football pitch. Now there's a good stretch on the left beside the A-15 to a

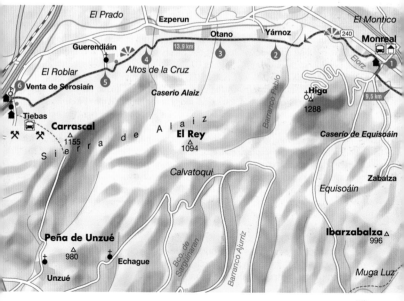

Santa María de Eunate.

large crossroads with a roundabout. Go through the tunnel to the right and through the underpass. At the information board turn off left. The terrain becomes noticeably flatter. After 1 hr. you reach **Muruarte (7)** and a small asphalt road brings you to **Olcoz (8**; ¼ hr.).

A broad, unsurfaced path then leads you downhill into the valley of the Río Lobo. First vines, olive trees and also fig trees are evidence of a mild climate. After an hour **Enériz (9)** is reached, after another ¾ hr. the remote small church of **Santa María de Eunate** seems to rise up out of the fields.

> [i] The eight-cornered pilgrimage church of **Santa María de Eunate** (end of the 12th century; see also photo on p. 1) is one of the most beautiful and curious examples of Romanesque architecture along the Way of St. James. It is attributed to the Order of Templar Knights on account of its similarities to the cathedral rock of Jerusalem. Other theories are that it once served as a graveside chapel of a princess or a queen. Excavations support the theory of its function as a pilgrim hospital, possibly of the Order of St. James.
>
> What is certain is that it was one of the three Navarian burial churches on the Way of St. James together with the chapel of Sancti Spiritus in Roncesvalles and the Santo Sepulcro church in Torres del Río. The name could also be derived from the Basque (Eunate, Basque for 100 doors), an illusion to the eight-cornered arcade around the building. Or it comes from 'eu nato', in English 'well-born'.
>
> The only decorations in the plain church are the capitals on top of the pillars with human and animal features, mythical beings and plant motifs. The figure of the Virgin Mary is an imitation of the missing Romanesque original. In 1943 Eunate was restored from top to bottom. The church is at its most beautiful at sunset (Tue.–Sun. 10.30–13.30 and 16.00–19.00). Pilgrimages: Easter Monday, 1st May, 24th August.

The route continues straight on from Eunate, crosses the country road and then goes left to **Obanos (11**; ¾ hr.; Obanos: see Stage 4 of Camino Francés). Alternatively continue left along the road (be careful of the traffic). After about 1.5km go left onto a farm track (marker stone) and about 2km along this track directly to Puente la Reina (total of 4.5km/good hour; arrows, markers stones).

Camino Francés in Navarra – from Saint-Jean-Pied-de-Port to Obanos and further to Logroño

The Navarra region (Comunidad foral de Navarra, in Basque Nafarroa) stretches over an area of 10,390km^2 and has about 620,600 inhabitants, roughly half of which live in the capital of Pamplona.

Independence of mind and self-determination characterise the history of Navarra. Around 75 BC the Roman commander Pompeius captured the largest Basque settlement, the future Pamplona. But after the fall of the Roman kingdom the Basque people were successful against Visigoth and Franconian invaders, and also the Arabs could never really gain a foothold in the region. In the 11th century the realm of Pamplona (from the 12th century the kingdom of Navarra) under King Sancho Garcés III experienced its largest expansion: it reached from Castilla y León to the county of Barcelona, in the north into the French Gascogne. Sancho Garcés was also a patron of the earlier pilgrim movement. The dynasty ended with the death of Sancho VII in the 13th century. Navarra forfeited a large part of its territory and came under French influence.

In the 16th century Fernando I of Aragón conquered the areas lying south of the Pyrenees for the Castilian crown. The part lying north of the Pyrenees (in French, Basse Navarre, lower Navarra) went to France. Although Navarra had been ruled by a viceroy, it received extensive privileges (fueros) such as its own political institutions and legislation.

Navarra has never relinquished its Basque inheritance. The second official language next to Castilian (high Spanish) is Basque (Euskera). Many towns and villages have two names (e.g. Roncesvalles/Orreaga, Pamplona/ Iruñea,

Delightful scenery characterises the start of the Pyrenean stage.

The red and white costume of Sanfermin in a souvenir shop in Pamplona.

Estella/Lizarra), but only a quarter of the population of the Basque country (Pais Vasco) and Navarra speaks Basque. They have never strived for independence in Navarra unlike the neighbouring Basque country.

ETA (*Euskadi Ta Askatasuna* – Basque homeland and freedom), founded in 1959, had been waging since the 1960s an armed struggle against oppression and for the independence of the Basque country. In the following 40 years 858 people lost their lives in ETA attacks. In the autumn of 2011 they declared a ceasefire.

Navarra today belongs to the richest and most expensive regions of Spain. Besides the service industry (also in the area of tourism, for example, especially in the Pyrenees), agriculture (vegetables, cereal, wine) is an important means of earning a living. Moreover, Navarra is one of the forerunners in the use of wind energy.

From Roncesvalles onwards the Way of St. James runs for about 140km through Navarra as the first section of the Camino Francés. The landscape as far as Pamplona is characterised by the very green Pyrenean mountain countryside with dense forests and extensive pastureland. In the foothills the terrain becomes flatter and the climate milder. Except for the area of Greater Pamplona, rural areas predominate and here the land is cultivated for arable farming and wine growing.

The rugged side of the Pyrenees when ascending the Route Napoléon.

In contrast to the Camino Aragonés the path in Navarra offers a whole series of historically significant landmarks (including Roncesvalles, Pamplona, Puente la Reina).

Thanks to the quite dense network of hostels the various stages in Navarra can be quite flexible – ideal for walkers who, at the start of the path, are not very sure of their capabilities.

7¾ hrs.
24,9 km

Saint-Jean-Pied-de-Port – Roncesvalles/Orreaga

1

Starting point: St-Jean-Pied-de-Port/France (169m, pop. 1,500). See p. 15.

Hostels: In **Saint-Jean-Pied-de-Port** there is a plethora of hostels and other accommodation so the following list in no way claims to be complete: **(1)** MH, ●●●, 32 B/8 € (incl. breakfast). Rue de la Citadelle, 55. Reception, information, pilgrim passport from pilgrim office (Accueil, Rue de la Citadelle, 39), 7.30–22.00, tel: 00 33 (0) 559 370 509. Beautiful old town house, kitchen, washing machine/drier. Pilgrims on foot have preference over those arriving by bus or train. Allowed access from 14.00 onwards, all year. **(2)** PH, ●●●, 14 B/half board 27,50 €. Gîte Azkorria, Rue de la Citadelle, 50, tel: 0033 (0) 559 370 053. Washing machine/drier, internet, garden. June–Dec. **(3)** PH, ●●●, 18 B/8 €. Esprit du Chemin, Rue de la Citadelle, 40 (opposite Accueil), tel : 00 33 (0) 559 372 468. Beautiful old town house, terrace, garden. Evening meal, breakfast/packed lunch on request. Two nights accommodation/reservation possible. April–end Sept. **(4)** PH, ●●●, 48 B/16 €. Aub. du Pelerin, Rue de la Citadelle, 25. Tel: 0033 (0) 559 491 086 or 00 33 (0) 678 446 210. Evening meal, breakfast, garden, internet. Reservation possible. 16–22.30, April–Oct. **(5)** PH, ●●●, 15 B/15 €, DR 20 €. Alb. Ultreia, Rue de la Citadelle, 8, tel: 0033 (0) 680 884 622. Kitchen, internet. 7.00–11.00 and 16.00–22.00. April–mid of Oct. **(6)** PH, ●●●, 14 B/12–14 €. Refuge Esponda, Rue du Trinquet, 9, tel: 0033 (0) 679 075 252. Kitchen, washing machine. All year. **(7)** PH, ●●●, 20 B/15 € with breakfast. Le Chemin vers les Etoiles, Rue d'Espagne, 21, tel: 0033 (0) 559 372 071. Kitchen, evening meal, washing machine/drier, internet, spacious old building. 14.00–23.00, Easter–Oct. **(8)** PH, ●●●, 12 B/donations (at least 15 €). Refuge Accueil Paroissial Maison Kaserna. Rue d'Espagne, 43, tel: 0033 (0) 559 376 517.

Communal evening meal, breakfast. About mid April–Sept. **(9)** PH, ●●●, 22 B/12 €, DR 40 €. Gîte Zuharpeta, Rue Zuharpeta, 5, tel: 0033 (0) 559 373 588, mobile 0033 (0) 621 300 305. Rest., internet, garden. Reservation possible. From 12.00, mid March–Oct. **(10)** PH, ●●●, 14 B/12,50 €, DR 30 €. Gîte Compostella, Route d'Arneguy, 6, tel: 0033 (0) 559 370 236. Kitchen. Reservation possible. All year. **(11)** PH, ●●●, 18 B/from 18 €. Gîte Zazpiak Bat, 13 bis Route Maréchal Harispe (just under 1km outside, south of the village, on the left of the Camino), tel: 0033 (0) 675 783 623. Kitchen (Nov.–March), washing machine, lots of space, terrace. All year. 'Route Napoléon': **Honto/Huntto** (492m), PH, ●●, 22 B/15 € (half-board 33 €). Ferme Ithurburia, tel: 0033 (0) 559 371 117. Kitchen, washing machine/drier, internet, quite roomy. All day, all year. **Refuge Orisson** (800m), PH, ●●●, 18 B/half board 32 €, tel: 00 33 (0) 559 491 303, mobile: 00 33 (0) 681 497 956 (better to phone beforehand). Washing machine, restaurant, terrace. All day, March–Oct. Route via Valcarlos: **Valcarlos-Luzaide** (350m, pop. 420), MH, ●●●, 24 B/10 €. Town hall: tel: 948 790 199, Plaza Santiago. Kitchen, washing machine, entrance with code, contact tel: 646 048 883, all year. **Roncesvalles/Orreaga** (962m, pop. 28), RH, ●●●, 180 B/10 €. Alb. de la Colegiata, tel: 948 760 000. Modern extension of the monastery. If necessary at least 120 B in the old pilgrim hospice and chalets, in the winter accommodation if necessary in former small hostel. Washing machine/drier, internet, kitchen/microwave, sale of ready meals, lockers. Exhibition of pilgrim passports.13.00–22.00, all year.

Grade and route: (1) France: red and white waymarkers of GR 65 (Chemin de St. Jacques de Compostela/Route Napoléon). In Spain yellow arrows. **(2)** Big variation in height but good paths.

Height difference: 1,270m in ascent, 480m in descent. Via Valcarlos: 1,080m ascent, 280m descent.

Critical points: none in fine weather. If the weather's bad and also in winter the alternative via Valcarlos is recommended (6½ hrs./ 22.5km). This route follows the little asphalt road or goes along the D-933/N-135, only 7km on woodland paths.

Scenery: in fine weather the 'Route Napoléon' can be a unique experience. Shortly after Saint-Jean-Pied-de-Port the path ascends with more and more lovely views into the valleys and the surrounding mountains. At the top it passes wide

alpine pastures of sheep and on the Spanish side penetrates forests again.

Local services: Saint-Jean-Pied-de-Port all services; Honto/Huntto ⌂ 🚐 🍴 @; Col de Bentarte (1,326 m) 🚐; Valcarlos 🍴 ⌂ 🗺 A € 🚐; Roncesvalles 🍴 ⌂ 🚐 i 🚌 @ € cash machine in Hostal La Posada, 🛏 with pilgrim blessings Mon.–Fri. 20.00, Sat.– Sun. 18.00 (info in the hostel).

Remarks: the height difference should not deter you from the Route Napoléon. Thanks to the good paths it can also be easily walked by less experienced hikers, provided sufficient time is allowed and you have taken plenty of food and water with you.

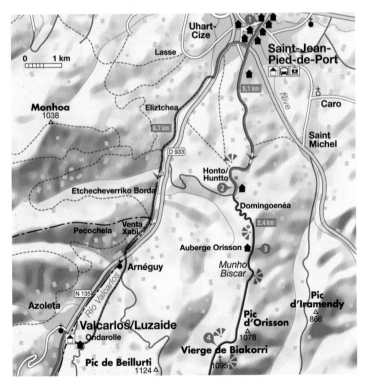

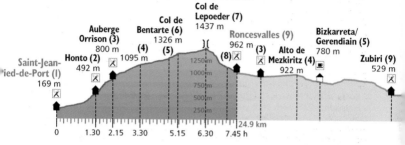

796.8   791.4 789.0 785.2   780.0 776.1 771.9 km

Col de
Lepoeder (7)
1437 m

Auberge   Col de
Orrison (3)   Bentarte (6)   Roncesvalles (9)   Bizkarreta/
800 m   1326 m   962 m   Gerendiain (5)
Honto (2)   (4)   (5)   (8)   (3)   780 m   Zubiri (9)
Saint-Jean-   492 m   1095 m   Alto de   529 m
ied-de-Port (I)   Mezkiritz (4)
169 m   922 m

1250m
1000m
750m
500m
250m

                                                                            24.9 km
0   1.30 2.15 3.30   5.15   6.30   7.45 h

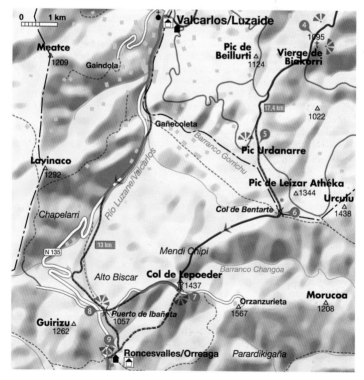

59

i **Saint-Jean-Pied-de-Port** (Basque *Donibane Garazi*) is the capital of the region of Basse Navarre in the French Basque country. The small town at the foot of Roncesvalles pass (also Cisa pass) is the last stopping place on the three pilgrim routes going through France before going over the Pyrenees to Spain. The Roman connecting road between France (Bordeaux) and Spain (Astorga) over the '**Summus Pyreneus**' followed the narrow valley of the Luzaide river via Valcarlos and the **Ibañeta pass**, a route already used by the Celts. For the march to Spain Napoleon's troops chose the strategically more favourable path over the **Lepoeder pass**, today known as the Route Napoléon. 6 HOURS

From the 12th–16th century **Saint-Jean-Pied-de-Port** belonged to the (Spanish) kingdom of Navarra until the region finally fell to the French in 1589. The Basque language is alive on both sides of the boundary with the same traditions as, for example, the ball game of pelote (Spanish 'pelota', a kind of cross between tennis and squash played with the hand). Saint-Jean-Pied-de-Port was declared a world heritage site by UNESCO in 1988. Pilgrims have been entering the old town with its elegant old buildings and little paved streets since the Middle Ages through the **Porte de St. Jacques** and go along the **Rue de la Citadelle**, named after the military site (citadel, 17th century) high above the town. The **Prison des Évêques** (prison of bishops) is on this street and its original function is uncertain. A small museum of the Way of St. James has been set up in the vaulted hall (13th century).

At the exit from the old town can be found the Gothic **Eglise Notre Dame de St. Jean Pied de Port** (13th/14th century); opening times from the tourist office, Place de Gaulle, 14.

Public holidays: saint's days middle of August. Cultural days end of September.
Gastronomy: fromage de brebis or Ossau-Iraty (sheep's cheese), pipérade (omelette with Bayonner ham and pepper pods), truite (trout).
Information: www.saintjeanpieddeport-paysbasque-tourisme.com.

Follow **Rue de la Citadelle (1)** downhill and come through the town gateway and over the river Nive into Rue d'Espagne. After the Porte d'Espagne you will see a sign for the Chemin de St. Jacques. In fine weather go straight ahead and take the steeply ascending Rué de Maréchal Harispe. (In bad weather, i.e. mainly snow, follow the sign to the right onto the Valcarlos route.) From now on the route is indicated by the red and white waymarkers of the GR 65 long distance path. After an hour follow the road sign for Roncevaux/Orreaga to the right uphill. After a good ½ hr. you reach the hamlet of **Honto/Huntto (2)**.

After that the path takes a small shortcut along a grassy path, but after ½ hr., just before a spring and an information board, joins the little road again. After ¼ hr. you reach the **Auberge Orisson (3)**, a café with a view, which is an inviting place to stop for a break. Following the road further uphill you come to a small crossroads after 1¼ hrs. and the **Vierge de Biakorri (4)** situated further on the left (1,095m).

*The small statue of the **Vierge de Biakorri** (also called d'Orrison) can just be seen on the precipitous rock formation diagonally left of the path. There used to be a pilgrim hospital close by in the Middle Ages. Not far away lie the ruins of the former Château Pignon, from which the Spanish used to control the area in the 16th century.*

*Here the path crosses wide pastureland where the longhaired **Manech sheep** are kept. The piquant Ossau-Iraty cheese is produced from their milk. The sheep (also horses, goats and beef cattle) move around freely and pasture fences are unusual. The animals have precedence over vehicles and walkers and are not to be disturbed!*

At the crossroads follow the small asphalt road to the right uphill. After 1 hr. the path leaves the asphalt road and continues as a beaten path past a stone cross (**Croix Thibaut, 5**) where many pilgrims have left behind mementos. The path crosses a small pass (a tiny stone shelter afterwards on the right) and ½ hr. later – along the French/Spanish border – in a small section of wood you reach Roland's spring and cross the official border into Spain/Navarra to arrive at the nearby **Col de Bentarte** (**6**; 1,326m).

From now on the yellow arrow becomes your constant and reliable companion on the route to Santiago de Compostela. At first along quite level, then ascending woodland and forest paths the highest point of this stage is reached after 1¼ hrs., the **Col de Lepoeder** (**7**; 1,437m), from where you can see a long way off onto the plain south of Roncesvalles. A wooden sign indicates the direct, but sometimes very steep and stony, path through the wood to Roncesvalles (1 hr.). The more comfortable route is on the right along the recommended (*recomendado*) Camino. Along this asphalt road, with a few shortcuts along beaten paths, you come to the **Puerto de Ibañeta** (**8**; 1,057m) in ¾ hr. It's now another half an hour along a lovely forest path to **Roncesvalles/Orreaga (9)**.

The pastures at high altitude belong to the long-haired Manech sheep.

On the way from the Col de Lepoeder to the Puerto de Ibañeta.

ℹ️ The path through the valley of the Río Luzaide over the **Ibañeta pass**, also known as Puerto de Roncesvalles, was the most important pass over the Pyrenees in the Middle Ages. Not only, because it brought together three pilgrim ways coming from France, but also because, at an altitude of 1,057m, it was less of a hurdle than the 1640m high Somport pass. The battle took place here in 778 on which the **song of Roland** was based dating from the 12th century (French 'Chanson de Roland', Spanish 'Canción de Roldán'). After his ill-fated campaign against the Moors in Zaragoza the army of Charles the Great (742–814) retreated from Spain. The rearguard under the command of the knight Roland was attacked on the Ibañeta pass by a Basque army in order to avenge the destruction of Pamplona by the Franks. Roland and several other knights were killed as a result. In the later epic tale the Basque attackers were transformed into Moors, Roland into the courageous hero and Charles the Great into the saviour of Christendom – a version which suited the world view of Christian Spain fighting against the Moorish rulers. At the top of the pass the modern **Capilla del Salvador** (1965) and the Roland monolith are a reminder of these events. A monastery stood here in the 11th century and the pilgrim hospital that was later transferred to Roncesvalles. A bell guided the pilgrims on their way in the fog since there was a high risk of getting lost in the wood and being at the mercy of the wolves. The tradition of putting a wooden cross into the earth at the Cross of Charlemagne (Cruz de Carlomagno) has continued to this day. See the following stage for information about Roncesvalles.

Hostels: 2.5km after Auritz/Burguete/1.5km before Espinal: in **Camping Urrobi**, ☕☕, 42 B/10,30 €. Reservation (11.00–20.00), tel: 948 760 200. Rest., shop, washing machine, drier. Apr.–Oct. **Aurizberri/Espinal** (868m, pop. 230), PH, ☕☕☕, 22 B/13 € with breakfast (also DR/3-bed room). Alb. Irugoienea, c/ Oihanilun, 2, tel: 649 412 487. About 600m on the left away of the path. Washing machine/drier, Wi-Fi, evening meal, provisions for journey. All day, March–Oct. **Zubiri** (529m, pop. 420), **(1)** PH, ☕☕☕, 24 B/10 €. Alb. Zaldiko, Puente la Rabia, 1, tel: 609 736 420. Microwave, washing machine/drier, internet. From 12.00, otherwise by telephone, March–Oct., rest of the year by reservation. **(2)** PH, ☕☕☕, 57 B/ from 15 € with breakfast (also SR/DR). El Palo de Avellano, Avda. Roncesvalles, 16, tel: 948 304 770 or 666 499 175. Washing machine, drier, rest., internet. 13.00–22.00 about April–Sept., Oct.–March only groups. **(3)** MH, ☕☕, 80 B/6 €. Tel: 628 324 186. Basic hostel in old school. Kitchen, internet. Reception 12.00–19.00, open until 22.00, Easter–Oct. **Larrasoaña** (499m, pop. 140), MH, ☕☕, 73 B/6 €. In the village, tel: 948 304 384. 3 buildings, kitchen, internet, pilgrim passport. Reception Apr.–May 15.00–19.30, June–Sept. 13.30–19.30, all year except 10th Dec.–10th Jan.

Grade and route: well marked, moderately difficult. Predominantly forest paths and farm tracks. Two small passes (Alto de Mezkiritz, 922m, and Alto de Erro, 801m).

Height difference: 410m in ascent, 870m in descent.

Critical points: none.

Scenery: a scenically beautiful stage through the foothills of the Pyrenees reminiscent of low mountains in central Europe. Dense forests, pastures and many small Pyrenean villages along the way. From Zubiri the path follows the Río Arga.

Local services: Auritz/Burguete (890m, pop. 290) 🅇 🏠 🖃 € 🅰 ✚ c/ Berexi, tel: 948 760 300; Aurizberri/Espinal 🅇 🖃 🏠 ✈ @; Bizkarreta/Guerendain (785m, pop. 95) 🖃 🖃 🏠 ✈; Linzoáin (745m, pop. 50) ✈; Alto de Erro (801m) snackbar; Zubiri 🅇 🏠 🖃 € 🅰 @; Ilarratz (558m, pop. 20) ✈; Ezkirotz (539m, pop. 20) ✈; Larrasoaña 🅇 🏠 🖃 @.

Remarks: (1) last opportunity in Zubiri for shopping until you reach Trinidad de Arre, corner shop in Larrasoaña. **(2)** The path crosses pastureland a few times that is secured with small wooden gates. The signs 'cierren el portillo' remind you to always close the gate behind you.

*ℹ The Augustine abbey of **Roncesvalles** (Basque **Orreaga**) founded in around 1130 quickly developed into an important and much praised stage destination along the pilgrim way. The reasons for this were partly geographical, but the proximity to the location of the colourful Roland legend might also have played a significant role. The generous food rations distributed in the monastery were also very popular. Pilgrims enter the complex of buildings across the courtyard of the new hospital built at the start of the 18th century, today the pilgrim hostel. A passageway brings you through to the Gothic collegiate church **Colegiata de Santa María** (13th/14th century, open 8.00–20.00). Be sure to see the impressive high altar with a Gothic figure of the Virgin Mary richly clad in gold and silver, **Nuestra Señora de Roncesvalles**. Adjacent to the church are the cloisters (**claustro**), a new building from the 17th century after its predecessor from the 12th century had collapsed under* the weight of too much snow. Behind it is the **Capilla de San Agustín**, the former Gothic chapter house where the remains of King Sancho VII are laid. The pilgrim office can be found on the ground floor of the **library** which contains 15,000 books (not open to the public) and the **museum**. One of the most valuable pieces in the museum is the splendid chessboard, the **Ajedrez de Carlomagno** (14th century, named after Charles the Great because of the divisions of the chessboard). (Daily 10.00–14.00 and 15.30–19.00 (Nov.–March until 18.00, closed Christmas and January. Entrance fee 4.20 €, pilgrims 3.20 €). The building behind is now used as holiday apartments. The Gothic **Iglesia de Santiago** (13th century) is below the monastery. Next door the oldest building of the complex has been preserved, the pilgrimage chapel, **Capilla del Espíritu Santo** (12th century), allegedly built by Charles the Great as a sepulchre for the knights who perished in the battle on the pass, but it had certainly served the same purpose since before the 12th century, www.roncesvalles.es.

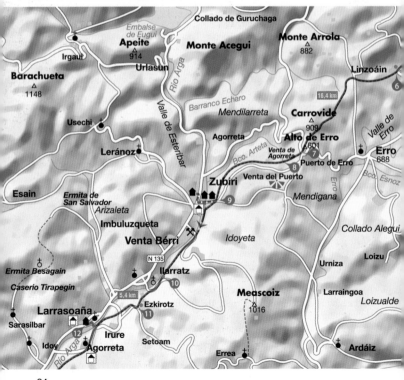

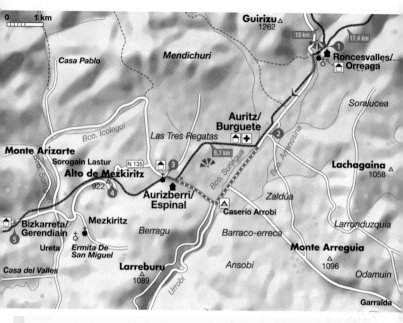

Public holidays: every Sunday in May and beginning of June there are pilgrimages of penitents in honour of the Virgin of Roncesvalles – a tradition dating from the 12th century – when some pilgrims wear garments of penitence.

Gastronomy: the cheese maker's, the Quesería SAT-Roncesvalles, produces and sells sheep's cheese with its Queso Idiazabal mark of origin.

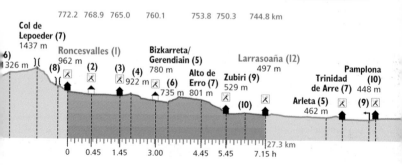

Frosty autumn morning in the Pyrenaen foothills.

A footpath starts at the **monastery (1)** next to the road. After about 300m you will see a stone pilgrim cross (14th century) on the left hand side of the road. Coming through a lush deciduous forest you reach **Auritz/Burguete (2; ¾ hr.).** In the village the Camino leaves the main road to the right (straight on to the campsite) and as a farm track winds its way through idyllic forest and pastureland. After coming to the top of a small pass descend to **Aurizberri/Espinal (3; 1 hr.;** about 600m left along the main road to the hostel). Go a short way through the village then leave it again to the left. Walk along forest paths and agricultural tracks over a hill to reach the **Alto de Mezkiritz (4; 922m, ½ hr.)** where the N-135 is crossed. There's a small sculpture of Nuestra Señora de Roncesvalles at the side of the road. The path enters a dense beechwood where there is little light even when the Sun is shining. After a little while the forest path becomes a concrete path. Along this path you come to **Bizkarreta/Gerendiain (5; ¾ hr.).** The concrete path becomes a gravel path again which brings you to **Linzoáin (6; ½ hr.).** From here a forest path first ascends, then continues up and down to finally lead downhill to **Alto de Erro (7; 801m, 1¼ hrs.).** Along the way can be found the 'Pasos de Roldán', large, longish erratic boulders that are said to correspond to Roland's stride. Down a steeply sloping forest path, past the ruins of the **Venta del Puerto (Agorreta, 8)** you come to **Zubiri (9)** in one hour. Go right across the bridge to the village and the hostels.

> *i* *Zubiri* bridge is also called In the vernacular **Punte de la Rabia**, bridge of rabies. It was thought that animals with the disease would be cured if they crossed the bridge three times.

Continuing straight ahead past Zubiri walk through the spoil area of a magnesium factory and after **Illaratz (10; ¾ hr.)** and **Ezkirotz (11; ¼ hr.)** you arrive at a fork before **Larrasoaña (12; ½ hr.).** Go across the bridge to the right and then turn left in the village to reach the hostel 300m away.

Hostels: Huarte (448m, pop. 6,000), MH, ●●●, 60 B/6 €. A good ¼ hr. after Arleta, from there 1.5km; Pl. San Juan, tel: 948 074 329. Roomy, disabled friendly facilities, kitchen, washing machine/drier, internet. Suitable for groups. 13.00–22.00, Apr.–Nov. **Trinidad de Arre/Villava** (431m, pop. 10,500), **(1)** RH, ●●●, 34 B/ 8 €. Order of Hermanos Maristas, tel: 948 332 941. Kitchen, washing machine, garden; mass in church of the Order: Sun. 11.00. From 14.00, all year. **(2)** MH, ●●●, 54 B/ 14 € € with breakfast. C/ Pedro de Atarrabia, 17–19, Reservation tel: 948 581 804. Washing machine/drier, Wi-Fi. Reception 11–20.00, all year. **Pamplona** (448m, pop. 197,500), **(1)** SH, ●●●, 24 B/6 €. Casa Paderborn, Paderborn (Germany) society of St. James pilgrims. Playa Caparroso, 6. Tel: 948 211 712. Located on the river bank 300m after Magdalena bridge on the left. Also open at Sanfermin. Washing machine/drier. 6.00–8.00 and 13.30–22.00. Mar.–Nov. **(2)** SH, ●●●, 112 B/7 €. In Iglesia de Jesús y María (near to the cathedral), tel: 948 222 644. Kitchen, washing machine/ drier, internet. 12.00–23.00, April–Oct. N.B. Open during Sanfermin (6th–14th July) but closed 25th Jan.–15th Feb.! **Cizur Menor** (462m, pop. 2,000) **(1)** RH, ●●●, 27 B/4 €. Order of the Knights of Malta, tel: 616 651 330. Spacious, kitchen with basic provisions, breakfast (donations), drinks machine. About 12.00–22.00, May–Sept./mid Oct. **(2)** PH, ●●●, 52 B/10 €. Alb. Maribel Roncal, tel: 948 183 885. Kitchen, internet, washing machine/drier, garden. 12.00 (winter from 14.00)–20.00, Dec.–Oct., phone to see if open the rest of the year.
Grade and route: well marked, easy. As far as Pamplona mainly on unsurfaced paths. In the municipal area you will find the yellow arrows on street lights, kerb stones or house walls (sometimes very high up).
Height difference: 250m in ascent,

270m in descent.
Critical points: at the end of the village of Burlada read the route description carefully.
Scenery: after some beautiful stretches in the valley of Río Arga the path from Trinidad de Arre onwards enters the area of Greater Pamplona. Although Pamplona is the town with the biggest population along the Way of St. James, the path through the streets is comparatively pleasant. Pilgrims enter Pamplona through the old part of the town, are guided through to the citadel park and leave the town very quickly again after a short section through the new town.
Local services: Akerreta (531m, pop. 10) 🏠; Irotz (477m, pop. 30) picnic area 🍴; Trinidad de Arre/Villava 🍴 🏠 🛏 € 🍴 ✉ 🚌 @ 🅰 ✚ Pl. Miguel Indurain s/n, tel: 948 335 022; Pamplona all public services, 🛏 information in hostels 🚌 bus station, 🚍 buses station 🚌 Yanguas y Miranda, 2, tel: 948 203 566. Autobuses Artieda, tel: 948 300 287 (bus route Pamplona – Roncesvalles) 🚉 Pl. de la Estación, Renfe, tel: 902 240 202 ✈ domestic flights, tel: 948 168 700, Iberia, tel: 948 317 955 ✚ Hospital Navarra c/ Irunlarrea, tel: 948 422 222, Clinica Universitaria, Avda. de Navarra s/n, tel: 948 255 400; Cizur Menor 🛏 🍴 @ 🅰 🛏 🍴 🚌 🚍 Iglesia de Malta Sun. 18.00, San Miguel parish church Mon, Wed, Fri. 10.00, Sun. 11.00, Sat. 20.00.
Remarks: during Sanfermin fiesta (6th–14th July) it's best to avoid Pamplona when it is overcrowded due to the fiesta and accommodation is very hard to find (alternative: Aragon route).

Change of scenery beyond Cizur Menor.

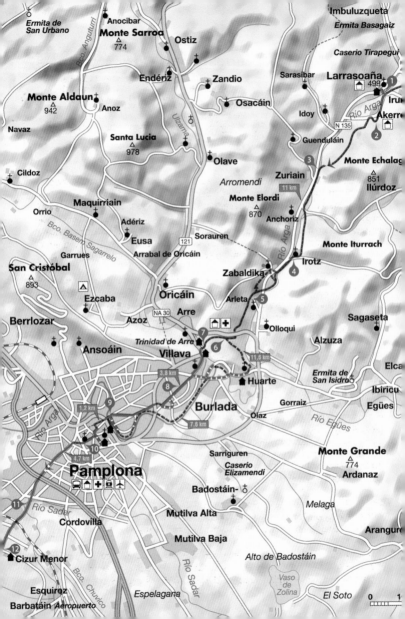

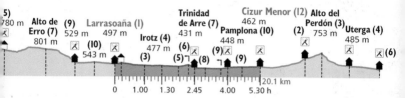

744.6 740.5 738.1 733.6   729.0 724.5 km

5) 780 m   Alto de   (9)   Larrasoaña (I)   Trinidad   Cizur Menor (I2) Alto del
           Erro (7)   529 m   497 m   de Arre (7)   462 m   Perdón (3) Uterga (4)
           801 m   431 m   Pamplona (I0)   753 m   485 m
                      (10)   Irotz (4)   448 m
                      543 m   477 m   (6)   (9)
                                   (3)   (5)   (8)   (9)   (6)

0   1.00   1.30   2.45   4.00   5.30 h   20.1 km

From **Larrasoaña (1)** first return to the bridge over the Arga, then turn right. A steeply ascending little road brings you to **Akerreta (2**; ¼ hr.). A lovely forest path then runs downhill again and meets the stream at the bottom. Next to the river you come to the hamlet of **Zuriain (3**; ¾ hr.). At the end of the village go across the bridge on the right and up to the N-135. Walk a short section along the side of the road before returning to the riverbank again to reach **Irotz (4**; ½ hr.). Just before the picnic area the path divides:

Main path: the new official route leads along the footpath beside the Arga past Zabaldika (on the way a sign indicates the village up to the right), then under the N-135 to a rest area. The path ascends here, bends to the left and then continues more on the level again to **Arleta (5**; ¾ hrs.).

Alternative: the old historic route keeps along a narrow path on the right above the footpath, crosses the N-135 by the houses and climbs up to **Zabaldika** with the **Iglesia de San Esteban** (a good ¼ hr.). The church dates originally back to the 12th century and was rebuilt many times until the 18th century. The altar is from the 17th century. The key can be obtained from the Sisters of the RSCJ (Society of the Sacred Heart) in the house next door, entrance twice to the right round the corner.

From the church follow the arrows and at the sharp left hand bend take the path straight ahead. It runs across the hillside above the road. At the small white house after about 600m keep straight on along the path (you could descend left, but the very steep and stony incline is not recommended). About 100m further on the path goes round a sharp left hand bend down to the main path. Continue along this path to **Arleta (5**; 20 mins. from Zbaldika).

The path continues across the slope, goes under the N-121 (shortly afterwards a turn-off left to Huarte, **6**) and after a good half an hour meets the medieval bridge across the Río Ulzama before **Trinidad de Arre/Villava (7)**.

*ℹ️ From **Trinidad de Arre** bridge your gaze falls on the **Iglesia de la Santísima Trinidad** (13th century) situated at the other end. Since the Middle Ages it has belonged to the convent of the Hermanos Maristas which still runs a pilgrim hostel today.*

69

On the medieval Trinidad de Arre bridge. In the background the church with the hostel.

The neighbouring town of **Villava** directly adjacent is the birthplace of Spain's great cyclist **Miguel Indurain** (*1964). The five times winner of the Tour de France is not only a freeman of the town, but a monument has been dedicated to him and also a square named after him.

The Camino is largely urban from now on. Following the main road you come directly to **Burlada (8)**. At the end of the village, at the corner house with the Michelin garage, follow the yellow arrow to the right into c/ Larrainzar to the N-121. (You could also go straight ahead to the next roundabout and turn left there onto the N-121). Another arrow points straight ahead; if you follow this (longer) alternative, turn right at the roundabout onto the N-121. Both ways bring you to a garden centre where you continue left onto a shady path through a park. This path joins the Camino de Burlada. You soon have your first view, across the allotments and trees, of the silhouette of medieval Pamplona. Go across the **Puente de la Magdalena** (9; left after that to the Casa Paderborn hostel) and through the old defensive moats directly into the old town of **Pamplona** (10; 1¼ hrs. from Trinidad de Arre).

ℹ️ **Pamplona** (in Basque, **Iruña** or **Iruñea**) is the capital of the autonomous region of Navarra. The town is said to be of Roman foundation dating back to the 1st century BC. A varied history followed with invasions by the Visigoths (5th century),

the Franks (6th century) and finally the Arabs (732). But already in 755 the Basques managed to shake off Moorish rule. In the year 778 Charles the Great, after an unsuccessful campaign against the Arabs at Zaragoza, had the previously Basque fortress razed to the ground to cut off his Moorish pursuers' path. The ensuing battle on the Ibañeta pass went down in history as the song of Roland. From the 9th century onwards the kingdom of Navarra was created with Pamplona as its capital, but the town's revival did not begin until the influx of pilgrims. Today Pamplona is a very nice place to live.

The unique and hair-raising bull running is world famous ('encierros'; the course, the Ruta de los Encierros, is waymarked in green on the town map) right through the centre of the old town at the time of **Sanfermin** (6th–14th July). Without Ernest Hemingway's novel 'The Sun. Also Rises' (1926) the spectacular and – especially for naïve foreigners extremely dangerous – bull running would have remained a totally standard patron saint's festival without any international popularity. In the 12th century French immigrants brought into the town the remains of Saint Firminius, who came from Pamplona but was sent as a missionary to France in the 3rd century. Since the 16th century the festival has been held in his honour at the start of July. The relics can be found in the **Iglesia de San Lorenzo**. (Mon.–Fri. 8.00–12.30 and 17.30–20.00, Sun. 8.30–13.45 and 17.30–20.00, free).

The festival begins on 6th July at 12.00 with the 'chupinazo', a volley of rockets and bangers let off from the balcony of the town hall (**Casa Consistorial**, façade 18th century). From then on the town transforms itself into a witch's cauldron through which there's a succession of parades with giant figures, numerous concerts and the whole community abandons itself into a collective frenzy of celebration and intoxication. Every morning, at 8.00 on the dot, the 'encierro' (bull running) takes place along the 850m long course from the Plaza de Santo Domingo to the bullring. Watching the daily live television broadcasts allow you to follow the not uncontroversial spectacle much more safely.

Statue of the bull running.

Pilgrims enter the old town quarter of **Navarrería** through the **Portal de Francia** or **Zumalacárregui**. The huge **Catedral de Santa María** stands close by. Behind the façade dating back to the 18th century lies hidden a beautiful Gothic church building from the 15th century. The founders of the cathedral, the royal couple Carlos III, the Noble, and Leonora de Trastámara, are buried in the chancel in an alabaster sarcophagus (around 1420). The choir stalls are worth noting (around 1530) as is the high altar in the Capilla Mayor. From the right hand aisle you come through an ostentatiously sumptuous gilded portal into one of the most beautiful cloisters (claustro) in Spain (built 1286–1419). High Gothic arches bestow it with a bright elegance. Next to the cloister you will find the Museo Diocesano. Amongst the inventory of the museum you will find a book of the gospels from the 13th century, a French reliquary casket from the Holy Tomb and also the Lignum Crucis, allegedly part of the cross of Jesus (cathedral: Mon.–Sat. 10.00–9.00, Sun./public holiday 10.00–14.00 and 18.30–21.00, museum and cloisters: 16th March–14th Nov. Mon.–Sat. 10.30–18.00, 15th Nov.–15th March Mon.–Sat. 10.30–17.00, Sun./public holidays closed, 5 €. www.catedraldepamplona.com).

Pamplona town hall.

A stroll through the streets between the town hall and the cathedral and along the remains of the town walls gives you a beautiful impression of the old town. There are numerous restaurants and cafés In the arcades around the **Plaza del Castillo**. The town fortress stood here until the building of the new citadel (**Ciudadela**, built between 1571 and 1645). Since the 17th century the 280,000m² **park** around the citadel has been the most popular place for a stroll amongst the inhabitants of Pamplona.

Gastronomy: in no way should you miss out on **pintxos**, fantastic small snacks (in other places know as tapas) which are enjoyed with a simple red wine in the many tascas and restaurants (especially in c/ Estafeta).

Information: www.turismodepamplona.es.

The way through Pamplona is well marked. After the old town walk along Calle Mayor which brings you into the citadel park. Then continue along C/ Puente del Hierro to reach the **university**, (**11**; ¾ hr. from the old town) at which point you leave Pamplona again. Following the footpath next to the country road you come to **Cizur Menor** (**12**; ¾ hr.).

i The small fortress-like Romanesque **Iglesia de San Miguel** at the eastern edge of the village of **Cizur Menor** was built in the 12th century by the Order of St. John which looked after a pilgrim hostel here. The church portal from the 13th century is worth seeing as well as the plain church tower.

The **Iglesia Parroquial** dedicated to the archangel Michael in the centre has a beautiful Romanesque portal.

Hostels: Zariquiegui (633m, pop. 160), PH, ◐◐◐, 16 B/10 € with breakfast. C/ San Andrés, 16, tel: 679 230 614. Washing machine, drier, microwave, internet, evening meal. 14.00–22.00, March–mid Oct., rest of time also for non-pilgrims. **Uterga** (499m, pop. 190), PH, ◐◐◔, 16 B/10 € (DR 50 €). Alb. Camino del Perdón, tel: 948 344 661. Bar/rest, internet. 8.30–21.30, closed 15th Nov.–15th Feb. **Obanos** (418m, pop. 950), PH, ◐◐◐, 36 B/7 €. Tel: 676 560 927 (Juan Irisarri). Comfortable old building. Microwave. 13.30–22.00, April–around mid Oct.

Grade and route: well marked. Predominantly farm tracks and hiking paths.

Height difference: 360m in ascent, 420m in descent.

Critical points: more than 1km on descent from Alto de Perdón, quite steep and stony.

Scenery: the hill of Alto de Perdón marks the change from the Pyrenean foothills to the mild climate of the part of Navarra characterised by winegrowing and agriculture. From the top of the pass you are afforded a view to the north across Pamplona to the Pyrenees and in the south across an idyllic hilly landscape to Uterga.

Local services: Zariquiegui ⌧⛺@; Uterga ⌧⛺🛏@; Muruzábal (452m, pop.) ⌧🅰; Obanos ⌧⛺🍴🛏🅰€@⛪ 🏠 parish church 19.00.

Remarks: (1) The ascent to Alto de Perdón is not as steep and unpleasant as it looks. (2) Remember to take water in the summer.

From **Cizur Menor (1)** the path keeps on the level for the first half hour on the plain before slowly ascending a farm track and woodland path. The wind farm on the mountain ridge can already be seen in the distance. Past the ruins of the fortified palace of the Dukes of Guendulain (16th century) on a hill on the right, you come to **Zariquiegui (2**; a good 1¾ hr.). The path runs on the right across the side of the mountain up to **Alto del Perdón (3**; ¾ hr.) which offers a marvellous panorama.

ℹ️ *At the top of the **Perdón pass** there's a memorial to the chapel and the pilgrim hospital of **Nuestra Señora del Perdón** or also **de Astrain**. In 1996 Navarra's friends of the Way of St. James erected an unconventional sculpture of a pilgrim caravan next to it. Just below the pass is the spring called the **Fuente de la Teja**. Tradition holds that the devil offered some pilgrims a drink from the spring in the*

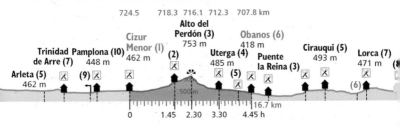

A pilgrim memorial on the Alto del Perdón ...

... and real pilgrims on the way to Obanos.

> hope that they would renounce God, the Holy Virgin or at least St. James. The brave pilgrims categorically refused the offer.

From the hill a very stony and steep path at first goes downhill, then becomes a pleasant hiking path to **Uterga** (**4**; a good ¾ hr.) and **Muruzábal** (**5**; ¾ hr.). In Muruzábal a little street turns left to the **Iglesia de Santa María de Eunate** ¾ hr. away (see Stage 6, Camino Aragonés). Continue straight ahead to **Obanos** (**6**; ½ hr.).

i *Obanos* *is where the pilgrim paths from Somport and Roncesvalles meet up, although Puente la Reina also claims to be that junction. In the 12th/13th century the village possessed one of the oldest democratic institutions in Spain: the Junta de Infanzones, a democratically elected council made up of members of the Klerus, the gentry, farmers and merchants. It functioned, amongst other things, as a court of law and represented citizens' rights against the monarchy, until the latter abolished the institution again.*

The place is famous for the ***Misterio de Obanos****, the lavish open-air theatre production of one of the most well known legends of the Way of St. James. With the participation of almost all the roughly 800 inhabitants of the village the story is told of the noble brother and sister, Felicia and Guillermo, children of the Duke of Aquitaine: after Felicia's pilgrimage to Santiago de Compostela she renounced her worldly title and riches and entered the convent. When she refused to obey Guillermo to go home and get married, he killed her. However, in remorse, he made a pilgrimage to Santiago, was converted and lived his life from then on as a devout hermit in the* ***Ermita de Arnotegui*** *on a mountain close to Obanos. Even if you do not understand any Spanish you are bound to enjoy the medieval atmosphere of this lively production in Obanos (every two years, next date: July 2014). Guillermo's skull is kept as a reliquary in a silver replica. Every Maundy Thursday water and wine are poured through the skull to be blessed.*

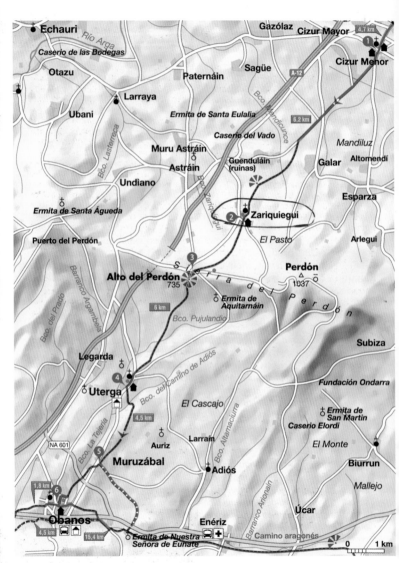

Echauri

Río Arga

Caserío de las Bodegas

Gazólaz

Cizur Mayor 4,7 km

1

Cizur Menor

Otazu

Paternáin

Sagüe

A-12

Bco. Mendicunce

Larraya

Ubani

Ermita de Santa Eulalia

6,2 km

Caserío del Vado

Mandiluz

Muru Astráin

Astráin

Bco. Lasterreca

Guendulain
(ruinas)

Galar Altomendí

Bco. Zariquiegui

Undiano

Ermita de Santa Águeda

2 Zariquiegui

Esparza

El Pasto

Arlegui

Puerto del Perdón

3

Alto del Perdón
735

Serie del Perdón

Perdón
1037

Barranco Argembela

Bco. del Prado

Ermita de
Aquitarnáin

Bco. Pujulandio

6 km

Subiza

Legarda

Bco. del Camino de Adiós

4

Uterga

El Cascajo

Fundación Ondarra

Ermita de
San Martín

Caserío Elordi

Bco. La Tejeria

4,5 km

Larrain

Bco. Altamaciurra

El Monte

Biurrun

NA 601

5

Muruzábal

Auriz

Adiós

Barranco Arañain

Mallejo

Úcar

1,8 km

6

Obanos

4,5 km

15,4 km

Ermita de Nuestra
Señora de Eunate

Enériz

Camino aragonés

0   1 km

Hostels: Puente la Reina (357m, pop. 2,800) **(1)** PH, ◐◐◐, 38 B/9–10 € (DR 36 €). Hotel Jakue, tel: 948 341 017. Washing machine/drier, internet, kitchen. Reception 12.00–20.00, mid Mar.–mid Oct. **(2)** RH, ◐◐, 100 B/4 €. Padres Reparadores, tel: 948 340 050. Kitchen, internet, garden. Very busy at peak times. 12.00–23.00, all year. **(3)** PH, ◐◐◐, 100 B/8 €. Alb. Santiago Apóstol, tel: 948 340 220. Washing machine, internet, pool, campsite, bar/rest., roomy; 650m from the centre. 12.00–23.00, Apr.–Oct. **Mañeru** (450m, pop. 420), PH, ◐◐◐, 12 B/10 € with breakfast. Alb. Lurgorri, c/ Esperanza 5, tel: 619 265 679. Kitchen, internet. Reception. 14.30–22.00, March–Oct. **Cirauqui** (495m, pop. 500), PH, ◐◐◐, 28 B/10 € (2 DR 40 €). Alb. Maralotx, tel: 678 635 208. Evening meal. From 13.00 onwards, Mar.–Oct. **Lorca** (469m, pop. 130), **(1)** PH, ◐◐◐, 14 B/7 € (DR 10 €). Tel: 948 541 190. Kitchen, internet, bar/rest., washing machine. Basic, but nice. All day, Apr.–mid Oct. **(2)** PH, ◐◐◐, 36 B/8 and 10 € (DR 25 and 40 €). Bodega del Camino, tel: 948 541 327. Washing machine/drier, kitchen, internet. Reception 12.00–20.00, all year. **Villatuerta** (422m, pop. 1,100) PH, ◐◐◐, 40 B/10 € with breakfast. Casa Mágica, tel: 948 536 095. Kitchen, washing machine/drier, internet. Spacious. 13.00–22.00, Apr.–Oct. (closed for 4 days mid-Aug. due to village fiesta). **Estella/Lizarra** (417m, pop. 14,000) **(1)** SH, ◐◐◐, 34 B/7 €. Alb. Anfas (society for the support of mentally handicapped people who, also as hospitaleros, look after the pilgrims). C/ Corderelos, 7, at the entrance to the village, sign to the right just before MH. Tel: 948 554 551. Kitchen, washing machine, internet. 13.00–22.00, June–Sept. **(2)** RH, ◐◐, 32 B/donations. C/ Mercado Viejo, 18, Parroquia de San Miguel, tel: 948 550 431. Kitchen, communal evening meal, internet. 12.00–22.00, all year. **(3)** MH, ◐◐, 98 B/5 €. Tel: 948 550 200. Kitchen, washing machine/drier, internet, breakfast; some beds too close together. Oct.–Apr. 14.00–22.00, May–June 13.30–22.00, July–Sept. 12.30–22.00. **(4)** YH, ◐◐◐, 150 B/pilgrims: 9,50 €/13 € in quiet room. Alb. juvenil municipal Oncineda, exit from the village about 200m on the right of Camino, tel: 948 555 022. Washing machine/drier, kitchen, evening meal/breakfast. 12.00–22.00, all year, Dec.–March groups only. **(5)** situated south of Estella, about 2km from the centre: Camping Lizarra, 250 B/from 9 €. Tel: 948 551 733. www.campinglizarra.com. Ideal for cyclists and groups.

Grade and route: moderate. Well marked. Little shade. Predominantly farm tracks and paths in a con-stant up-and-down.

Height difference: 350m in ascent, 330m in descent.

Scenery: delightful countryside with gently undulating hills, vineyards and cornfields. Small villages like Mañeru or Cirauqui date back to the Middle Ages. The motorway can be noisy between Puente la Reina and Lorca.

Critical points: none.

Local services: Puente la Reina ▱ ✗ € ✉ ⌂ ☐ Ⓐ @ ⌀ ▱ ⌂ Iglesia de Santiago Mon.–Sat. 10.00 and 19.30, Sun. 9.00, 12.00, 19.00 ✚ c/ San Pedro, tel: 948 348 003; Mañeru ✗ ⌁ ⌂ ☐ Ⓐ ▱ @; Cirauqui ▱ € ✗ Ⓐ ⌂ ▱; Lorca ✗ ⌁ ⌂ ▱ @ ▱; Villatuerta ⌂ ▱ ✗ Ⓐ ⌀ € ✚ c/ Ozalder, tel: 948 536 007; Estella/Lizarra ▱ ✗ € @ ⌂ Ⓐ ✉ ⌂ ▱ ⌀ ⌂ Igl. San Pedro de la Rúa Sun. 9.00 and 12.30 ✚ Paseo de la Inmaculada, 35, tel: 948 556 350.

Remarks: very busy in Puente la Reina in July/Aug.

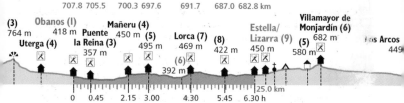

(3)	Obanos (I)		Mañeru (4)						Estella/	Villamayor de Monjardín (6)	
764 m	418 m	Puente	450 m	(5)	Lorca (7)	(8)		Lizarra (9)	682 m		
Uterga (4)		la Reina (3)		495 m	469 m	422 m		450 m	(5)		Los Arcos
		357 m							580 m		449
					(6)						
					392 m						

707.8 705.5   700.3 697.6   691.7   687.0 682.8 km

0   0.45   2.15   3.00   4.30   5.45   6.30 h   25.0 km

The path out of **Obanos (1)** goes left past the church. After that do not descend the road on the left, instead go the right along the front of the houses and down a path. Cross over the road at the bottom and walk through some allotments to reach **Hotel Jakue (2**; ½ hr.) and **Padres Reparadores hostel (3)** shortly afterwards at the start of **Puente la Reina**. To reach the **hostel of Santiago Apóstol** go along the Way of St. James through the village, over the bridge and on the other side of the road, up the little road diagonally right (¼ hr. from the centre).

i *The origins and development of **Puente la Reina** are closely connected with the elegant bridge (puente) from the 11th century which gave it its name. At the start of the 12th century Alfonso I, king of Navarra and Aragón, gave this place, located on the Río Arga, town status. More and more merchants and craftsmen, amongst them many French, settled on the left and right of the Pilgrim route. Still today the **Calle Mayor** runs in a straight line through the well preserved old town to the bridge over the Arga. It is said to have been built on the wishes of a queen (probably Doña Mayor, widow of Sancho Garcés III), hence the name: bridge of the queen (reina). Road and bridge construction was so important in the Middle Ages and made social and economic growth possible in many regions, also along the Way of St. James.*

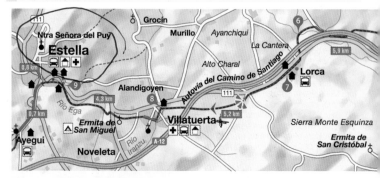

The former Templars' church, the **Iglesia del Crucifijo** (11th century, about 9.00–20.00), is named after the unusual pilgrim cross (12/13th century). The **crucifix** in a **Y-shape** is said to be a gift from Rhineland pilgrims. This and a second one in Carrión de los Condes are the only ones of their type in Spain. An archway connects the church with the monastery of St. John situated on the other side of the road. In the centre of town lies the **Iglesia de Santiago** (12th–14th century, redesigns in the 16th and 18th centuries) with the sculpture of **Santiago Beltza**, depicted on many postcards, the 'black' St. James due to the dark colour of his face (Mon.–Sat. 9.40–13.30 and 17.00–20.00, Sun./public holidays 18.40-20.10, winter until 19.40).
Public holidays: 24th–30th July patron saint festival in honour of Santiago, processions, fairs and bull running; last weekend in September fair and Carrera de layas (kind of stilts competition but on pitchforks).
Gastronomy: Sept./Oct. sale and preparation of pimientos del piquillo in the market at the edge of town (also available ready pickled in the supermarket). At this time the whole place smells of roasted peppers.

Leave Puente la Reina across the famous bridge and at the end of the bridge go left and then take a farm track on the right between the Río Arga and the N-111 in the direction of Logroño. After a good ¾ hr. there's a short but steep ascent that begins up to the right in the direction of the motorway. When you reach the top take the gravel path to the left next to the motorway to reach **Mañeru** (4; ¾ hr.; pilgrim cross at the start of the village, 16th century). Continue through cornfields and vineyards towards **Cirauqui** (5; ¾ hr.). Already from a distance you can see the cone-shaped medieval looking village as it rises up above the horizon. The path ascends steeply up through the village to the fortress-like Iglesia de San Román (13th century, portal modelled on that of the Iglesia de Santiago in Puente la Reina).

Going downhill again, the path leaves the village where a short section of an old Roman road (*calzada romana*) and a little old Roman bridge remain.

Keep going west ...

Then cross the motorway to the right. Steadily up and down for a quarter of an hour through fields and vineyards, you then cross the motorway to the left, go a short way between the A-12 and the old main road and straight afterwards under the A-12 to the right. Follow the road for a short way signposted 'Alloz/Canal de Alloz' , but you need to look out immediately for the turn-off left. Walk across the twin-arched medieval bridge over the **Río Salado** (**6**; in English salty river), spoken about in the Codex Calixtinus which says that the poisonous water will kill 'every horse on the spot'. After that you make a start on the ascent to **Lorca (7)** which brings you under the motorway again (1½ hrs. from Cirauqui). The shady village square is a welcome place to make a stop with its cool drinking fountain water and small bars. On your way out of Lorca follow the N-111 for a short while until the Camino turns off left again as a farm track parallel to the road. There's now a lovely view south of the 1044m high Montejurra. After an easy walk across flat terrain you come to **Villatuerta** (**8**; 1 hr.).

i In **Villatuerta** it's worth visiting the **Iglesia de la Asunción**. Originally Roman-esque it was rebuilt in Gothic style after its destruction in 1378. The high altar (middle of 17th century) decorated with gold makes a striking contrast to the plain inside of the church with its elegant vaulted ceiling.
The **Ermita de San Miguel** (10th century) lies in a remote position along the path just after Villatuerta. It once belonged to a monastery.

From Villatuerta leisurely tracks bring you into the valley of the Río Ega and to **Estella/Lizarra** (**9**; ¾ hr.).

i King Sancho Ramírez was instrumental in making **Estella** in around 1090 into a significant stopping place along the Way of St. James. He summoned in particular French settlers into the Basque village of **Lizarra**, gave the new settlement on the Río Ega town status and altered the course of the pilgrim way which originally ran further south. The town grew and quickly flourished. In the 13th century its wealth was comparable only to that of Burgos. The many magnificent civic and religious buildings earned Estella nicknames like 'Toledo of the north' and 'Estella, the beautiful' (Estella la bella). Aimeric Picaud praised Estella in the Codex Calixtinus as a welcoming town with 'good bread, excellent wine and meat and fish in abundance'. During the war of independence in the 19th century the star of Estella finally went down.

At the entrance to the village pilgrims pass the **Iglesia del Santo Sepulcro** (14th century). The one-nave, early Gothic building is certainly in a sorry state, but the portal still remains worth seeing. The showpiece of Estella is the late Romanesque church, the **Iglesia de San Pedro de la Rúa**. Elegant steps accentuate the impact of the raised building. You should see the church portal (13th century) and the cloister (12th century; Mon.–Sat. 10.00–13.30 and 18.30–20.30, free entry. Information about guided tours tel: 948 550 070). A beautiful Romanesque portal adorns the **Iglesia de San Miguel** (12th–14th century). The **Palacio de los Reyes de Navarra** (late 12th century, former king's palace, today Museo Gustavo de Maeztu) is the only example of civic Romanesque architecture in Navarra (Tue.–Sat. 9.30–13.00, Sun./public holidays 11.00–14.00, free entry). Next to it, the Renaissance fountain, the **Fuente de los Chorros** (16th century).

Public holidays: from 1st Friday in Aug. a one week patron saint festival (San Andrés) with large cattle market etc. On 25th May they celebrate the Virgen del Puy.

Gastronomy: asado de gorrín (suckling pig), rocas del Puy (roasted hazelnuts covered in chocolate), conchas del Camino (chocolate St. James shells).

If the fields have been harvested, the countryside is swathed in warm brown tones.

Hostels: Ayegui (477m, pop. 1,300) MH, ●●, 80 B/6 €. Left of the Camino, in sports hall, with about 22 beds being built in 2012. **Villamayor de Monjardín** (682m, pop. 140), **(1)** new pilgrim hostel with about 22 beds being built in 2012. **(2)** RH, ●●●, 25 B/7 €. Hogar de Monjardín. Dutch protestant foundation Oasis Trails, tel: 948 537 136; Renovated old building, quiet atmosphere, evening meal/breakfast, grace. Appropriate price-performance-ratio. 16.00–23.00, Apr.–Oct. **Los Arcos** (450m, pop. 1,290) **(1)** PH, ●●●, 54 B/8 € (price of DR on request). Alb. de la Fuente/Casa de Austria, tel: 948 640 797. Kitchen, washing machine/drier, internet, drinks machine, inner courtyard, fireplace. From 12.00 onwards, all year (except Christmas and Jan.). **(2)** PH, ●●●, 30 B/8 € (3 DR 35/45 €). Alb. Casa de la Abuela, Pl. de la Fruta, 8, tel: 948 640 250 and 630 610 721. Also for non-pilgrims, reservation possible. Kitchen, internet, washing machine/drier. From 12.00–22.00, March–Oct. **(3)** M/RH, ●●●, 70 B/6 €. Alb. Isaac Santiago, managed by volunteers from the Flemish association of St. James. tel: 948 441 091. Large, well equipped kitchen, drinks machine, telephone, internet, lots of room (old school house), garden, tents (max 8 people) allowed. 12.00–22.00, Easter–Oct. **(4)** PH, ●●●, 29 B/10 € (2 DR 35 €).(Near MH), Casa Alberdi, tel: 948 640 764 and 650 965 250. Washing machine/drier, kitchen, internet, Wi-Fi, space for tents. 14.00–23.00, all year except Jan./Feb. **Sansol** (496m, pop. 110) PH, ●●●, 14 B/5 €. Tel: 680 679 065. Kitchen, washing machine/drier. Internet. 12.30–23.00, Easter–Oct. **Torres del Río** (463m,

pop. 150), **(1)** PH, ●●●, 54 B/7 €. Casa Mariela, tel: 948 648 251. Kitchen, washing machine/drier, internet, bar/rest. 10.00–22.30, all year. **(2)** PH, ●●●, 40 B/10 € (4 DR 60 €, three 3-bed rooms 75 €). Alb. La Pata de Oca, c/ Mayor, 5, tel: 948 378 457. Kitchen, washing machine/drier, lockers, restaurant, internet. All day, all year. **(3)** PH, ●●●, 26 B/7 €, Casa Marí, tel: 948 648 409. Kitchen, washing machine, telephone, coffee/drinks machine, terrace, large separate bathrooms, masseur, lockers, paddock. Rather narrow rooms. 10.00–22.30, all year.

Grade and route: easy stage, well marked, predominantly broad gravel roads, flat terrain. Little shade.

Height difference: 420m in ascent, 410m in descent.

Critical points: there's a fork in the path after Irache monastery: the alternative on the left to 'Los Arcos via Luquín' does not go via Monjardín! To Monjardín follow signs for 'Los Arcos via Azqueta' on the right.

Scenery: scenically attractive. Reddish-brown earth paths between vineyards and cornfields with beautiful wide views. Unfortunately the idyllic landscape is spoilt by the noise of the new motorway in the first 45 mins. from Villamayor de Monjardín.

Local services: Ayegui ⊠ 🖾 🅰 @; Azqueta (580m, pop. 60) 🖾 🖾 🖾; Villamayor de Monjardín 🖾 @ 🖾 🖾 🗶 Wed/Fri. 9.30, Sun. 13.00; Los Arcos ⊠ 🖾 🖾 @ ➕ 🛈 🖾 🖾 🖾 Igl. de Santa María Mon.–Sat. 20.00, Sun 19.00 (with pilgrim blessings) ➕ c/ del Paseo, 4, tel: 948 640 860; Sansol 🅰 🖾; Torres del Río ⊠ 🖾 🖾 🖾 € @.

Remarks: no water or places for refreshments between Monjardín and Los Arcos (12 km), take water and food with you!

Leave the old town of **Estella (1)** by carrying straight on along the old pilgrim route. You come directly into the suburb of **Ayegui (2)**. From a long way off you can see the vineyard with the **wine fountain (3)** and the **monastery of**

Between heaven and earth, a pilgrim on his way to Sansol.

Irache (**4**; ¾ hr.) on the other side of the N-111, at the foot of Montejurra (1044m).

ℹ️ The **Monasterio de Santa María la Real de Irache** (also: Iratxe) is one of the oldest religious institutions in Navarra. It was first mentioned in writing in the year 958 and in the 11th century the Benedictine monks began the building of the new monastery on the foundations of a monastery that had already existed in the 8th century. The monastery experienced its heyday under Abbot Veremundo at the end of the 11th century. In Irache he founded (in Basque, iratze means fern) one of the first pilgrim hospitals on the Way of St. James and dedicated his whole life to it. St. Veremundo is the patron saint of the Way of St. James in Navarra. The huge monastic building combines architectural styles of Romanesque (main entrance and Portal de San Pedro), Renaissance (the 32 x 37m large cloister) and Baroque styles (church façade). The monastery has not been used since 1985, but there are plans to turn it into a Parador Nacional (state-run luxury hotel). Open Wed.–Sun. 10.00–13.15 and 16.00–19.00, free entry. Mass: Sun./public holidays 11.00.

The former monastery winery of **Bodegas Irache** is well known, not least for its **Fuente de Vino** (wine fountain, see photo). Pilgrims are invited to drink water as refreshment and to revive themselves with a sip of wine. If you are more thirsty you have to buy the wine. The wines from Irache, except for the Rosé wines, are not amongst the great wines of Spain, but they are quite respectable.

Just after the monastery take the slightly ascending footpath and then follow signs for 'Los Arcos vía Azqueta' on the right. Cross over the main road and you come past the campsite into a small wood. First ascending then descending you reach **Azqueta (5)** in about 1¼ hrs. After that there's a short ascent, past the Fuente de los Moros (13th century) of **Villamayor de Monjardín (6**; ½ hr.).

i *The Bodega Castillo de Monjardín in **Villamayor de Monjardín** has made a name for itself with its white wine. Above the village on the 894m high Pico de Monjardín can be found the ruins of the defensive castle (10th century). The Baroque church tower of the Romanesque **Iglesia de San Andrés** is quite striking (summer 8.00–20.00).*

The path leaves Monjardín downhill in a southerly direction. At first it runs close to the motorway, then you walk along broad, remote and well marked agricultural tracks to **Los Arcos (7**; 2¾ hrs.). The hiker is presented with a softly undulating landscape modelled by man and nature with cornfields, vineyards and forests. Depending on the time of year you can enjoy a spectacle of colours with fresh green tones in spring and summer to earthy brown shades in autumn and winter.

i *The most significant building of **Los Arcos** is the **Iglesia de Santa María** (12th–18th century), situated in the central square of the same name. It combines architectural styles from the Romanesque and Gothic to the Baroque. Worth seeing*

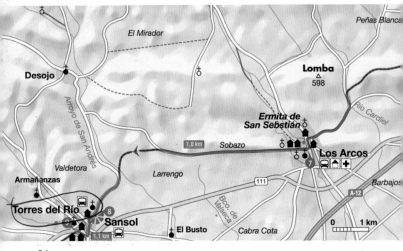

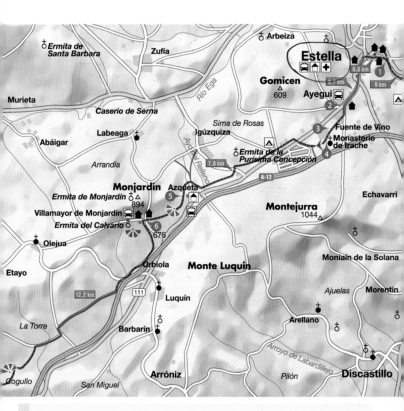

are the plateresque (adorned with finely chiselled decorations) church portal, the Gothic cloister, the choir stalls from the 16th century, the Baroque high altar and the Rokoko organ. Amongst the civic buildings the town hall (**Ayuntamiento**, 18th century) is particularly striking with its Baroque façade.

Public holidays: Monday before WhitSun. small fiesta with bull running and street celebrations; 14th–20th Aug. patron saint festival.

Gastronomy: rosquillas de Los Arcos (pastries made with flour, eggs, sugar and orange juice fried in olive oil).

Now you are walking to a large extent along gravel roads without shade through a wide and quite flat countryside. With **Sansol (8)**, already in your sights situated on a hill, turn left onto a little used country road and walk up

85

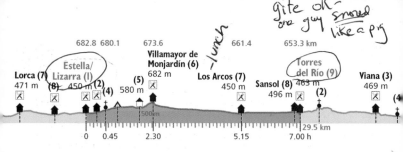

*gite ok -
one guy snored
like a pig*

682.8 680.1   673.6   661.4   653.3 km

Estella/   **Villamayor de**
Lorca (7) Lizarra (1)   **Monjardín (6)**   Los Arcos (7)   Torres
471 m   (8) 450 m (2) 682 m   450 m   Sansol (8) del Río (9)   Viana (3)
              (5)   496 m   463 m   469 m
              580 m   (2)

              0   0.45   2.30   5.15   7.00 h

                                                              29.5 km

into the village (1½ hrs. from Los Arcos). From the terrace of the Iglesia de
San Zoilo (17th century) you are afforded a lovely view of **Torres del Río (9)**
lying below on the Río Linares (¼ hr.). A path on the left of the main road
leads you through a small valley into the little village.

> *i* The **Iglesia del Santo Sepulcro** *(church of the Holy Grave) from the end of the
> 12th century is worth visiting in* **Torres del Río**. *Although there are no reliable
> sources, it has been attributed to the Order of Templars. Like Santa María de Eu-
> nate the tower-like construction has an eight-cornered layout and appears to have
> also been a graveside church. The inside is beautifully simple. Light only comes
> through a few small slit windows into the unadorned high interior. The church
> dome clearly shows Moorish influences. The cross above the altar dates back to
> the 13th century. The church can be found in its original state and it was only dur-
> ing the Spanish civil war thatsome of the paintings and wall pillars were taken
> away. Viewings 9.00–13.00 and 16.30–19.00, information in the hostels.*

You will not usually experience a frenzy of activity in the charming village of Torres de Río.

Hostels: Viana (469m, pop. 4,000), **(1)** RH, ☕☕☂, 15 B/donations, priest's office, Hospital Santa María, old building directly next to the church. Kitchen, communal evening meal with grace, small, but fine. From about 12.30, roughly June–Sept. **(2)** MH, ☕☕☂, 54 B/6 €. Alb. Andrés Muñoz, tel: 948 645 530, c/ San Pedro s/n; follow the main road past the church and the town hall square straight on almost to the end, then look for signs to the left. Large kitchen, dining room, washing machine, drier, internet. Bunks on three levels. 15th March–15th Oct.: 12.00–22.00, rest of the time tel: 609 141 798. **Logroño** (377m, pop. 148,000), **(1)** MH, ☕☕☂, 68 B/7 €. Tel: 941 248 686, c/ Rúavieja, 32. Dining room, washing machine/drier, internet, terrace; lots of room. 16.00–21.30, mid March–Oct. **(2)** RH, ☕☕, ca. 30 M/donations. In Iglesia de Santiago (entrance on the Camino/c/ Rúavieja). Basic hostel in the Christian sense, large area for mattresses. Communal evening meal, breakfast. Ring the bell, June–Sept. **(3)** east of the route: PH, ☕☕☂, 40 B/10,50 €. Alb. Puerta del Revellín, Pl. Martínez Flamarique, 4, tel: 941 700 832. Washing machine/drier, micro-

wave. 11.00–22.00, all year.
Grade and route: well marked. A lot of up-and-down from Torres del Río to Viana, sometimes along uncomfortable stony paths, little shade, no water, at times along a country road. Easy from Viana to Logroño. From the border Navarra – La Rioja the path goes along asphalt for 11km way after the town.
Height difference: 250m in ascent, 350m in descent.
Critical points: none.
Scenery: sections next to the N-111 interfere with the natural experience. After Viana begins the area of Greater Logroño, a wide, flat plain.
Local services: Viana 🏧 🕮 € ✉ A ⓘ 🏠 🚌 @ ⌧ 🖳 Iglesia de Santa María, summer Mon.–Sat. 19.30, Sun. 12.00, winter Mon.–Sat. 20.00, Sun. 12.00 ✚ c/ El Hoyo, 2, tel: 948 646 207, Virgen de las Cuevas ✚; Logroño all services 🚌 Avda. de España, tel: 941 235 983, 🚉 Plaza de Europa, tel: Renfe 902 240 202 🖳 see p. 88 ✚ Hospital General de la Rioja, Avda. de Viana, tel: 941 291 194.
Remarks: take water with you between Torres del Río and Viana.

After **Torres del Río (1)** the path first goes onto a high plain. After just under ¾ hr. you cross the N-111 to the right and shortly afterwards passes the chapel of the **Virgen del Poyo (2)**. According to legend, there were many attempts to take the statue of the Virgin Mary (14th century) to Viana, but it kept returning to the chapel and so was finally left there. After the chapel go for a short way on

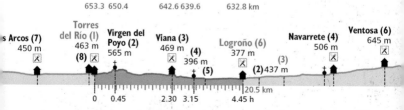

653.3 650.4   642.6 639.6   632.8 km

s Arcos (7) — Torres del Río (I) — Virgen del Poyo (2) — Viana (3) — Logroño (6) — Navarrete (4) — Ventosa (6)
450 m — 463 m — 565 m — 469 m **(4)** — 377 m — 506 m — 645 m
(8) — **(4)** 396 m — **(2)** 437 m — **(3)**
(5)

0   0.45   2.30 3.15   4.45 h   20.5 km

the right of the N-111 and then follow the broad, but later steep agricultural track (sign: 10% incline) downhill. For a while follow the bottom of the valley of the Barranco de Cornava and then ascend roughly 60 vertical metres again. The terrain is now flatter, but further on there's a short section along the busy N-111 before a path turns off left parallel to the road and brings you to **Viana (3)**, the last town on the Camino in the region of Navarra (1¾ hrs. from Virgen del Poyo).

i *King Sancho III, El Fuerte (the Strong) of Navarra, in 1219 bestowed trade privileges, amongst other things, upon **Viana** which at that time lay on the border with Cas-*

*tilla. The town developed into a well-known stopping place on the Way of St. James. The principality of Viana was founded in the 15th century. Prince Felipe, Spain's heir to the throne, still carries the title of Prince of Viana today. At the start of the 16th century **Cesare Borgia** died here (son of the later Pope Alexander VI). He is buried in the church of **Iglesia de Santa María de la Asunción** (13–18th century, May–about Sept. Mon.–Sat. 10.00–13.30, as well as 30 mins. before mass; mass: Mon.–Sat. 20.00, Sun. 11.00 and 12.00). Many Baroque and Renaissance palaces are proof of Viana's economic and cultural heyday from the 16–18th century. The most beau-*

tiful civic building is the town hall (**Casa consistorial**, see photo) opposite the Iglesia de Santa María with baroque façade (17th century). The oldest church in the town, **Iglesia San Pedro** (13th century), has remained in ruins since its collapse in 1844.
Public holidays: end of July, festival in honour of the patron saints María Magdalena and Santiago.
Gastronomy: embutidos (air-dried sausage); rancho (fried lamb and potato).

The first kilometres after Viana are pleasant. The path goes on the level through allotments at first, then after ¾ hr. there's a resting place at the chapel of the **Virgen de las Cuevas (4)** where you can take a break. Shortly afterwards the path swings to the right and a good 20 mins. later leads to the right through a small pine wood across a footbridge **(5)** over the N-111. After that walk along the right hand side of the N-111 and at an industrial building reach the border with the autonomous region of La Rioja. Along the asphalt path

The town hall of Viana.

All that's missing is the speed limit ...

you walk under the N-11 to the left. The sign '2km to Logroño' indicates the town boundary, but it's roughly another 4km to the centre of **Logroño (6)**. For many years, Doña Felisa stamped the pilgrim passports on the footpath down to the Ebro. Sadly she died in 2002 at the age of 92 and now her daughter stamps your pilgrim passport with the beautiful inscription *'Higos – agua y amor'* (figs – water and love).

ℹ️ **Logroño** *is the capital of* **La Rioja** *wine region. Besides the trade of wine and other agricultural products, the town makes its living from the production of metal and textiles. Celts and Romans had already settled on the banks of the* **Río Ebro***, the largest of Spain's rivers. It is said that the town's name today came from ‚gronio', the Celtic word for ford. In the 11th century King Sancho of Navarra routed the Way of St. James through the town thereby providing the booster for economic and cultural progress.*

The **Concatedral de Santa María de la Redonda** *(16/18th century) is worth a visit with its Baroque façade and two towers on which storks make their nest in the spring. The two very beautifully carved altars are interesting (16/17th century) and the choir stalls (16th century); (Mon.–Sat. 8.00–13.00 and 18.00–20.45, Sun. 9.00–14.00 and 18.30–20.45; mass: daily, 9.00, 10.00, 11.00, 12.00 and 20.00, also 13.00 on public holidays).*

The **Iglesia Imperial de Santa María de Palacio** *(11/12th century) stands next to the hostel. Its pointed pyramid-shaped tower – called Aguja (needle) by the locals – is the emblem of the town (daily 9.00–13.30 and 18.30–20.30, mass: Mon.–Sat. 9.30, 19.45, Sun. 10.00, 12.00 and 19.00).*

Above the main entrance of the **Iglesia de Santiago el Real** *(16th century)* **Santiago Matamoros** *(Santiago, the Moor slayer) is depicted riding into battle on* his white steed. In the church (open 8.15–13.15 and 18.30–19.00; mass: Mon.–Sat. 8.15, 9.00, 12.10 and 19.30, Sun. 9.30, 12.30 and 17.30) he is portrayed in a much more peaceful way as a pilgrim. In the church square a huge **Juego de la Oca** (game of the goose, similar to snakes and ladders) has been set into the ground, a very popular children's game in Spain, the origin of which has been linked with, amongst others, the Way of St. James – it being just as difficult to get to the end of the game as to make a pilgrimage to Santiago.

Juego de la Oca is still a popular game.

Public holidays: around 11th June patron saint festival of San Bernabé (in memory of the French siege in 1521). Around 21st Sept. large wine festival (vendimia).

Gastronomy: typical cuisine in La Rioja with verduras (all kinds of vegetables), pimientos rellenos (peppers stuffed with minced meat), chorizo (spicy sausage) and cordero (lamb). And of course red wine from Rioja. C/ Laurel is famous for its tapas bars.

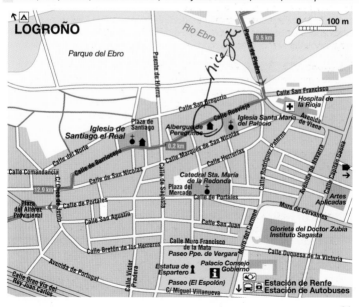

The autonomous region of La Rioja

The region of La Rioja (pop. 321,700, 5,045km², capital Logroño) has made Spain's reputation throughout the world as an excellent wine region. However, this small agricultural region has not played a large role in the political history of Spain. After long regional battles with Navarra, La Rioja fell into the hands of the Castilian crown in the 11th century. Not until the democratic reformation of Spain after the end of the Franco dictatorship did La Rioja become an independent region in 1978.

More interesting is the 2,000 year long history of the wine growing in La Rioja. Romans and Phoenicians brought the vines into the upper Ebro valley basin which is as much favoured by the Atlantic as by the Mediterranean climate. The importance of wine growing in La Rioja was documented in written form for the first time in the 11th century. King Sancho of Navarra gave Rioja wines official recognition by law in the 12th century. One century later Rioja became the cradle of the first words written in the Spanish language. In the Yuso monastery at San Millán de Cogolla the secular priest and poet Gonzalo de Berceo composed his worked, the Miracles of Our Lady'. The wine inspired him to the following lines: ,I would like to write in the language with which people speak to each other, for I'm not so learned as to do it in Latin. Therefore, I think I deserve a good glass of wine'. In 1560 winegrowers from Logroño furnished their wineskins destined for export with a seal of origin, a novelty in those days. Since soon an over production threatened the

The two faces of La Rioja: green vines in Rioja Baja ...

... and earthy brown cornfields in Rioja Alta.

market, in the 17th century the planting of new vines was prohibited for the first time. The prime objective was always the quality.

In 1632 wine growers demanded, for example, a ban on carts with metal fittings in Logroño since 'the vibration damaged the vines'. After an infestation of mildew in the middle of 19th century they started to plant more resistant types of vines which lead to a close and fruitful collaboration with the French winegrowers who had been ruined by the plague of phylloxera.

Since 1892 quality and export have been controlled centrally and since 1925 the wines have borne the mark of origin D.O. La Rioja (officially recognised since 1947) and in 1991 they received the highest quality category of DOC. But more and more wine regions are entering into competition with La Rioja (e.g. Ribera de Duero in Castilla y León). Today there's an annual production of 280 million litres of Rioja wine over 60,000 hectares, 85 % of which is red wine. Wine growing, agriculture and the industry of canned foods provide La Rioja, together with the Basque country and Navarra, with one of the highest per capita incomes in Spain.

The Way of St. James runs for little more than 60km across the Rioja region. It starts not very picturesquely in the area of Greater Logroño, leads through the town to the nearby recreation area of La Grajera where the countryside of La Rioja begins. Through the Rioja Baja (lower Rioja) characterised by vineyards and red soil via Navarrete you reach the former royal seat of Nájera. Afterwards, in the Rioja Alta (Upper Rioja), the vineyards recede and the cornfields around Santo Domingo de la Calzada give you a foretaste of the expanses of the Castilian Meseta.

Hostels: Navarrete (506m, pop. 2,800), **(1)** PH, ●●● , 20 B/8 € (DR 25 €). La Casa del Peregrino, c/ Las Huertas, 3, tel: 630 982 928. Immediately after crossing the broad road before entering the village take the first street right (paved in places), after 100m sharp right again. Kitchen, microwave, washing machine/drier, internet, Wi-Fi, 13.30–22.00, April–mid Oct. **(2)** MH, ●●● , 40 B/7 €. Tel: 941 440 776. Kitchen, washing machine/drier. 13.30–22.00, Easter–Oct. **(3)** PH, ●●● , 16 B/10 € (DR 30–40 €). El Cántaro, c/ Herrerías, 16, tel: 941 441 180. Kitchen with mi-

crowave, washing machine. Reservation possible. About 11.00–22.00, all year. **Ventosa** (645m, pop. 170), PH, ●●● , 42 B/9,5 €. Alb. San Saturnino, tel: 941 441 899. Kitchen, washing machine/drier, Wi-Fi, small shop (not even one in the village any more). 13.00–22.00 (winter from 14.00), all year. **Nájera** (488m, pop. 8,400), **(1)** PH, ●●● , 32 B/10 € (DR with bed/bunk bed 15 €, 4-bed room 60 €). Alb. Puerta de Nájera, Ribera del Na-jerilla, 1, tel: 941 362 317 and 683 616 894.

Diagonally right after bridge over river. Washing machine/drier, microwave, drinks/ snack machine, internet, Wi-Fi. Beautifully renovated old town house. From 11.00, all year. **(2)** PH, ●●● , 9 B/8 € (4 DR/25 €). Alb. Calle Mayor, c/ Dicarán, 5 (straight on after bridge, 2nd street on left by the café on the corner.), tel: 941 360 407. Hostel without bunkbeds. Reserve by email: calle-

mayor@grupostar.com. From 10.00, East-er–Oct. **(3)** MH, ●● , 92 B/donations, St. James society of Nájera; Pl. Santiago, after bridge a good 300m on the left beside the river, tel: 941 360 675. Kitchen, large dormitory. Prayers 21.30. 13.00 (winter 14.00) –22.00, all year. **(4)** PH, ●● , 10 B/8 € (4 DR 15 €/person). Alb. de Peregrinos Sancho II, reception in La Judería restaurant, in the centre on the Camino, left at the monastery of Santa Maria de la Real, hostel at C/ San Marcial 8 tel: 941 361 138 (reservation possible). 11.00–22.00, Mar.–Oct. Double room available all year. **(5)** PH, ●●● , 32 B/8 € (SR 20 €, DR 40 €, 3-bed rm.50 €). Alb. Alberone, c/ San Marcial, 8 (next to PH 4), tel: 674 246 826. Washing machine/drier, kitchen, few bathrooms. Functional hostel in normal block of houses. All day, all year.

Grade and route: easy. Asphalt to recreation area of Grajera, then mainly farm tracks, small height difference.

Height difference: 360m in ascent, 240m in descent.

Critical points: none.

Scenery: from La Grajera more in the countryside with cornfields and vineyards. The main road is a nuisance up to Ventosa. After that Rioja-type vineyards on red soil.

Local services: Parque la Grajera ⚡ 🍴 🚰; Navarrete ⚡ 🍴 🏧 @ € 🅰 🚑 ✉ 🚰 ➕ Crta. de Entrena, tel: 941440 638; Ventosa ⚡ 🍴 (small shop in hostel); Nájera ⚡ 🍴 🏧 € ✉ ⓘ @ 🚰 ✂ 🅰 🖎 Parroquia de Santa Cruz Mon.–Sat. 9.00/20.00, Sun./ public holidays 9.30/13.00, Iglesia de Santa María la Real Sat./Sun. 19.00 ➕ Avda. de la Rioja s/n, tel: 941 360 975.

Remarks: beyond Ventosa, after the Alto de San Antón, just before reaching the N-120, you could theoretically walk south of the main path via Tricio and Alesón to Nájera. The roughly 1km long stretch of path is not well marked, however.

Along the Alto de San Antón.

The Way of St. James goes along the Ruavieja through the old town of **Logroño (1)**, past the Iglesia de Santiago into c/ de Barriocepo, at the end turns left into c/ Once de Junio and bends right just after that into c/ de Portales. This road leads to a large roundabout (Plaza del Alférez) across which you come to the big arterial road c/ del Marqués de Murrieta. Follow this road until it becomes the Avda. de Burgos after crossing the railway lines. At the crossroads with c/ de Portillejo the path turns to the left and becomes the asphalted path through the **Parque de San Miguel (2)** to the recreation area of La Grajera. You finally leave the town after 1½ hrs., at the reservoir **Embalse de la Grajera (3)**.

A hiking path goes along the partly wooded shoreline of the lake until it joins an ascending gravel path. Parallel to the N-120 it goes over a small hill and across the plain towards **Navarrete (4)** which rises up ahead like a cone (1½ hrs. from La Grajera).

---

i Before **Navarrete**, after crossing the motorway, the Way of St. James passes the ruins of the pilgrim hospital **San Juan de Acre** (founded in 1185).
The small old town of Navarrete has been quite well preserved. The **Iglesia de la Asunción** (16th century) stands in the attractive central square, with its plane trees and drinking fountain?, above the hostel. The extravagant Baroque altar is worth seeing. Navarrete is well known for its **pottery** (alfarería).

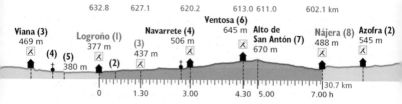

From Navarrete follow the N-120 at first. After the **Ermita de Santa María de Jesús** (**5**; 16th century, beautiful Romanesque portal from the 12th century) you leave the road to the left and walk through vineyards. The path unfortunately soon turns right and then runs next to the motorway. If you are following the signs to the hostel before **Ventosa** (**6**; 1½ hrs.), you can avoid the motorway sooner, otherwise the direct route past Ventosa is a bit shorter. Both alternatives join up again just before the many cairns erected by pilgrims, then walk uphill to the **Alto de San Antón (7)**.

Continue straight on afterwards past the house (sign says Dinastía Vivanco; on the left the alternative via Alesón, as yet still not waymarked) and immediately down to the left and under the N-120. First close to, then further north of the N-120 you reach a gravel factory where you keep right and then left after the slip road to the motorway,.The waymarkers lead you further along the N-120, past the *polideportivo* (sports hall) and into the new part of town. Carry straight on and cross the **Río Najerilla**.

The municipal hostel is left after the bridge, about 300m along the riverbank. The Camino, on the other hand, turns diagonally right after the bridge, passes the Puerta de Nájera hostel, then goes left through the old gateway, then right and left to the monastery in the old town of **Nájera** (**8**; 2½ hrs.).

---

i *There is little remaining today to give you a sense of the once flourishing capital of the kings of Navarra. Originally a Roman stronghold, **Nájera** was first occupied by the Visigoths, later seized by Arabs. In 923 King Sancho Garcés the Elder conquered the town. After the destruction of Pamplona by the Arabs in 924 the residence of the kings of Navarra was moved to Nájera. In 1045, after the wonderous*

find of a Madonna, King García Sánchez III established the **Monasterio de Santa María la Real** as the bishopric and royal burial ground and in 1079 it was ascribed to the Order of Cluny. The town where the miracle took place and the **Panteón real**, the royal crypt, are the only elements of the original monastery still preserved today. The Romanesque sarcophagus of Doña Blanca de Navarra (12th century) is particularly sumptous. The building of the church was started in 1432. The beautifully carved choir stalls are impressive (15th century) and the cloisters with their Gothic tracery worked with filigree (16th century). (Easter–Oct. Tue.–Sat. 10.00–13.00* and 16.00–19.00*, Sun./public holidays 10.00–12.30* and 16.00–18.00*, winter in the afternoon until 17.30*. *Last entry, after that only half an hour an hour allowed for visit; Aug.–Sept. open Mon.; 3 €. www.santamarialareal.net). From the 17th century Nájera lost its military and therefore also its economic and cultural significance. During the War of Independence (1808–1814) French troops destroyed large parts of the town.

Public holidays: 24th–29th June San Juan and San Pedro, Nájera's most popular fiesta, high points are the vueltas, when thousands of people dance and sing in the streets to brass band music. The second half of July: evocaciones, lavish drama productions about the history of the town. 16th–19th Sept. festivals in honour of the patrons of San Juan Martír and Santa María la Real.

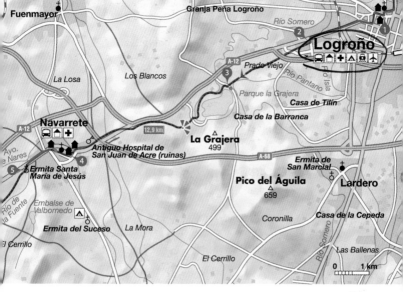

Hostels: Azofra (545m, pop. 260), MH, ●●○, 60 B in main building (extra space available at busy times with 50 B)/7 €. Tel: town hall 941 379 220. Washing machine/drier, kitchen, drinks machine, internet, 2-bed rooms, garden. 13.00–22.00, all year, smaller hostel in winter. **Cirueña** (741m, pop. 90), PH, ●●○, 25 B/13 €. Alb. Virgen de Guadalupe, c/ Barrio Alto, 1, tel: 638 924 069. Washing machine. 13.30–22.00, 15th March–15th Oct. **Santo Domingo de la Calzada** (640m, pop. 6,700), **(1)** RH, ●●, 33 B/donations, in the Cistercian monastery, tel: 941 340 700. Small cooking area, very basic hostel, some rooms rather narrow, 11.00–22.00, May–Sept. **(2)** RH, ●●●, 229 B/donations. Cofradía (brotherhood) del Santo, tel: 941 343 390. Oldest hostel, newly refurbished, kitchen, internet. Pilgrim passport. 11.00–22.00, all year.

Grade and route: easy, well marked.

Mostly broad farm tracks. Short ascent after Nájera onto plateau, long ascent before Cirueña, otherwise flat. No shade.

Height difference: 280m in ascent, 120m in descent.

Critical points: none.

Scenery: the plateau of La Rioja Alta with its flat expanses gives you a foretaste of the plains of the Meseta between Burgos and León. Grain is cultivated here instead of vines. The Tierra de Campos begins here, the granaries of Spain.

Local services: Azofra ⓧ ⊟ 🖬 🔜 @; Ciriñuela ⓧ; Cirueña ⓧ 🖬 🔜 @; Santo Domingo de la Calzada ⓧ 🏠 (also Parador Nacional) ⊟ 🅰 🔜 @ € 🖬 ✕ 🛈 🅰 🖬 cathedral Sat. 20.00, Sun. 13.00 and 20.00 ✚ c/ Margubete, 1, tel: 941 342 173.

Remarks: without shade, be sure to take enough water and something to cover your head in high temperatures.

Past **Nájera monastery (1)** walk for about one kilometre up a wooded slope onto the plateau of La Rioja Alta. It's 1¼ hrs. to **Azofra (2)** along broad farm tracks and level ground. After Azofra the stone *Cruz de los Peregrinos* (16th century, also *picota*, once served as a waymarker and pillory) indicates the route to the pilgrims. A long incline takes you up to the golf course before Cirue-

ña, or Ciruñuela (both 2 hrs.). Going straight on brings you to **Cirueña (3)** where you turn right in the village, go left at the roundabout and carry straight on. To go to **Ciriñuela** turn off right before the new housing development and then go straight on. Continue left as far as the road, go left there and immediately right onto the farm track. Continue along this track to the Camino and turn right to **Santo Domingo de la Calzada (4**; 1¼ hrs.) on the plain which is already visible from a long way off.

Having a chin-wag in Azofra.

ℹ️ ***Santo Domingo de la Calzada*** *is one of the most prominent stopping places on the Way of St. James. Its existence is thanks to Domingo de Viloria (1019–1109). The erstwhile hermit devoted his life to the pilgrim way. He cleared the then dense forested area around the Río Oja, built the bridge and surfaced the road (Calzada) that has characterised the linear town until today. He founded a hostel and a hospice and looked after sick pilgrims himself. Thanks to his considerable charisma he won the favour equally of clerics, noblemen and the people for his work. Shortly after his death Domingo was declared a saint. His disciple Juan de Ortega carried on his life's work. Since 1930 Santo Domingo has been the patron saint of the Spanish road and bridge builders. The Romanesque-Gothic* **cathedral** *was built between 1158 and 1235. The monumental high altar and the choir stalls are extremely ornate (both 16th century, Renaissance). The tomb of the founder of the town is also worth seeing in the church (daily 9.00–19.10 (winter from 10.00) apart from during mass, entrance to pilgrims 2.50 €. Info about guided tours at www.catedralsantodomingo.es, link Visita cultural). The free-standing Baroque church tower dates*

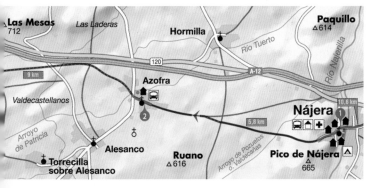

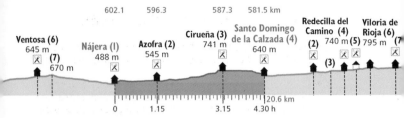

| | | 602.1 | 596.3 | | 587.3 | 581.5 km | | | | |

Ventosa (6)
645 m
(7)
670 m

Nájera (I)
488 m

Azofra (2)
545 m

Cirueña (3)
741 m

Santo Domingo
de la Calzada (4)
640 m

Redecilla del
Camino (4)
(2) 740 m (5)

Viloria de
Rioja (6)
795 m (7

(3)

20.6 km

0   1.15   3.15   4.30 h

back to the 18th century. The pair of white **chickens** kept in the church is in memory of the miracle of Santo Domingo, one of the most popular legends along the Way. First versions date back to Toulouse in the 12th century. Around the 14th century the German pilgrim Hugonell and his parents are said to have made a stop in Santo Domingo. When the young man spurned the love of the innkeeper's daughter, the offended party accused him of robbery. The young man ended up on the gallows. On the return from Santiago the parents found their son at the entrance to Santo Domingo – hanging from the rope, but still alive, on the shoulders of Santo Domingo. When they reported this to the judge who was sitting at table, he told them, 'Your son is as dead as the roast chickens on my plate.' But while he was speaking, the birds rose up with a loud crow. The judges of the town wore a rope around their necks for a long time as a reminder but this was later replaced with a more comfortable band. The chickens are exchanged every 21 days. Diagonally opposite the cathedral is the pilgrim hospital founded in the 11th century by Santo Domingo which was operational into the 18th century; today it is a Parador Nacional, an elegant state-run hotel.

Also worth seeing: the old town, the Plaza Mayor and the Convento de San Francisco (16th century; church is closed due to renovation work).

Public holidays: end April–15th May: big fiesta in honour of Santo Domingo. Middle of Aug. drama productions of the town's legends.

Gastronomy: ahorcaditos (little hanged men), pastries filled with cream in the shape of St. James shells and little hanged men.

A cycling pilgrim between Cirueña and Santo Domingo de la Calzada.

The autonomous region of Castilla y León

Castilla y León (pop. 2.6 million, 94,226km²) consists of nine provinces: Ávila, Burgos, León, Palencia, Segovia, Salamanca, Soria, Valladolid, Zamora. Valladolid is the capital.

The huge central Spanish region of Castilla y León is the cradle of modern Spain and high Spanish, Castilian. It has certainly been a long journey that has led to the unity of this autonomous region, the largest as regards surface area in Spain. The Asturian kingdom was founded after the occupation of the Visigoth capital of Toledo (714) by the Arabs. The Reconquista, the rebellion of Christian Spain against the Arab ruling powers, began a little later (722).

The kingdom of León was founded at the start of the 10th century. Shortly afterwards the earldom of Burgos separated and from then onwards called itself Castilla (derived from castillo, castle). The two kingdoms united and separated from each other many times until, in 1230 under King Fernando III, they finally came together to become the kingdom of Castilla y León with Burgos as its capital. Through the marriage of Isabella I of Castellon with Ferdinand II of Aragón (1469) the new Spanish state was created out of the two mightiest king-

doms in the country; with the capture of Granada in 1492 the Reconquista was concluded. The Way of St. James also became an important instrument in the broadening and security of the power of the Catholic church.

Seen historically and geographically the central Spanish regions of Castilla y León (also Castilla la Vieja, old Castillon), Castilla la Mancha (Castilla la Nueva, new Castillon) and the region of Madrid form a unified whole. A harsh, continental climate prevails on the often barren plateaus with hot summers and cold winters. Nevertheless history has left behind some of its most impressive traces here: in fabulous towns like Burgos and León directly on the Way of St. James, but also in Salamanca, Ávila or Valladolid, to name just the largest ones.

The Way of St. James runs for over 400km through the provinces of Burgos, Palencia and León. The name of *Campos Góticos*, meaning Gothic fields, dates back to the former Visigoth settlers. The wide, level, often uninviting landscapes of the Meseta require the pilgrims to have a strong willpower. However, there is a great richness of sites with cultural-historical interest whether San Juan de Ortega, Burgos, Castrojeriz, Frómista, León, Astorga or Ponferrada. From Astorga the way offers insights into the, rather unfairly, little known Spanish regions like the Maragatería, the mountains of the Montes de León and El Bierzo, that give you a foretaste of Galicia with lovely green stretches of countryside. The pilgrim hostels in the region are governed by a new law, see p. 19.

Hostels: Grañón (724m, pop. 315), RH, ◖◗, about 40 B/donations. Hospital de Peregrinos San Juan Bautista, in Grañón church. Mattresses on the floor, if necessary also in the chancel of the church. Communal evening meal, breakfast, prayers. All day, all year. **Redecilla del Camino** (740m, pop. 130), MH, ◖◗◖, 40 B/donations, town hall: tel: 947 580 283. Kitchen, evening meal, washing machine, internet, inner courtyard, friendly rooms. All day, all year. **Viloria de Rioja** (795m, pop. 50), PH, ◖◗◗, 12 B/5 €. Acacio and Orietta, tel: 947 585 220. The Brazilian author Paolo Coelho is patron to the hostel. Communal evening meal/breakfast for a donation. Lots of useful info about the Camino. Washing machine, internet. From 13.00 onwards, Mar.–Oct. **Villamayor del Río** (791m, pop. 50), PH, ◖◗◗, 26 B (extendable)/5 €. Alb. San Luis de Francia, tel: 947 562 566. Good alternative if the other hostels are already full. Washing machine/drier, internet, large separate bathrooms, garden, snacks, evening meal, breakfast, possible to reserve. 12.30–22.00, Easter–Oct. **Belorado** (783m, pop. 2,000), **(1)** PH, ◖◗◖, 98 B/5 € (SR 30 €, DR 40 €). A Santiago, tel: 947 562 164. About 700m from the centre. Kitchen, washing machine/drier, internet, garden, pool, restaurant. All day, all year. **(2)** RH, ◖◗, 24 B/donations. Rectory, in summer run by Swiss volunteers, tel: rectory 947 580 085. Kitchen/dining room, former theatre, narrow rooms, quite basic but charming hostel. 13.00–22.00, mid Apr.–Oct. **(3)** PH, ◖◗◗, 22 B/5 € (2 DR 45 €, 2 SR 35 €). El Caminante, c/ Mayor, tel: 947 580 231. Internet, washing machine/drier, small garden, restaurant. Quite roomy. 10.00–22.00, March–Oct., after that groups of 10 or more by reservation, tel: 656 873 927. **(4)** PH, ◖◗◗, 62 B/5 €. Alb. Cuatro Cantones, tel: 947 580 591. Kitchen, restaurant/communal evening meal, barbecue site, covered pool, washing machine/drier, internet, garden, massages, renovated old building. About 12.00–22.00, all year. Alternative accommodation: **(5)** Alb. rural El Corral, tel: 947 580 683, www.beloaventura.org. 14,50 €. **(6)** Casa Waslala, B&B only for pilgrims (diagonally opposite PH 3), tel: 947 580 726, www.casawaslala.com.

Grade and route: easy, only moderate height differences, well marked. Gravel paths, asphalt in places. The path runs parallel to N-120 before Belorado.

Height difference: 240m in ascent, 100m in descent.

Critical points: possible diversion due to motorway works beyond Santo Domingo.

Scenery: the path forges its way further into the granaries of Spain. Huge cornfields characterise the gently rolling landscape, the monotony of which is only broken by a few small villages.

Local services: Grañón ▯▯▯€✗▯▯; Redecilla del Camino ✗▯ⓘ (with WC and ⓐ) ▯▯; Castildelgado (767m, pop. 55) ✗▯▯▯; Viloria de Rioja ▯▯ⓐ; Villamayor del Río ✗▯▯▯▯ⓐ; Belorado ✗▯€▯✉ⓘⓐ▯▯ Capilla de Santiago (Iglesia de Santa María, next to the hostel) 20.00 with pilgrim blessing ▯ Las Cercas, 2, tel: 947 580 558.

Remarks: (1) Many hostels along the way allow flexible stage planning. **(2)** It is extremely hot in summer in the area with virtually no trees.

As for almost 1,000 years the Way of St. James runs in a totally straight line through **Santo Domingo (1)** as the Calle Mayor. At the exit from the town it crosses the Río Oja, keeps for a short way on the right of the N-120, crosses over it to the left and then runs parallel to it. Now walk along a broad farm track up a gentle hill and then back down again. At the bottom shortly after the wayside cross (1 hr. from Santo Domingo) the Camino turns left and then immediately right. You are walking across extensive fields to finally reach **Grañón** situated on the right in just under ¾ hr. The **hostel (2)** can be found in the **Iglesia de San Juan Bautista** (14th century) in the centre of the village. The former community priest José Ignacio was, at the end of the 80s, one of the driving forces behind the new pilgrim movement in the 20th century.

An angel looks down on pilgrims from the church portal in Grañón.

The start of the Castilla y León region.

In Grañón either walk straight on to the end of the village (lovely viewpoint), turn right there and then sharp left onto the steeply sloping farm track. Or turn right into the first road after the church and at the T-junction swing right onto the main path. After nearly ½ hr. a border stone marks the start of the autonomous region of **Castilla y León/ Burgos province (3)**. After another ½ hr. you reach **Redecilla del Camino (4)**. The beautifully crafted Romanesque font is worth seeing (Pila bautismal, 12th century) in the parish church of Santa María (opposite the hostel).

Welcome refreshment in Redecilla del Camino.

The small villages of **Castildelgado (5; ½ hr.)** and **Viloria de Rioja (6; ½ hr.)** follow on only a short distance after each other. Here Santo Domingo, the later founder of Santo Domingo de la Calzada, saw 'the light of the world'. Afterwards you came downhill through **Villamayor del Río (7; ¾ hr.)**. The hostel lies on the right of the main road roughly 300m further on. Straight on, walking close to the road, brings you comfortably in one hour to **Belorado (8)**.

| | 581.5 | 574.7 | 570.4 566.9 | 563.2 | 558.0 km |

Santo Domingo de la Calzada (1) 640 m

Cirueña (3) 741 m

Grañón (2) 724 m

Redecilla del Camino (4) (5) (6) 795 m (3)

Villamayor del Río (7) 791 m

Belorado (8) 783 m (2) (3) (4)

Villafranca Montes de Oca (6) 948 m (7) (8)

23.5 km

0   1.45   2.45   3.40   4.30   5.30 h

ℹ️ Pilgrims used to discover physical and spiritual well-being in **Belorado** in two hospitals and nine churches. The **Iglesia de Santa María** (next to the hostel) from the 16th century with some remarkable altars and the **Iglesia de San Pedro** (18th century) in the **Plaza Mayor** are well preserved. The former border town between Navarra and Castilla is dominated by the hill where the remains of the medieval fortress can be found. The **monastery of Santa María de la Bretonera** of the Order of Clarissa, re-established in the 14th century, stands at the exit from the town.

Gastronomy: embutidos (air-dried sausage) and morcillas (blood sausage).

Shopping: Belorado is well known for its leatherware (peleterías). On Mondays there's a large weekly market in the central square, the setting up of which was granted in 1116 by Alfonso I. It is one of the oldest in Spain.

Tourist office and information for pilgrims: Pl. Mayor, 1, Mon.–Fri. 12.00–15.00, Sat./Sun. 11.00–14.00, afternoons daily except Wed: 16.30–20.30.

Hostels: Tosantos (821m, pop. 50), RH, ◖◗, about 15 M/donations, rectory, tel: 947 580 371. Mattresses on the floor, kitchen, communal cooking and clearing up, prayers. 13.00–22.00, April–Oct. **Villambistia** (860m, pop. 50) MH, ◖◗◠, 14 B/5–6 €. Alb. San Roque, tel: 680 501 887. Plaza Mayor, right at the church down to the centre of village. Washing machine/drier, internet, bar, communal meals. All day, all year except Christmas to Three Kings. **Espinosa del Camino** (900m, pop. 36), PH, ◖◗◠, 10 B/price on request when you're there. Albergue La Campana, José Mir, tel: 678 479 361. The hostel is up for sale, therefore changes possible. Evening meal and breakfast. Small private museum. 13.00–22.00, March–Oct. **Villafranca Montes de Oca** (948m, pop. 130), **(1)** MH, ◖◗, 60 B/6 €. Tel: 947 582 124. Large dormitory, microwave, washing machine/drier, internet, Wi-Fi. From 11.00, mid March–Oct. **San Juan de Ortega** (1,008m, pop. 18), RH, ◖◗, 60 B/5 €. San Juan de Ortega monastery, tel: 947 560 438. Often full in July/Aug.

Some renovations, now with heating and warm water, kitchen, washing machine. 13.00–22.00, Mar.–Oct., possibly all year.
Grade and route: easy to moderate. Well marked, paths and farm tracks. Easy up to Villafranca, but after that an incline and 12km without services along a forest track .
Height difference: 440m in ascent, 230m in descent.
Critical points: rather than walking along the N-120 before Villafranca Montes de Oca, it's better to follow the beaten path on the right of it.
Scenery: from Belorado the landscape becomes greener again. The path to Villafranca ascends imperceptibly to over 900m. Then it goes steeply uphill into the wooded area around Montes de Oca. Moss covered oak trees and thick ferns create a magical atmosphere until the path runs along a broad firebreak.
Local services: Tosantos ▣▦@; Villambistia ✕ ✚▦@; Espinosa del Camino ▣▦▦; Villafranca Montes de Oca ✕ ▤♦✚▦Ⓐ@; San Juan de Ortega ♦ ✕▦▙ 18.00.
Remarks: take water and food with you for the long stretch from Villafranca Montes de Oca to San Juan de Ortega.

From the end of **Belorado (1)** walk as far as the petrol station, walk straight through and then take the farm track on the left of the road. After the rather monotonous stages walking through cornfields, a broad path now leads to **Tosantos (2**; 1¼ hrs.) on the left hand side of an overgrown streambed. Just

before Tosantes you come past an inviting and shady picnic spot to stop for a rest. A little way outside the village (to the north) lies the hermitage, the Ermita de Nuestra Señora de la Peña, with a statue of the Virgin Mary from the 12th century (information about visits to the hermitage in the hostel).

The route out of Tosantes continues along a leisurely farm track slightly uphill. Although always within hearing distance of the N-120, you are distracted by lovely views of the surrounding countryside, and then you come through **Villambistia** (**3**; ½ hr.), **Espinosa del Camino** (**4**; ½ hr.) and **Villafranca Montes de Oca** (**6**; ¾ hr.) in quick succession. The remains of **San Félix de Oca** church (**5**; 9th century) are passed just before reaching Villafranca.

> *i* *Villafranca Montes de Oca* *is where pilgrims used to recover their energies for the long and dangerous crossing of the Oca mountains (oca means goose), in whose woods robbers and bandits did their foul work. Villafranca was a bishopric until the seat was transferred to Burgos in 1075. At the end of the 14th century, the* **Hospital de la Reina** *(or de* **San Antonio Abad***) was built at the command of Doña Juana Manuel, wife of King Enrique II (Henry II of Trastámara). It is said to have been popular with pilgrims due to large servings of food. In the centre of the village stands the* **Iglesia de Santiago** *(originally, Romanesque, end of the 18th century). A baroque statue of St. James inside the church is very striking and so too the font made from a huge St. James shell originating from the Philippines (15th June–30th Sept., 10.00–14.00 and 17.00–20.00).*

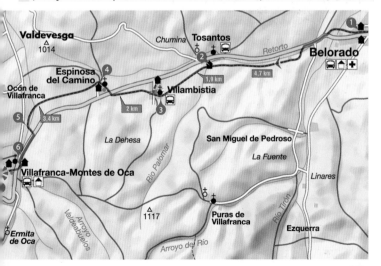

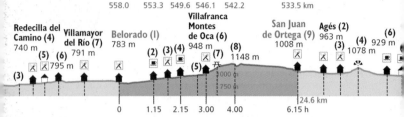

558.0   553.3   549.6   546.1   542.2   533.5 km

Villafranca
Montes
Redecilla del   Belorado (I)   de Oca (6)   San Juan   Agés (2)   (6)
Camino (4)   Villamayor   783 m   948 m   de Ortega (9)   963 m   (4)   929 m
740 m   del Río (7)   1008 m   (3)   1078 m
             791 m   (2)   (3)(4)   (8)
(5)   (6)   795 m   1148 m
(3)   (5)
                                                            1000 m
                                                            750 m
                                                                    24.6 km

0   1.15   2.15   3.00   4.00   6.15 h

Already in the village the at first tough, then less steep ascent onto the **Montes de Oca** starts along a hiking path. After about ½ hr. you can catch your breath at a small **resting place (7**; 1,080m, *área de descanso*). According to the sign (*agua no potable*), however, the water is not for drinking. Another half an hour, this time up a moderate incline, the highest point with an antenna at 1,155m is reached. There's a lovely panoramic view across the extensive forest area.

Shortly afterwards you walk along the broad firebreak to the **memorial (8)** for the Republicans shot in 1936 in the Civil War. The inscription is as follows: 'It was not their deaths, but the manner of their deaths that was senseless. May they rest in peace'. Immediately afterwards a deep ravine forces you into a short but steep descent and ascent. Then continue along a broad forest path to **San Juan de Ortega (9**; 2¼ hrs.).

You reach Tosantes along a broad agricultural track.

View of San Juan de Ortega.

ℹ️ The later canonised **Juan de Ortega** (1080–1163) was, together with Santo Domingo, the second largest patron of the Way of St. James. After a pilgrimage to Jerusalem the student of Santo Domingo retreated into the inhospitable Oca mountains in 1115. In thanks for the amazing rescue during a storm on the journey back he built Saint Nicholas of Bari the **Capilla de San Nicolás**. To resist the Oca bandits he later opened a pilgrim hostel around which a small monastic community was founded. After Juan's death the village was neglected. Just like his role model, Santo Domingo, he also improved the Way of St. James by building roads and bridges. In the 15th century the monastery started to fall into disrepair. The interior of the **Iglesia Monacal** (previously a monastery church, 12th–19th century) combines Romanesque, such as the three apses with very beautiful capitals (12th century), and Gothic elements from the 14th century, like the finely worked **tomb of San Juan** with a Gothic canopy over the Romanesque-Gothic sarcophagus. The simple plain tomb chamber is to be found beneath.

The **Milagro de la Luz**, the miracle of light is an architectural masterpiece. On the equinox (21st March: 18.00, 22nd Sept.: 19.00, also one or two days before and after) a ray of Sun. falls for a few minutes onto the capital on the left of the altar which depicts the Christmas story from the Annunciation to the Epiphany.

A pilgrimage to the church was for a long time the last hope of childless women. However, Queen Isabella of Castilla, wife of Fernando of Aragón, brought three children into the world after her visit to San Juan. To show her gratitude she made a gift of the canopy above the Saint's tomb.

Hostels: Agés (963m, pop. 65), **(1)** PH, ♛♛♛, 10–12 B/10 € (DR 45 €, SR 36 €). Tel: 947 430 392 and 661 263 289. Alb. San Rafael, c/ Adobera, 18 (start of the village). Bar/rest. Washing machine/drier, internet, Wi-Fi. 12.00–22.00 (or telephone), all year. **(2)** PH, ♛♛♛, 34 B/9 €. El Pajar de Agés, tel: 947 400 629 and 699 273 856. Washing machine/drier, Wi-Fi, internet, evening meals, breakfast. All day, Mar.–Oct. **(3)** MH, ♛♛♛, 36 B/7 €. Alb. Municipal la Taberna de Agés (on the left next to PH 2), tel: 947 400 697, 660 044 575. Bar/rest., washing machine/drier, Wi-Fi, internet, roomy, disabled friendly. 11.00–22.00, all year. **Atapuerca** (962m, pop. 150), ♛♛♛, 36 B/8 € (DR 35 €). Alb. de Atapuerca El Peregrino, centre of village, tel: 661 580 882. Kitchen, washing machine/drier, drinks machine, garden. From about 12.30–22.00, all year. **(2)** PH, ♛♛♛, 18 B/ 6 €. La Hutte, belongs to Centro de Turismo Rural Papa Sol, tel: 947 430 320. Washing machine, internet. 13.00–22.00, all year. **Cardeñuela-Riopico** (929m, pop. 100), MH, ♛, 15 B/donations. All day, all year. **Burgos** (865m, pop. 173,700), **(1)** RH, ♛♛♛, 20 B/donations. Casa Emaús, Casa parroquial para peregrinos, spaces in rectory San José Obrero, c/ San Pedro Cardeña, 31 Bis (on edge of town, see route description/town map). Christian hostel, communal cooking and clearing up, prayers. 14.00–22.30, Easter–Oct. **(2)** SH, ♛♛♛, 18 B/donations. Alb. Divina Pastora. C/Laín Calvo, 10 (centre), tel: 947 207 952. Washing machine, internet. For mass time see sign outside the hostel. 11.00–21.00, Easter–12th Oct. **(3)** MH, ♛♛♛, 150 B/5 €. Casa de Cubos. C/ Fernán Gómez, 32 (on Camino, just before the cathedral), tel: 947 460 922. Washing machine/drier, internet, roomy. June–Sept. 12.00–22.30, Oct.–May 16.00– 22.00.

Grade and route: mostly well marked until just before Burgos. After Atapuerca

small, at times steep pass, otherwise easy. A lot of asphalt. There are two alternatives to Burgos (see Remarks): the better one via Castañares is also marked with yellow arrows.

Height difference: 120m in ascent, 270m in descent.

Critical points: the path may be badly marked in places around the town area of Burgos. Check the de-scription/town map carefully.

Scenery: continue through forests as far as Agés. After that you are afforded a lovely view across the plain of Atapueraca. From the 1078m high Matagrande after Atapuerca you can see Burgos in the distance which is reached across fields and through small villages.

Local services: Agés ⊗ 🖪 ⊡ @; Atapuerca ➕ ⊗-🖪 @ ⊡; Villalval (946m, pop. 30) ➕; Cardeñuela-Riopico ▣ ➕ ⌂; Orbaneja-Riopico (912m, pop. 175) ▣ ➕ ⌂ Casa Rural Fortaleza, tel: 947 225 354, www.casaruralfortaleza.com; Villafría (884m, pop. 870) ⊗ ⌂ ⊡ 🖪 ⊡; Castañares (892m, pop. 310) ➕ ⊗ ⊟; Burgos all services, 🚉 cathedral: Capilla de Santa Tecla: Mon.–Fri. 10.00 and 11.00, Sat. 19.30, Sun./ public holiday 9.00–14.00 hourly as well as 19.30. Capilla de Santísimo Cristo Mon.–Fri. 9.00 and 19.30, 🚍 c/ Miranda, 4, tel: 947 288 855 🖪 Est. Rosa de Lima, Avda. Príncipe de Asturias s/n, tickets: c/ Moneda, 4, tel: 947 209 131 ➕ domestic flights ➕ Hospital General Yagüe, Avda. del Cid, 96, tel: 947 281 300, Hospital San Juan de Dios, Paseo de la Isla, 41, tel: 947 257 730.

Remarks: the original historical route leads via Villafría to Burgos, but runs for 10km through the industrial area and the new town. Some pilgrims there¬fore take the bus from Villafría.The alternative via Castañares is more pleasant and leads along the green banks of the Río Arlanzón directly into the old town.

View of Agés.

From **San Juan de Ortega (1)** continue through the forests of Montes de Oca. Then the view opens out over the wide valley in which **Agés** (2; a good ¾ hr.) and **Atapuerca (3**; just under ½ hr.) lie.

i *Since the sensational finds in 1994 of the 800,000 year old remains of the 'first European', the homo antecessor, **Atapuerca** has been one of the most important archaeological excavation sites in the world. Until the discovery of a 1.2 million year old jaw bone (2007) it was considered to be the oldest confirmed hominid in Europe and thus the forerunner of homo sapiens and Neanderthal man. Cave paintings had already been found at the start of the 20th century in the Sierra de Atapuerca. In the 60s scientists came across fossils on the track of a former mine. In 1976 the first human remains emerged. The large number and the good condition of the findings are a stroke of luck for research. Since 2000 the excavation site has been declared a World Heritage site by UNESCO.*

The places of discovery lie 12km away from Atapuerca in a military area. A visit to the excavations: groups all year round, but only by prior arrangement. Individuals Jan.–June and Oct.–Dec. only Sat./Sun., July–Sept. daily, 5 € (with Museo de la Evolución Humana 16 €). Tel: 902 024 246, departures from Atapuerca and Ibeas (one hour earlier from Ibeas). More information about times in the Visitor Centre in Atapuerca: Apr.–Oct. 9.30–14.00 and 15.30–20.00, Nov.–Mar. 10.00–14.00 and 16.00–18.30; see also www.visitasatapuerca.com.

*Many of the findings of Atapuerca are on display in Burgos (**Museo de Burgos**), Casa de Miranda, c/ Calera, 25. July–Sept. Tue.–Sat. 10.00–14.00 and 17.00–20.00, Sun. 10.00–14.00, Oct.–June Tue.–Sat. 10.00–14.00 and 16.00–19.00, Sun. 10.00–14.00, 1.20 €, free Sat./Sun. and for people over 65. www.museodeburgos.com.*

After Atapuerca there's a sometimes wearisome, roughly ¾ hr. long ascent, in places stony, onto the high **Matagrande** plain (4; 1,078m). Just after the wooden cross the view opens out towards Burgos. After a stony descent the Camino becomes a broad agricultural track which leads to **Villaval (5**; ½ hr.). From there it follows a small country road to **Cardeñuela-Riopico (6**; ½ hr.) and **Orbaneja-Riopico (7**; ½ hr.). After crossing the motorway you have to make a decision when you reach the housing estate **(8)**: the path straight on goes via **Villafría** (¾ hr.) through the industrial zone to **Burgos** (2¼ hrs. from Villafría).

The nicer alternative leads left at first towards the motorway and then away from it as far as the access road (N-120) just before **Castañares (9**; ¾ hr.). Follow the path next to the road into the nearby village. At the traffic lights go left across the N-120 and through c/ de la Iglesia straight on past the church (southwards, with the N-120 behind you). At the gravel works turn right and follow the surfaced path. It leads over a blue footbridge and then next to the motorway through the wood. After a good ¼ hr. it goes left under the motorway and at the fork, right (arrow on the board). After just under 500m there's a wooden railing beside the footpath. Follow this for a short way round its left hand bend and then carry straight on along the path. Keep heading towards the electricity pylon and take the path diagonally right from there. The path becomes clearer as it follows the power lines parallel to the Río Arlanzón through the Fuentes Blancas recreation area. Past **Fuentes Blancas campsite (10)** you come to the river swimming pool of **Playa Fuente del Prior (11**; a good ½ hr.). At the end of the small beach you walk under a new bridge and after about 25 mins. under a broad road. Shortly afterwards pass a footbridge over the river and a second one a little later on. You can turn off left here to the **Casa-Emaús-hostel**: walk left away from the river and over

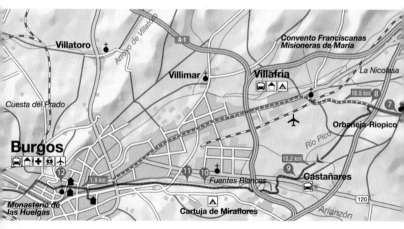

112

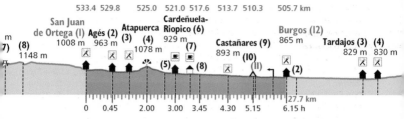

533.4 529.8   525.0   521.0 517.6   513.7 510.3   505.7 km

San Juan
de Ortega (I) Agés (2) Atapuerca Cardeñuela-
(3) (4) Riopico (6) 929 m Castañares (9) Burgos (12)
m 1008 m 963 m 1078 m (7) 893 m 865 m Tardajos (3) (4)
7) (8) (5) (8) (10) 829 m 830 m
1148 m (II) (2)

0 0.45 2.00 3.00 3.45 4.30 5.15 6.15 h
27.7 km

the road into c/ Padre Diego de San Vitorés. Carry straight on to c/ San Pedro Cardeña and left there to the square with the large parish building where the hostel can be found.

To walk directly into town continue along the promenade beside the river as far as the road bridge (Puente Gasset), cross over this to the right and then walk left past the Colegio público (school) and the Museo Santa María into the Plaza de San Juan (the Iglesia de San Lesmes is diagonally to the left). Turn left here onto the waymarked Way of St. James to reach the old town and the **Catedral de Santa María (12)** in **Burgos** (½ hr. from the Emaús turn-off).

i *In hardly any other town along the Way of St. James have political, economic and religious powers left behind such remarkable traces as in **Burgos**. Founded in 884 by Duke Diego Rodríguez Porcelos, in 1037 Burgos became the capital of the earldom of Castilla (founded in 951) and was the royal capital of the united kingdom of Castilla y León until the end of the Reconquista (1492). Thanks to the huge*

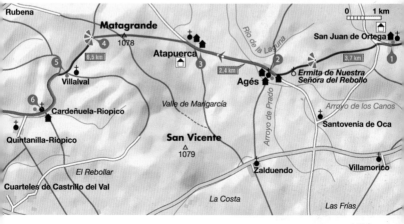

herds of sheep on the broad expanses of the Meseta it was, right into the 16th century, the centre of the Castilian wool trade. The relocation of the capital to Madrid (1561), plague epidemics and the expulsion of the last Moors (1609) led to its economic and thus also its demographic decline at the beginning of the 17th century. During the civil war (1936–1939) Burgos was the seat of the nationalistic government of Franco. The textile, chemical and rubber factories (Firestone) established during Franco's dictatorship make Burgos today an important industrial location. The most remarkable building in Burgos in all respects is the **Catedral de Santa María**. The church, begun in 1221 under King Fernando III and completed in the 16th century, is an impressive example of Gothic architecture. International architects like Felipe de Borgoña (Burgundy), Gil de Siloé (Flanders) and Juan de Colonia (Hans of Cologne) as well as his son Simón and grandson Francisco created the architectural and sculptural artisitic unity of the church.

The two 84m high towers of the west façade, designed according to plans by Juan de Colonia, are the emblem of Burgos. Several richly decorated portals adorn the cathedral from the outside like, for example, the Puerta de la Coronería (around 1250, north transept), the Puerta de la Pellejería (1516, Francisco de Colonia, facing east) and at the south transept the Puerta de Sarmental (around 1230). The huge interior of the church is just below 84m – not including the Capilla del Condestable (15th century, Simón de Colonia) behind the choir ambulatory. As in many Spanish cathedrals the choir and high altar are separated by a highly decorated screen. Above the nave on huge 59m high pillars is the splendid domed ceiling (Cimborrio) (1568, Juan de Vallejo). The bones of Rodrigo Díaz de Vivar, in short El Cid, (1043–99), the Spanish national hero, has lain beneath the dome

since 1921 and also that of his wife Doña Jimena. In the Capilla del Santísimo Cristo can be seen El Cristo de Burgos, the much worshipped statue of Christ made out of wood, leather and hair (Mon.–Fri. 17.00–19.30). The Escalera dorada (golden staircase, due to the gilded handrail) spans the 8m height difference to the Puerta de la Coronería. High above the western portal the curious figure of Papamoscas, the flycatcher, strikes the hours. In the south of the church you come to the two-storied cloister (Claustro) from the 13th century (19th March–Oct. 9.30–19.30, last entry 18.30, Nov.–18th March 10.00–19.00, last entry 18.00. 7 €, pilgrims with passport 3.5 €. Internet: www.catedraldeburgos.es, link: horarios/cultos/turismo for information about mass).

Pilgrims have been entering the old town of Burgos for centuries along the **Calle de las**

Calzadas which goes past the **Iglesia de San Lesmes** (14th century), tomb of San Lesmes, in the 11th century benefactor of pilgrims and patron saint of the town. The Reyes Católicos, Fernando and Isabella, received Christopher Columbus after his second journey to America in the splendid palace of **Casa del Cordón** (15th century). The utterly plain and simple **Iglesia de San Gil** (13th–5th century) is the most beautiful Gothic building in Burgos after the cathedral. Diagonally opposite the cathedral the **Iglesia de San Nicolás de Bari** (15th century) houses an unusual high altar for Spain, made of coloured alabaster by Simón and Francisco de Colonia (July–Sept. 10.00–13.30 and 17.00–19.00, Oct.–June 12.00–13.30 and 17.00–19.00). The **Iglesia de San Esteban** (13th/14th century) is home to the Museo de Retablo in which altar pieces from the 16th–18th century can be seen (visit to the museum on application, information from the tourist office). Pilgrims leave Burgos through the **Arco de San Martín** (13th/14th century), the former entrance into the Jewish quarter. The **Hospital del Rey** (from the end of the 12th century) is situated/located before the town, once one of the biggest pilgrim hostels along the Way of St. James. The Gothic monastery complex of the **Monasterio de las Huelgas Reales** can be found near to El Parral park. Around 1187 Alfonso VIII and his wife Leonor Plantagenet, daughter of

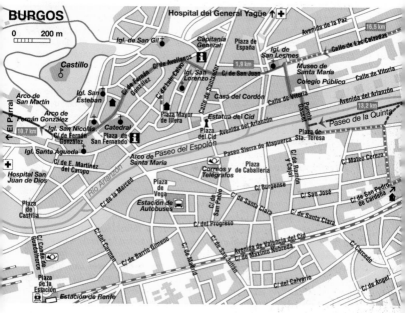

Henry II of England, made a Cistercian convent out of the royal pleasure palace (huelga used to mean recovery, today, strike) (Tue.–Sat. 10.00–14.00 and 16.00–18.30. Sun./public holidays 10.30–15.00, 7 €, Wed. afternoon free, sale of tickets up to 1 hr. before closing). The Carthusian monastery of **Cartuja de Miraflores** lies outside the town, a late Gothic masterpiece, at the end of the 15th century commissioned by Isabella la Católica as a tomb for her parents (daily Mon.–Sat. 10.15–15.00 and 16.00–18.00, Sun./public holidays 11.20–15.00 and 16.00–18.00, Mass: Mon.–Sat. 9.00, Sun./public holiday 10.15. Free entrance, in summer a tourist train takes you from the centre to the Cartuja).

As you walk around the town it's worth making a detour to the **Plaza Mayor** and taking a stroll along the **Paseo de Espolón** by the river. The **Arco de Santa María** is one of the twelve town gateways in the past. It was designed by Juan de Vallejo and Francisco de Colonia in the 16th century as a triumphal arch (Tue.–Sat. 11.00–13.50 and 17.00–21.00, Sun. 11.00–13.50, closed Mon/public holidays, free entry).

The harsh continental climate has earned Burgos the nickname of 'la fría', the cold. In fact the short summers are very hot, whereas it can still be quite cool into June.

Public holidays: end of January: San Lesmes in honour of the town's patron saint. On the Friday after Corpus Christi, Festividad de el Curpillos, around the Huelgas Reales and in El Parral park. At the end of June, San Pedro and San Pablo processions including gigantillos, enormous human figure (see photo above).

Gastronomy: quesos de Burgos (fresh cheese, popular with honey and nuts as postre del abuelo – granddad's pudding), morcilla (black pudding enhanced by rice, onions and pepper, made into fritters, served boiled or fried). A hearty dish which Sancho Panza, Don Quijote's travelling companion, used to enjoy is olla podrida, a bean stew, with, amongst other things, spicy sausage and black pudding, but also pig's ear, knuckle and rib of pork as well as bacon and sometimes cecina, dried beef. An acquired taste. Wine: D.O. Ribera del Duero.

Information: www.aytoburgos.es and www.turismoburgos.org.

Hostels: Tardajos (829m, pop. 850), MH, ☕, 18 B/donations. Basic, but decent sleeping accommodation. 16.00–22.00, Mar.–Oct. **Rabé de las Calzadas** (830m, pop. 220) PH, ☕☕, 28 B/from 8 €. Alb. Liberanos Domine, Pl. Francisco Riberas, 2, tel: 655 116 901. Washing machine/drier. 12.30–22.00, all year. **Hornillos del Camino** (826m, pop. 60), MH, ☕☕, 32 B (if necessary space in town hall and sports hall)/7 €. Next to the church, tel: 947 411 050 Casa Manolo. Kitchen/dining room, coffee machine, washing machine. Rather cramped. From around 13.00–22.00, all year. **San Bol** (896m), MH, ☕☕, 15 B/5 €. Remote house, evening meal/breakfast. All day, Apr.–Oct. **Hontanas** (871m, pop. 60), **(1)** PH, ☕☕☕, 50 B/4 € (3 DR 24 €, one 3-bed room 30 €). El Puntido, tel: 947 378 597. Bar/rest., breakfast from about 6.00, internet, washing machine/drier. 6.00–22.00, Apr.–Oct. **(2)** PH, ☕☕☕, 14 B/5 €. Alb. Santa Brígida, tel: 628 927 317. Washing machine/drier, kitchen, meals, small shop. Lots of room. From 12.00, Mar.–Oct. **(3)** MH, ☕☕☕, 21 B (two extra lodging places with 14 and 20 B)/5 €. Tel: town hall 947 377 021. Renovated, former pilgrim hostel, drinks/snack machine, telephone, kitchen. Extra accommodation more simply equipped, but quite roomy. Open from around 13.00, all year.

Grade and route: easy, well marked. A lot of asphalt at times to Rabé de las Calzadas, after that farm tracks and dirt paths.

Height difference: 290m in ascent and descent.

Critical points: none.

Scenery: the Tierra de Campos starts at Burgos, the seemingly endless cornfields of the Meseta, the central Spanish plateau. A sometimes wearying flatness and monotony characterise the walk as far as León, so many pilgrims avoid it and take the bus to León. But then they are missing out on a unique natural experience in which the beauty lies in the detail, in the changing play of colours, the bright red carpets of summer poppies and the vastness of the sky.

Local services: Tardajos 🖥️ € ✚ ✗ 🏪 🅰️ 🛏️ @; Rabé de las Calzadas 🛒 🏠 🛏️ 🏪 @; Hornillos del Camino ✗ 🏠 🏪 🛏️; Hontanas 🛏️ ✗ @ 🏠 🚲 🛏️ (small shop in the Santa Brígida hostel).

Remarks: in summer it is best to avoid the midday heat since there is hardly any shade in spite of the newly planted trees. Remember to take water with you.

Sheep farming is still an important occupation in the central Spanish highlands.

Pass the north side of the **cathedral (1)** and go down the long c/Fernán González, then diagonally left through c/ Emperador into c/ Benedictinas de San José. Cross over the Río Arlanzón and leave Burgos through **El Parral park (2**; ½ hr.). At the end of the park turn right and soon afterwards, go left. After the *Escuela Superior Politécnica* (technical college) take the road diagonally right and now continue straight ahead.

You come past a new housing development (on the right), go under the railway, over the 4-laned N-120, follow it for a short while to the left and go under the motorway one last time. Shortly afterwards take the road on the right to **Tardajos (3**; 2¼ hrs.) and from there it's just a short way to **Rabé de las Calzadas (4**; ½ hr.).

You have finally left the area of Greater Burgos behind and the path leads again through small, medieval looking villages that adapt well into the countryside with their massive stone houses.

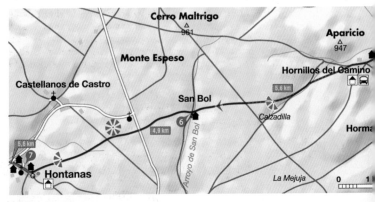

Farm tracks bring you through cornfields across a softly undulating land-scape to **Hornillos del Camino** (5; 1¾ hrs.).

i *In the Middle Ages **Hornillos del Camino** was an important stopping off point for pilgrims with several pilgrim hospitals and a leper ward founded in the 12th century. The name originates from 'Forniellos' (kilns) and dates back to the Middle Ages when the production of limestone and pottery was an important line of business in the village. The Gothic **parish church of San Román** dates back to the 16th century. The caring of pilgrims with volunteer hospitaleros started in Hornillos del Camino in 1989, on the initiative of Lourdes Lluch, a woman from Catalonia.*

Continuing across the fascinating wide, gently undulating high country you reach the **turn-off (6)** left to the remote **San Bol** hostel lying in a hollow (1½ hrs.). The former small hamlet of San Bol was deserted by its inhabitants for reasons unknown in 1503.

From the hollow ascend again onto the plateau where not a single settlement can be seen for a long time, just one or two wind farms, until you are standing directly above **Hontanas (7)** which lies tucked into a valley (a good 1 hour). The locals maintain that the water from the church drinking fountain is very healthy. The name of the place also comes from the ancient word for fountain, *fontanas*.

Hostels: San Antón (807m), PH, ☕, 12 B/donations. Basic hostel in the ruins of the monastery church, cold water, no electricity, sleeping area separated from the outside only by a curtain, can be cold at night; communal evening meal. 7.00–21.00, June–Sept. **Castrojeriz** (816m, pop. 570), **(1)** PH, ☕☕, 30 B/6 €, DR 37 €, 4-bed room 80 €, 6-bed room 90 €. Large hall in campsite at entrance to village about 1km before the centre, to the entrance as indicated on the left and turning right three times around the campsite. Washing machine/drier, small shop, internet, bar/restaurant. All day, roughly mid March–mid Oct. **(2)** PH, ☕☕☕, 20 B/6,50 €. Casa Nostra, c/ Real del Oriente, 54, tel: 947 377 493. Restored, spacious old house, kitchen, washing machine/drier, internet, 10.00–23.00, Easter–Oct./Nov. **(3)** MH, ☕☕◠, 30 B/donations. Alb. de San Esteban, tel: town hall 947 377 001. Large dormitory with bunk beds and mattresses, internet, microwave. 13.00–22.30, all year. **(4)** MH, ☕☕, 28 B/donations. Alb. de San Juan, tel: 947 377 400. Opposite El Lagar bar, i.e. on the Camino, after Casa Nostra, sign to the left, at the bottom first right and just under 400m straight on.

Breakfast, garden. 15.00–22.30, about April–Oct. **San Nicolás de Puente Fitero** (769m), RH, ☕☕, 11 B/donations. Confraternita di San Japoco di Compostela (Italian). Basic hostel in the small Gothic chapel of San Nicolás, dormitory and dining room in the church, separate showers and WC. From about 16.00, around May/June–Sept. **Itero de la Vega** (770m, pop. 180), **(1)** PH, ☕☕◠, 24 B/8 € (7 DR 40 €). Hostal-rest. Puente Fitero, tel: 979 151 822. Washing machine/drier, internet, bar/restaurant, shop. All day, all year. **(2)** PH, ☕☕, 14 B/6 € (2 DR 8 €). Alb. La Mochila, tel: 979 151 781. Village centre. Internet, meals/breakfast. Washing machine/drier. All day, all year. **(3)** MH, ☕, 12 B (+M)/5 €. Left at Bar Tachu/PH 2, opposite church. Basic sleeping accommodation. Open, someone comes to stamp pilgrim passport/collect money. All day, all year. **Boadilla del Camino** (780m, pop. 130), **(1)** PH, ☕☕☕, 12 B/7 €. Alb. Putzu. Kitchen, washing machine, garden. Serafin who runs the hostel only accepts 'genuine' pilgrims and exercises his right of refusal or ejection. From 13.00. All year except Christmas. **(2)** MH, ☕, 12 B/4 €. Basic sleeping accommodation in the old school house. 13–22.00, all year. **(3)** PH, ☕☕☕, 48 B (+ 12 B if necessary)/6 €. Alb. En el Camino, Plaza del Rollo, tel: 979 810 284. Washing machine/drier, internet, drinks machine, bar/restaurant, lovely day room garden, pool. All day, March–Oct.

Grade and route: easy except for the short ascent after Castrojeriz; well marked, unmistakable farm tracks on wide plains.
Height difference: 220m in ascent, 310m in descent.
Critical points: none.
Scenery: the limitless expanses become even more endless from the province of Palencia onwards, broader and flatter. The path goes through a remarkably bare landscape for middle Europeans.

Local services: Castrojeriz 🍴 🏨 🛏 ✂ @ ✈ A € ♿ ℹ 🚃 🛒 Iglesia de San Juan Mon.–Sat. 18.00, Sun. 13.00, Convento de las Clarisas Sun. 8.30 ✚ c/ Cruz de la Riviera s/n, tel: 947 372 595; Itero de la Vega 🍴 🛏 🏨 @; Boadilla del Camino 🍴 🏨 @.

Remarks: (1) You can lose all sense of time across this almost treeless plain where time appears to stretch forever. **(2)** Avoid the midday heat in summer, hardly any shade, remember to take water with you. **(3)** There is a spring and resting place just before San Nicolas Punte Fitero.

First follow the road out of **Hontanas (1)** and just after the village turn off right. Continue along the dirt path at the edge of the mountain and then you come back to the road. This brings you in a good 1¼ hrs. to **San Antón (2)**.

ℹ *San Antón is one of the oddest ruins along the way (see photo above). Since today's country road follows strictly the historic pilgrim route, it runs right through the middle of the archway that once connected the monastery with the church. The monastery was established in the 12th century as a pilgrim hospital of the Order of St. Anthony. The few remaining walls of the church date from the 14th/15th century. In the Middle Ages there was talk of the miracles of the monasteries of the Order of St. Anthony since many pilgrims were cured of '***St. Anthony's fire***' (ergotism). The poisoning was caused by the fungus claviceps, a parasite on rye, which usually ended in death. The disease occurred mainly in northern Europe after poor harvests whenever bad corn was used to make bread. They found out that the 'miracle healing' simply came from the fact that pilgrims on the Iberian peninsula started eating wheat bread which was customary there.*

*Closely connected to San Antón and the nearby Castrojeriz is the T-shaped '**Tau**'. Its origins lie in Egypt. It is the last letter of the Hebrew alphabet and corresponds to the Greek letter 'Tau'. In the bible it is mentioned as a symbol of protection and Pope Urban IV named it a symbol of Christian devotion. The monks of the Order of St. Anthony wore it as a sign of recognition and gave it to the pilgrims to take with them as protection against evil and sickness. So it became the **Cruz del Peregrino** and is still today one of the mystic symbols of the Way of St. James.*

San Antón Abad is the patron saint of animals who is always depicted with a pig. On the 17th January farm animals and pets in the whole of Spain are taken to church to be blessed and, of course, in San Antón too.

Continue along the country road to the church of **Nuestra Señora del Manzano (3; 1 hr.)** and turn right to reach **Castrojeriz (4)** roughly 1km away.

i **Castrojeriz** is one of the longest places along the Camino. Founded by the Visigoths, Castrum Sigerici was in the 9th/10th century an important stronghold in the battle of the Christians against the Arabs. (The town charter granted in 974 is the oldest in Castilla.) In the 11th century it was a royal residence and had up to nine churches and seven pilgrim hospitals. Castrojeriz played no further role in the course of history.

At the entrance to the village lie the monastery buildings and the former collegiate church of **Santa María del Manzano** (11th–13th century). A pictorial representation of the Virgen del Manzano (virgin of the apple tree) can be found, amongst other things, in the interior of the three-nave church (daily 15th June–15th Sept. 10.00–14.00 and 17.00–20.00, Sept.–June Tue.–Sun. 10.00–14.00 and 17.00–19.00). The **Iglesia de Santo Domingo** (16th century) is situated in the village. On the exterior façade there are two stone skulls as a reminder of the past ('O

On the way to Castrojeriz.

Arroyo de Villajos ó de San Martín
Ayo. de Garbanzuelo
4,9 km
Hontanas
Ermita de Espinosa
as Cántaras
913
5,6 km
Alto de Carroalcarro
△ 918
Juan Andrés
1 km
2,8 km
San Miguel
△ 951
Convento de San Antón
Convento de Santa Clara
0   1 km

Mors') and eternity ('O Aeternitas'). As you walk out of the village you walk past the **Iglesia de San Juan** (13th–16th century). The church tower with a Romanesque base and a Gothic border is very striking (June–Sept. Tue.–Sun. 10.00–14.00 and 17.00–19.00). The castle (castillo) above the town was founded in the 9th century and from the 18th century used as a quarry. In the **Convento de Santa Clara** located outside (founded in the 14th century) the nuns make cakes and biscuits as well as Tau crosses out of wood. On sale: 9.30–14.00 and 16.00–20.00.

Public holidays: weekend before 25th July: Fiesta del Ajo, garlic festival. On Saturdays competition in making garlic plaits (ristras de ajo), afterwards garlic soup (sopa al ajo) and garlic chicken (pollo al ajillo).

The path leaves Castrojeriz in the direction of the table mountain of **Alto de Mostelares (5)**. After ½ hr. the ascent begins along a broad gravel path. In half an hour it goes onto the roughly 910m high plateau from which there are lovely views back towards Castrojeriz and the table mountains opposite. Cultivated with cornfields, the plain spreads out below you on the descent.

0   1 km
Tardantes
Itero de la Vega   8   Itero del Castillo
San Nicolás   1,9 km
9,1 km
Arroyo del Barco
Arroyo de la Robrixa
Otero Largo
△ 857
Arroyo de Chamadilla
Casas de la Dehesa
8,3 km
6 km
Los Cascajares
Ayo. de la Sangre
Provincia de Palencia / Provincia de Burgos
9   Boadilla del Camino
Melgar de Yuso

Plain after the Alto de Mostelares on the Camino towards San Nicolás.

After a good hour you come to a small resting place along the way with a drinking fountain **(6)**. Continue along the small asphalt road, then left along the farm track to the chapel/hostel of **San Nicolás** (7; 13th century; ¼ hr.). When you have crossed the bridge over the Río Pisuerga you come into the province of Palencia. Immediately after the bridge take the field path on the right to reach **Itero del Castillo** (8; ½ hr.). Then walk along broad farm tracks across the wide, gently undulating plain to **Boadilla del Camino** (9; 2 hrs.).

> *i* *The stone column of justice is worth visiting (**rollo jurisdiccional**, 16th century). The finely worked column adorned with St. James shells and other things, is one of the most beautiful of its kind along the Way of St. James. Judgement was once administered here. The church of **Nuestra Señora de la Asunción** dates from the 16th century, but was redesigned many times, the last time in the 18th century.*

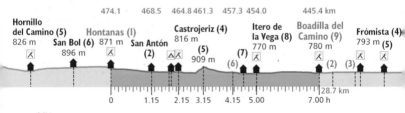

Hostels: Frómista (793m, pop. 820), **(1)** PH, ●●, 40 B/7 € (accommodation, evening meal, breakfast 17 €), (4 DR 30 €, SR 25 €). Alb. Canal de Castilla, c/ La Estación, 2, tel: 979 810 193. After going under the railway bridge turn right at the sign: go back along the sidewalk, turn right over the bridge and straight on to the former railway building. Washing machine/drier, internet, restaurant. From about 12.00, all year (possibly closed in winter). **(2)** MH, ●●, 56 B/7 €. behind Iglesia de San Martín, tel: 979 811 089, *hospitalera* Carmen, tel: 686 579 702. Reservations, washing machine/drier. Summer: 12.00–22.30, winter: 13.30–21.30 (no heating!), closed 20th Dec.–31st Jan. **(3)** PH, ●●▲, 32 B/from 7 €. Alb. Estrella del Camino (right at San Martín church, near Hostal Camino de Santiago), tel: 979 810 053. Internet, washing machine./drier, garden. 12.00–23.00 (summer), 13.30–21.00 (winter). **Población de Campos** (780m, pop. 150), MH, ●●, 18 B/4 €, tel: 979 811 099 and 625 469 326. Cooking facilities, washing machine. Garden, internet. Hostel managers also run Hotel/Casa Rural with SR/DR next to the hostel. All day, all year. **Villarmentero de Campos** (798m, pop. 10 PH, ●●●, 18 B/6 €, 6 hammocks/3 €, 8 B teepee/6 €, 2 B in hut/18 €. Alb. Amanecer, tel: 629 178 543. Kitchen, breakfast with donation, communal evening meal, bar. All day, Mar.–Oct. **Villalcázar de Sirga** (808m, pop. 180) **(1)** MH, ●●, 19 B+M/donations. Town hall, tel: 979 888 041. Kitchen, slot machine for warm water, basic, but acceptable. About 13.00, but definitely 15.00–22.00, April–Nov. **(2)** PH, ●●●, 7 B/7 €. Alb. Casas Aúrea, tel: 979 888 163 and 620 399 040 (towards exit from village). 2 bunk beds, 3 normal beds, washing machine, internet, bar/restaurant. Garden. All day, April–Sept./Oct. **Carrión de los Condes** (830m, pop. 2,200), **(1)** RH, ●●, 30 B/5 €, (guesthouse/*hospedería*: DR

44 €/SR 22 €). Alb. del Convento de Santa Clara, Order of Clarissa, tel: 979 880 837. Microwave, narrow rooms, not very comfortable. Reception 11.00–15.00 and 17.00–20.00, closed Dec.–Feb. **(2)** RH, ●●, 102 B/5 €. Alb. Espíritu Santo. Hijas de la Caridad de San Vicente. C/ San Juan, bei left at Bar España, right at the fork, past Conde Garay café-bar, then right along the street (just under 150m from Bar España). Tel: 979 880 052. Clean, quiet. Small patio. About 10.00–22.30, all year. **(3)** RH, ●●, 52 B/5 €. Rectory Santa María del Camino, tel: 979 880 072. Washing machine/drier, internet, kitchen. 12/13.00–22.00, March–Oct.

Grade and route: easy and flat, well marked. Frómista to Carrión de los Condes, gravel path parallel to the P-980. Alternative route away from the road between Población de Campos and Villalcázar de Sirga there's an alternative away from the road.

Height difference: 80m in ascent, 20m in descent.

Critical points: none.

Scenery: continue through endless sea of cornfields in the Tierra de Campos. In places the typical mud brick construction (adobe) of the area can still be seen, then the water-abundant and green lined Canal de Castilla just before Frómista.

Local services: Frómista everything ✚ Avda. Ejército Español s/n, tel: 979 810 065; Población de Campos ⊠ ☑ ✚ 🏠 🚌 @ ✚; Revenga de Campos (782m, pop. 160) 🍴✚; Villovieco (781m, pop. 90) 🍴 🍴; Villarmentero de Campos 🍴 🍴; Villalcázar de Sirga 🍴 ☑ 🏠 🚌 🚌 19.15; Carrión de los Condes 🍴 🏠 ℹ️ ⊠ 🚌 🅰 @ 🚐 🔋 Igl. de Santa María del Camino Mon.–Sat. 20.00, Sun. 12.00 and 19.00 🚌 (tickets in Bar España), ✚ Pl. Conde Garay s/n, tel: 979 880 245.

Remarks: do not be put off by the 'endless' wide-open spaces which are some of the most impressive aspects of the path.

About ½ hr. after **Boadilla (1)** the path meets the **Canal de Castilla (2)** and continues for ¾ hr. along the old tow path to the **weir (3)** at the entrance to the village of **Frómista**. The village centre **(4)** lies 1km/¼ hr. away.

ℹ️ The **Canal de Castilla** (See photo on the right) was built from 1753–1859, with some interruptions, along a 207km long stretch of water. With 49 weirs the canal overcomes 150 vertical metres. Corn was transported along the canal from the Tierra de Campos into the north of the region and further to the Atlantic coast. The weir at **Frómista** overcomes 14 vertical metres. Up to 400 laden ships pulled by mules travelled daily along the canal. Since 1959 it has been used only for the irrigation of agricultural land – and by canoeists as a long distance route.

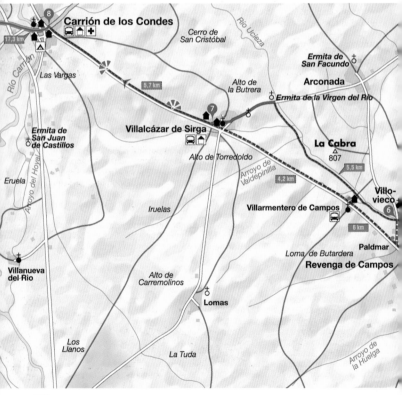

The **Iglesia de San Martín** was consecrated in 1066 and is, with a rarely attained harmony of proportions and masterly sculptures, a beautiful example of the Spanish Romanesque period. Nothing remains of the adjoining Benedictine monastery. Moderate restoration was carried out from 1896–1904. The exterior façade appears plain and unadorned, but on closer inspection, you will see the chessboard frieze and the 315 decorative corbels in the shape of people, plants, animals, demons, mythical beings and some erotic figures. The column capitals inside the church with biblical and everyday motifs give an insight into the medieval world of pictures (10.00–14.00 and 16.30–20.00, winter: 15.00–18.30).

Less known are the **Iglesia de San Pedro** (15th century, Renaissance portal 16th century, daily 10.00–14.00 and 17.00–20.00) and the **Iglesia de Santa María del Castillo** (16th century; daily video about Frómista and the Camino, May–Oct. 12.00, 13.00, 18.00 and 19.00, 3 €).

A son of this arid region is, surprisingly, the patron saint of seafarers; in the 13th century **San Telmo** is said to have walked on the waters of the Río Miño. There is a celebration in his honour on the Monday after Easter with, amongst other things, the rather noisy El Ole procession which is a night time affair with dancing and singing, and the brandishing of sticks, brooms and streamers.

Text book Romanesque style – the Iglesia de San Martín in Frómista.

A gravel path parallel to the country road leads from Frómista to **Población de Campos (5**; ¾ hr.), **Revenga de Campos** (1 hr.) **Villarmentero de Campos** (¼ hr.) and **Villalcázar de Sirga (7**; 1 hr.).

The somewhat longer, but nicer alternative goes from **Población de Campos (5)** away from the road and parallel to the stream to **Villovieco (6**; ¾ hr.). Walk over the bridge at the left hand end of Población de Campos and then right and beside the stream past **Villarmentero de Campos** (½ hr.). Following the stream (arrows on footbridges) you reach a road (¾ hr., straight on to the Ermita de la Virgen del Río), turn left there to **Villalcázar de Sirga (7**; just under ½ hr.).

i *The **Iglesia de Nuestra Señora de la Virgen Blanca** (12th–13th century) rises up large and powerful above **Villalcázar de Sirga** (Villasirga, for short; camino de sirga = tow path). Miracle cures are said to have taken place here in the Middle Ages below a statue of the Virgin Mary which Alfonso X el Sabio (the Wise) immortalised in his cantigas (songs). The Templar Knights extended the church to its present day size. The striking entrance portal is situated cornerwise below the portico. The portal and the interior are adorned with sculptures. The colourful Gothic tombs of Don Felipe (brother and rival of Alfonso the Wise) and his second wife Doña Leonor Ruiz de Castro are very beautiful (Easter-15th Oct.10.30–14.00 and 16.30– 19.00, rest of the year Sat./Sun./public holidays 12.00–14.00 and 17.00–18.30).*

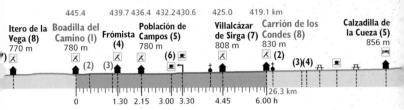

	445.4	439.7 436.4	432.2 430.6		425.0	419.1 km		

Itero de la Vega (8) 770 m · Boadilla del Camino (1) 780 m · Frómista (4) · Población de Campos (5) 780 m · Villalcázar de Sirga (7) 808 m · Carrión de los Condes (8) 830 m · Calzadilla de la Cueza (5) 856 m

26.3 km

0   1.30 2.15 3.00 3.30   4.45   6.00 h

There's now an almost endless stretch to walk next to the road to reach **Carrión de los Condes** (8; 1¼ hrs.).

ℹ️ There is not much left of the former splendour of the capital of Tierra de Campos, **Carrión de los Condes**. The settlement founded by the Romans on the Río Carrión in the Middle Ages belonged to the kingdom of Castilla y León and was the seat of the Duke (condes) Beni Gómez. Court assemblies, court hearings and councils were held in Carrión de los Condes. Aimeric Picaud in the Codex Calixtinus praised 'the excellent town where there was bread, wine, meat and all kinds of products in abundance'. In the 15th century there were 14 pilgrim hospitals. Two sons of the the count and countess of Gómez enjoy an inglorious, if also fictional mention in the heroic epic Cantar de Mio Cid. They are said to have been married to two daughters of the Spanish national hero El Cid. They paid with their lives for the attempted murder of their wives who were not befitting their social station. The most well known monument is the Benedictine monastery, **Real Monasterio de San Zoilo**. It is probably of Mozarabic origin and in 1077 affiliated itself to the order of Cluny. The Romanesque west façade (11th century) and the plateresque cloister (16th century) are worth seeing. The counts of Carrión are buried in the monastery church (17th century). The monastery houses a hotel today (daily 10.30–14.00 and 16.30–20.00, winter only Tue.–Sun. and only until 19.00, pilgrims 1.50 €). Also of interest is the **Iglesia de Santa María del Camino** (also de la Victoria, 12th century) in the centre of the village. The south portal alludes, amongst other things, to the 100 virgins ('Tributo de las 100 doncellas') surrendered to the Moors in tribute every year: bulls rescue four girls from the village before the handing over to the Moors. In the church you will find the second of the Y-shaped crucifixes, the work of a Rhineland artist. The other is to be found in Puente la Reina. The Romanesque frieze depicting figures at the entrance of the **Iglesia de Santiago** (12th century) is interesting. The parish museum is located in the church (info in Iglesia de Santa María del Camino: 15th April–Sept. daily 10.00–13.00 and 17.00–19.00, rest of the year by appointment). The **Convento de Santa Clara** founded in 1255 is the oldest Convent of St. Clarissa in Spain. **Public holidays:** at Corpus Christi the main street is festooned with carpets of flowers. Second half of August: patron saint festival in honour of San Zoilo with processions and street celebrations. Large market every Thursday since 1618.

129

Hostels: Calzadilla de la Cueza (856m, pop. 55), PH, ◐◐, 70 B/7 €. Alb. Camino Real, tel: 979 883 187 and 616 483 517. Washing machine/drier, internet, small pool. 12.00–22.30, all year. **Lédigos** (878m, pop. 75), PH, ◐◐▲, 50 B/from 6 € (5 DR 18 €), El Palomar, tel: 979 883 605. Well-equipped kitchen, washing machine, garden, small pool, internet, bar, shop, bunk-beds and normal beds in several rooms, lots of space. 10.30–23.00, March–Dic. **Terradillos de los Templarios** (880m, pop. 80), **(1)** PH, ◐◐◐, 46 B/from 7 € (also SR/DR). Alb. Los Templarios, tel: 667 252 279. Before the village, on alternative road. Bar/Rest., internet, laundry service, large complex, reservations possible. All day, Apr.–Oct., rest of time. **(2)** PH, ◐◐◐, 49 B/8 € (bunkbed), 10 € (normal bed). Alb. Jacques de Molay, in centre of village, tel: 979 883 679, Washing machine/drier, bar/restaurant, terrace, internet, small shop. 7.00–23.00, all year except Christmas.

Grade and route: easy, well marked. After Carrión de los Condes short section on country road, otherwise farm tracks. Alternative possible from Lédigos by side of road.

Height difference: 130m in ascent, 90m in descent.

Critical points: none.

Scenery: between Carrión de los Condes and Calzadilla de la Cueza the Way of St. James goes for 12km along the original route, the old Roman road of Vía Aquitana: dead straight and with absolutely no shade. Lots of storks in early summer.

Local services: after roughly an hour along the Vía Aquitana, May–Oct., 7.00–16.00 ▣; Calzadilla de la Cueza ⊠ ▣ ▣ @; Lédigos ▣ ➤ ▣ @; Terradillos de los Templarios ⊠ ▣ ▣ @.

Remarks: make sure to take water, food and something to cover your head! It's best to walk in the morning in summer.

The path through **Carrión (1)** goes along the old main road to the square in front of the Iglesia de Santiago and at Los Condes restaurant (diagonally left below) follow the sign for the Monasterio San Zoilo. After the **Monasterio de San Zoilo** (**2**; ¼ hr.) you come onto the country road. The ruins of the **Abadía de Santa María de Benivívere** (**3**) can be found after 1 hr. lying on the right.

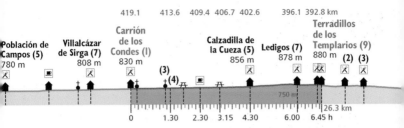

			419.1	413.6	409.4 406.7 402.6		396.1 392.8 km

Población de Campos (5)
780 m

Villalcázar de Sirga (7)
808 m

Carrión de los Condes (I)
830 m

(3)
✝(4)⍭ ▣ ⍭

Calzadilla de la Cueza (5)
856 m

Ledigos (7)
878 m

Terradillos de los Templarios (9)
880 m (2) (3)

750 m

26.3 km

0   1.30   2.30   3.15 4.30   6.00   6.45 h

ℹ️ *The Franciscan abbey founded in 1169 was well known for its opulance (benivívere: something like 'good living'). The **Vía Aquitana** begins shortly afterwards along which the Romans used to transport the gold extracted in the mines of Las Médulas from Astorga to Bordeaux. It runs as straight as a ramrod across the almost treeless plain. The path crosses the **Cañada Real Leonesa**, a meadow path, hundreds of years old, that goes from Andalucía into the north of the province of León. These sorts of meadow paths have existed all over Spain since the 12th century and are still used to some extent. One goes right through Madrid and it's quite possible that you will even come across a herd of sheep in Astorga. Due to the lack of stones in the region the traditional building method was with **adobe** clay, with air-dried clay bricks, and later also with bricks that were fired in a kiln. Many of these houses are today either falling into disrepair or the façades have been covered with more durable materials. You will find quite striking a marked tendency to use the diminutive for place names, as for example, calzadilla (small street), terradillos (small estates), almost as if they wanted to emphasise the diminuitive presence of humans in these wide expanses.*

The **Vía Aquitana (4)** begins about ¼ hr. after the abbey and runs dead straight across the almost treeless plain that is cultivated with cornfields, but

On the Vía Aquitana – nothing to challenge the eye or the mind.

there are a few resting places, some with shaded areas, for a well-earned break. After about 2¼ hrs. the belltower of **Calzadilla de la Cueza (5)** cemetery finally comes into view, but it's still another ¾ hr. to get there. Just after the village the yellow arrow at a fork indicates the original route to the right, a footpath next to the N-120. After a good quarter of an hour you pass the turn-off to the ruins of **Santa María de las Tiendas monastery (6)**. After just under 1¼ hrs. **Lédigos (7)** is reached.

There are two alternatives from here, both about ¾ hr., to Terradillos de los Templarios: the path continuing along the road passes the **first hostel (8)**. To avoid the road, cross over the N-120, walk in the direction of Población de Arroyo and turn right after the bridge onto the farm track (shell, arrows). After the farm go left and straight on to **Terradillos de los Templarios (9)**.

i **Terradillos de los Templarios** *once belonged to the **Order of the Knights Templar***. *The French knights Hugo de Payens and Godefroy de Saint Omer had founded the religious and military order after the first crusades in 1119 for the protection of Christian pilgrims in Palestine. The official name was the 'Order of the poor knights of Christ'. Equipped with papal proof of identity and privileges such as, for example, exemption from taxes and tolls, the Order rose to become the most important Order of Knights in the Middle Ages for a time. Together with the large Spanish Orders of Calatrava and Santiago the Templars looked after the pilgrims' safety along the Way of St. James. It was the power and wealth of the Order (especially in France) that led to their abolition by the church on 13th October 1307 under pressure from the French King, Philipp IV. Their members were persecuted by the inquisition and executed under the pretext of heresy, blasphemy and fornication. In 1314 the last Grand Master of the Order, Jacques de Molay, was burnt at the stake. However, this legendary Order has not completely disappeared. Some members joined Christian Orders of lay knights after the dissolution. After the 2nd World War the Order of Templars was revived as a charitable Christian organisation in Germany and other places.*

Hostels: Moratinos (856m, pop. 20), PH, ❂❂❂, 16 B/9 € (1 DR 45 €). Alb. San Bruno, c/ Ontanón, 9, tel: 979 061 465 and 672 629 658. Washing machine, internet, garden, bar, italian food. All day, mid March– mid Jan. **San Nicolás del Real Camino** (845m, pop. 50), PH, ❂❂❂, 20 B/8 € (DR 30 €). Alb. Laganares, tel: 629 181 536. Washing machine/drier, internet, Wi-Fi, terrace, restaurant. Taxi service. 7.00– 22.00, mid March–Oct. **Sahagún** (830m, pop. 2,400), **(1)** PH, ❂❂◢, 60 B/7 € (SR+ DR 15–30 €). Alb. Viatoris, Travesía del Arco (at the edge of town directions to the right), tel: 987 780 975. Online reservations www. viatoris.es. Kitchen, washing machine/drier, internet, bar; lots of room, rather draughty in cooler weather. All day, easter–Oct. **(2)** MH, ❂❂, summer: 64 B/4 €. Alb. de Peregrinos de Cluny, tel: 987 782 117. IIn former church, next to the community events room, at times very noisy and asked to be quiet when there are concerts. Washing machine, internet. Reception Mon.–Thur. 12.00–14.00 and 18.00–21.00, Fri.–Sun. 11.00–14.00 and 16.00–21.00, Mar.–Oct. Winter small hostel in c/ Antonio Nicolás, 55 (on the Camino, just before CH): 16 B/4 €. Kitchen, washing machine. 12.00–21.00, Nov.–Feb. **(3)** RH, ❂❂, 14 B/donations, Monasterio de Santa Cruz (Christian accommodation through Benedictine nuns), on the Camino almost at the exit from the village. Tel: 987 780 078. Breakfast, washing machine, prayers and pilgrim blessings. 12.00–21.30, 12th April– 12th Oct.

Grade and route: easy, well marked. Predominantly agricultural paths.

Height difference: 60m in ascent, 100m in descent.

Critical points: none.

Scenery: unspectacular, running chiefly beside the road. Just before Sahagún you leave the province of Palencia and reach León. Softly rolling hills and solitary patches of greenery liven up the countryside.

Local services: Moratinos ⊟ ⌂ ✗; San Nicolás del Real Camino ⊟ ✗ ⌨ @; Sahagún ✗ ⌂ ✉ ℹ ✉ @ € ⛁ ⌨ ⌷ ✚ c/ Constitución s/n, tel: 987 781 291.

After **Terradillos (1)** the Camino continues as a track through corn-fields across softly rolling hillsides. For the first time in a long while you can enjoy the sight of groups of trees again. After ¾ hr. you reach the ham-let of **Moratinos (2)**. Walking just a little away from the N-120 you arrive in **San Nicolás del Real Camino (3;** ½ hr.). Walk through the village to a storage depot. To the right brings you to the route that runs next to the main road and the motorway, but go straight on along the gently ascend-ing farm track. This brings you round a wide bend in a good hour to the N-120. Go left and after the bridge,

Just before San Nicolás del Real Camino.

Calzadilla de la Cueza (5) 856 m

Ledigos (7)

Terradillos de los Templarios (1) 880 m

392.8   387.0   382.0 379.4 km

San Nicolás del Real Camino (3) 845 m

(2)

Sahagún (5) 830 m

(4)

812 m

(2)

Bercianos del Real Camino (3) 850 m

El Burgo Ranero (4) 882 m

0   1.15   2.30   3.00 h

13.4 km

right (clearly marked with yellow arrows as the main route) onto the farm track to the **Ermita de la Virgen del Puente** (4; ¼ hr., straight on: next to the N-120 to Sahagún). From there, gently ascending again, walk in ¾ hr. to **Sahagún** (5). Signposts just after the edge of the village guide you on the right to the Viatoris hostel, If you carry straight you come into the centre.

i *The small brick chapel of the **Ermita de la Virgen del Puente** (12th century; see photo on the right) combines Romanesque and Arabic elements (Mudéjar style). Every 25th April a pilgrimage is held there (romería) 'de pan y queso', where there's bread and cheese and they perform the tantárigas (typical dances). Only a few traces remain of the former political, religious and cultural greatness of **Sahagún**. The **Abadía de San Benito el Real de Sahagún**, founded at the end of the 9th and and affiliated to Cluny in the 11th century, was the most important Benedictine monastery in Spain into the 19th century. Only the **Capilla de San Mancio** (12th century), the **Arco de San Benito** archway (17th century) and the **Torre del Reloj**, a tower dating from the last chapter in the monastery's history, remain today.*

*Due to the lack of stones for building they created in Sahagún some very interesting brick constructions in Romanesque style with Arabic influenced **Mudéjar elements** such as the horseshoe arches. These can easily be seen on the **Iglesia de San Lorenzo** (13th century, exceptional four-storey church tower), San Tirso (12th century) and the shrine of **Nuestra Señora la Peregrina** (17th century) lying outside. It houses 'La Divina Peregrina' (the divine pilgrim), also called 'La Roldana' for short, the statue of the Virgin Mary made by the sculptress Luisa Roldán (Sevilla 1654–1704). In the Benedictine monastery, the Monasterio de las Madres Benedictinas,*

134

can be found a small museum (Tue.–Sat., guided tours 10.00, 11.00, 12.00, 16.00 and 17.00, Sun./public holidays 10.00, 11.00 and 12.00). The **Iglesia de la Trinidad** (13th and 16th–17th century) has been a pilgrim hostel since 1993.

Public holidays: 2nd July Fiesta de la Peregrina in honour of the patron saint of the town. Procession with the Virgin made by the sculptress Roldana, festival with sweet cakes and pastries and lemonade and a (belated) midsummer eve bonfire.

Gastronomy: puerro (leek, introduced by French monks), e.g. as a sauce for trout (trucha). Last weekend in October: Feria del Puerro, a fair with agricultural products.

Sahagún – Reliegos via Calzadilla de los Hermanillos

7½ hrs.

31,6 km

Hostels: Calzada del Coto (828m, pop. 200) MH, ◎, 24 B/donations, Alb. San Roque. Very basic. Open all year. **Calzadilla de los Hermanillos** (872m, pop. 150), **(1)** PH, ◎◎◎, 20 B (plus extra beds)/15 € (DR 35 €). Alb. Vía Trajana, c/ Mayor, 57; tel: 987 337 610 and 600 220 104. Washing machine/drier, internet, bar, rest. 7.00–22.00, Easter–Nov., otherwise when necessary. **(2)** MH, ◎◎, 22 B/donations. Run by town hall of El Burgo Ranero, tel: 987 330 023. Cooking facilities, washing machine, drier. Basic, but acceptable. Easter–Nov. **Reliegos** (827m, pop. 190) **(1)** MH, ◎◎◎, 45 B/5 €. just after you enter the village in the small street on the right, tel: 987 317 801. Well-equipped kitchen. 12.00–22.30, all year. **(2)** PH, ◎◎◎, 36 B/7 € (2 DR 30 €). Alb. La Parada, tel: 987 317 880. Past MH and right. Kitchen, washing machine, drier, internet, small shop, bar, rest. All day, mid Jan.–mid Dec. **(3)** PH, ◎◎◎◎, 12 B/10 € (2 DR 45 €). Alb. Piedras Blancas II, tel: 987 330 094. On the Camino coming from El Burgo Ranero. Washing machine/drier. Bar, rest. All day, Mar.–Oct.

Grade and route: easy. Farm tracks.
Height difference: 100m.
Critical points: none.
Scenery: this little used and very remote alternative proves to be a very special scenic experience. It resembles overgrown African steppes at the start, then later on the extensive plateau after Calzadilla de los Hermanillos you can only see the Cantabrian mountain range, its peaks covered in snow right into spring, to the north in the distance. Sometimes there are no traces at all of human habitation. You feel totally alone and at a certain point you may even begin to doubt if you will ever reach another village.
Local services: Calzada del Coto ⊠ ☑; Calzadilla de los Hermanillos ⊡ (2km before the village) ⊠ ☑; Reliegos ▣ ⊠ ⊡ ☷ @.

Remarks: (1) for the start of this stage see map on p. 134 and 139. **(2)** Be sure to take plenty of water and food with you. There is no shop in Reliegos.

A hint of Africa – the start of the Vía Trajana just after Calzada del Coto.

The wide, often uninhabited regions, as here on the path to Calzadilla de los Hermanillos, are a paradise for storks.

From **Sahagún (1)** the path goes beside the road to the crossroads and goes over the bridge on the right to **Calzada del Coto (2**; ¼ hr.). Walk through the village and then leave it along the **Vía Trajana (3**; Roman road Astorga-Bordeaux, also called *Calzada de los Peregrinos*, Pilgrim road) which, depending on the weather is either dusty or muddy. After ½ hr. the route goes over a railway bridge. 1 hr. later you come to a **shady resting place with a spring (4)** on the right of the path. ½ hr. later you reach **Calzadilla de los Hermanillos (5)**.

After the village continue along the country road. After 1 hr. the road to El Burgo Ranero turns off left. However, continue straight on along the **Calzada romana (6**; writing). At the fork after about 1½ hrs. continue straight ahead

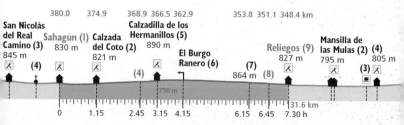

137

A shady resting place before Calzadilla.

(not diagonally left to the railway) and diagonally towards the railway tracks to a **level crossing** (**7**; ½ hr.). Stay on your side of the rails and carry straight on for a few paces along a well-trodden path (or onto the dirt road on the right and then immediately left) and follow the farm track on the left of the railway line (signpost). After ½ hr. walk down through a hollow with poplars and a

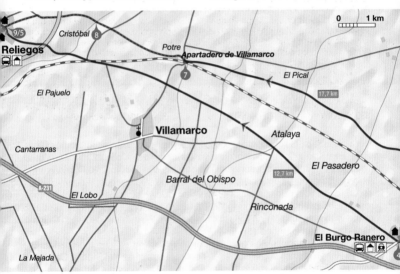

bridge over a stream (**Arroyo del Valle de Valdearcos, 8**). After that go up-hill again and through fields. After just under ½ hr. you meet a broad road under construction (just afterwards to the right is the direct alternative to Mansilla de las Mulas). Continue straight ahead and you will soon see the first roofs and, after ¼ hr., you are standing in the main square of **Reliegos** (**9**). The municipal hostel can be found on the right in the narrow street and past it, La Parada hostel, before the small park. To reach the Piedras II hostel carry straight on past the park, then go diagonally left to the main road and about 200m along to the left (total of a good 400m from the centre).

Hostels: Bercianos del Real Camino (850m, pop. 200), **(1)** PH, ◍◍◍, 7 B/donations. Alb. de María Rosa, c/ Iglesia, 3, tel: 987 784 314. Kitchen, washing machine, drier, Wi-Fi, breakfast, communal evening meal. Garden. All year. **(2)** RH, ◍◍, 48 B+M/donations. Tel: 987 784 008. Follow signs to the left at the start of the village; internet, communal evening meal, breakfast. All day, April–Nov. Winter 5 B, key with Señora Tina, c/ Santa Rita. **El Burgo Ranero** (882m, pop. 250), **(1)** SH, ◍◍◍, 28 B/donations. Alb. Doménico Laffi, tel: 987 330 047. At the church in the centre of village. Follow the signs on the right, adobe house. Kitchen, washing machine/ drier, telephone, internet. 13.00–22.00, al year, in winter key at Autoservicios Pili. **(2)** PH, ◍◍◍, 20 B/8 € (DR 40 €, SR 30 €). Alb. La Laguna, tel: 987 330 094. Kitchen, internet, bar/rest. Washing machine/drier. All day, March–Oct. **(3)** About 1km outside PH, ◍◍◍, 15 B/10 €. Alb. Ébalo Tamaù, c/ la Estación, 37, tel: 679 490 521. Kitchen, washing machine, garden, room for tents. From 15.30, April–mid Oct. **Reliegos** see Stage 18a.

Grade and route: easy. Footpath lined with trees next to the old country road.

Height difference: 90m.

Critical points: none.

Scenery: broad cornfields with only a few small clumps of trees. Quite unspectacular to monotonous stretches of path where only the croaking of countless frogs can be heard.

Local services: Bercianos del Real Camino ⨯ ▭ ⌂ ▭ ⊞ El Burgo Ranero ⨯ ⌂ Ⓐ ▭ ⊞ @; Reliegos see stage 18a.

Remarks: for the start of the stage see map on p. 134. Take water with you.

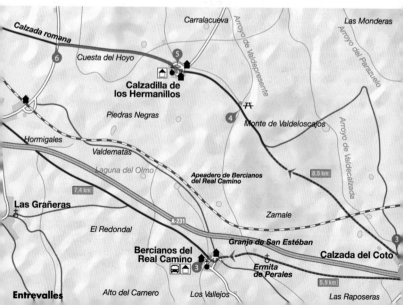

The rather unvaried path to Reliegos.

Leave **Sahagún (1)** as in stage 18a but instead of turning off right at the road bridge **(2)** in the direction of Calzada del Coto (hostel), follow the '*Real Camino Francés*' (the royal French way) straight ahead. Along the quite monotonous footpath next to the old country road you come to **Bercianos del Real Camino (3**; 1½ hrs.), **El Burgo Ranero (4**; 1¾ hrs.) and eventually **Reliegos (5**; 3 hrs.). To find both the hostels in the centre go left after the park area.

i *The hostel of **El Burgo Ranero** is named after **Doménico Laffi**, a priest from Bologna and pilgrim in the 17th century. In his report he mentioned the village by recounting a dreadful experience: Laffi was a witness to an attack by a wolf on one of the pilgrims. Today the most noticeable animals in the flat landscape are the frogs. They live in the small lagoon at the western edge of the village from where you can see some magnificent sunsets. The name of the village is also said to have come from frogs (ranas). Other theories maintain that Ranarius, the founder of the village, was the origin of the name.*

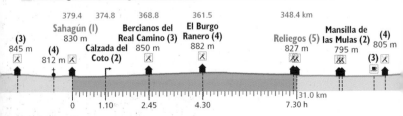

Hostels: Mansilla de las Mulas (795m, pop. 1,900), **(1)** PH, ⚫⚫◠, 36 B/8–10 €. Alb. El Jardín del Camino, tel: 987 310 232. Washing machine/drier, Wi-Fi, bar, rest. From 12.00, all year except Christmas and New Year. **(2)** MH, ⚫⚫◠, 70 B/5 €. Tel: 987 310 791. Kitchen, washing machine/drier, internet, Wi-Fi, inner courtyard. 12.30–23.00, all year except Dec. **Puente Villarente** (805m, pop. 190), **(1)** PH, ⚫⚫, 30 B/5 €. Alb. El Delfín Verde, ctra. General, 15 (immediately after the bridge on the right), tel: 987 312 065. Kitchen, washing machine, normal beds and bunkbeds, internet, pool. 12.00–23.00, March–Oct. **(2)** PH, ⚫⚫⚫, 66 B/8 € (also SR/DR). Alb. San Pelayo, c/ El Romero, 9 (after PH 1 on the right away from the road), tel: 650 918 281. Converted, large farm, kitchen, Wi-Fi, washing machine/drier, internet, garden, rest. 12.00–22.00, all year. **Arcahueja** (851m, pop. 200), PH, ⚫⚫◠, 22 B/7–8 €, HP 18 € (DR 35 €, 3-bed room 45 €). La Torre, tel: 987 205 896. Internet, Wi-Fi, restaurant. 11.00–22.00, all year (except mid–end Dec./Feb.). **León** (840m, pop. 130,000), **(1)** MH, municipal YH, tel: 987 081 832, c/ Campos Góticos, at the edge of town. Recently closed, uncertain if open again, ask when there for up-to-date info. **(2)** RH, ⚫⚫, 132 B/5 €. Alb. de las Carbajalas (Benedictine nuns), tel: 987 252 866. Washing machine/ drier, breakfast. Issuing of pilgrim passport, mass Mon.–Fri. 19.00, Sat. 8.30, Sun. 12.00. Pilgrim blessing 21.30, singing of evening prayers. 11.00–21.30, Feb.–Dec., open Christmas.

Grade and route: easy, well marked. Predominantly unsurfaced footpaths. Shortly before León there's an unpleasant stretch next to a very busy road. The long awaited pedestrian bridge has meanwhile been completed. The path into Léon is also marked, but at times not very obvious.

Height difference: 120m in ascent, 100m in descent.

Critical points: none.

Scenery: the path after Reliegos leaves the Tierra de Campos and heads for the mountain chain of Montes de León. From Mansilla de las Mulas the catchment area of León begins without any outstanding natural experiences.

Local services: Mansilla de las Mulas 🏧 🛏🍴🛒€🏧@ⓘ🏪▨⛲🖼 Igl. Parroquial de Santa María Mon.–Sat. 9.30 and 20.30 (winter 20.00), Sun. 9.30 and 12.00, Ermita de la Virgen de Gracia July/Aug. Sun. 13.00 ✚ c/ Villa de Lil s/n, tel: 987 311 175; Villarmoros de Mansilla (799m, pop. 105) 🏪 🛒📨🚌; Puente Villarente 🏧🏪🅰€🏪 🚌@; Arcahueja 🏧@🏪🚌; León all services, ✈ domestic flights, 🏪 c/ Astorga, 11, tel: Renfe 902 240 202 🚌 Paseo Saénz de Miera, s/n, tel: 987 211 000 🖼 Cathedral and San Isidoro: see description of the buildings , ✚ Hospital Princesa Sofia, Altos de Nava, tel: 987 237 400.

Cloister in the Basilika of San Isidoro.

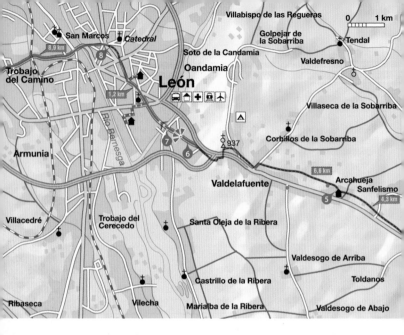

From **Reliegos (1)** a footpath goes along the left hand side of the country road straight on to **Mansilla de las Mulas** (**2**; 1¼ hrs.).

i *Mansilla de las Mulas on the Río Esla was already an important intersection before the medieval 'pilgrim boom'. The Vía Trajana had an intersection with north-south trade paths at the former country estate. Around 70 AD the Romans fortified the town with a wall. In the following centuries it fell under Gothic, Arab and finally Spanish rule. In the 12th century Fernando II, King of León, brought settlers into the town and granted it a town charter in 1181. In the 12th/13th century Mansilla was the largest and richest market town in the region. Its by-name 'de las mulas' (of the mules) was derived from the cattle markets. At the end of the almost endless Meseta there were five churches, three pilgrim hospices and numerous hostels and inns for pilgrims.*

Today the traces of former splendour have faded away. The oldest church is the ***Iglesia de Santa María*** *(18th century, beautiful Baroque high altar and some paintings from the ruined churches. 15th June–15th Sept. 10.00–14.00 and 16.00–20.00). The* ***Iglesia de San Martín*** *(13th century) serves as an arts centre today. Still preserved are the early Gothic portal and parts of the Mudejar style roof (15th century, only open during events/exhibitions). From the* ***Convento de San Agustín****, the convent founded around 1500, only parts of the plateresque* chapel have survived the destruction by French troops in the 19th century. Now-adays it houses the ethnographic museum of the province of Léon (April–Sept., Tue.–Sun. 10.00–14.00 and 17.00–20.00, Oct.–Mar., Tue.–Sun. 10.00–14.00 and 16.00–19.00). The brick construction of the **Santuario de la Virgen de la Gracia** (shrine of the Virgin of Grace, patron saint of the town; 15th June–Sept. 10.00–14.00 and 16.00–20.00) dates from the 18th century.

Public holidays: end of July Feria medieval, medieval festival with jousting and tournaments. 25th July: Día del Peregrino, festival in honour of St. James' pil-grims. End of August Feria del Tomate, 'tomato fair', folkloric performances and sale of tomatoes. 1st Sun. in Sept. pilgrimage from León to Mansilla in honour of the Virgen de la Gracia, patron saint festivals the following Sunday.

Gastronomy: bacalao de ajoarriero (arriero = muleteer), also called bacalao al es-tilo mansilles, dried cod in garlic sauce; callos and mollejas (tripe and sweetbreads).

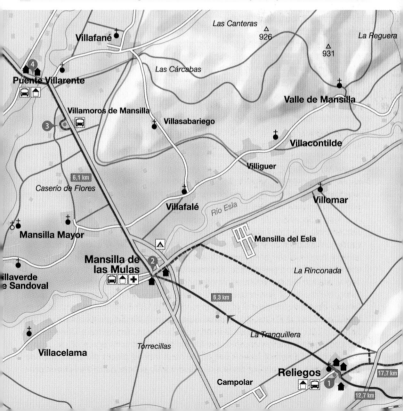

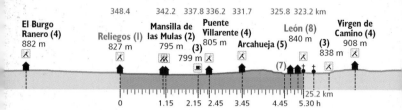

El Burgo Ranero (4) 882 m — 348.4 — Reliegos (I) 827 m — 342.2 — Mansilla de las Mulas (2) 795 m (3) — 337.8 — 336.2 799 m — Puente Villarente (4) 805 m — 331.7 — Arcahueja (5) — 325.8 — León (8) 840 m (3) 838 m — 323.2 km — Virgen de Camino (4) 908 m — (7)

0   1.15   2.15 2.45   3.45   4.45   5.30 h   25.2 km

From Mansilla de las Mulas the area of Greater Léon disturbs the tranquil and charming nature of the walk. First you pass the small hamlet of **Villar-moros de Mansilla** (3; 1 hr.), straight after wards **Puente Villarente** (4; ½ hr.). After the last houses of the town the Camino changes over onto the right hand side of the main road and leads slightly away from it. It's an easy incline up to **Arcahueja** (5; 1 hr.; to the hostel: go about 100m left at the fountain in the centre).

Carry straight on out of the village and after just under ½ hr. turn down left to the N-601. On the right of the road go as far as the roundabout, follow the path that goes round it up to the right and then leads down again to the N-601 (¼ hr.). Cross the N-601 over the footbridge and then over the foot-bridge before the Caja España. At roughly the same height as the place-name sign for **Puente Castro** (6; ¼ hr.) you can see the towers of the cathe-dral on the right. A tourist information place can be found at the bridge over the **Río Torío** (7). Pilgrims are led into town along the Avda. Alcalde Miguel Castaño.

The municipal hostel is signposted to the left at the crossroads with Avda. de Fernández Ladreda (¼ hr., *Albergue municipal*). A good quarter of an hour later, at the corner of c/ Puerta Moneda/ and c/ Escurial, go right to the hostel of the Benedictine nuns. Carry straight on into the old town and to **Léon** ca-thedral (8; just under ¼ hr.).

---

i *The last big town and cultural highpoint before Santiago is **León**. The military stronghold founded by Roman soldiers in 68 AD developed into the political and military centre of the north-western Iberian peninsula until the 3rd century. The town name of León (which also, coincidentally, means lion) came from the Latin 'legio'. Under the command of Almansur, Moorish armies destroyed the settle-ment in 996, but it was rebuilt by Alfonso V (999–1027) and up until the 12th century León was the capital of the kingdom of the same name that reached from the Atlantic to the Rhône. With the amalgamation of the kingdoms of Castille and León in 1230, León became less important. León was the centre of the iron ore and coal fields in the region up to the middle of the 20th century.*

*The bright **old town** of León is one of the most inviting places along the Camino francés. The traffic calming devices of a few years ago have given the historic cen-*

Early morning in the streets of León.

tre back its medieval flair. The bars and restaurants of Léon seethe with nightlife in the **barrio húmedo**, the 'humid quarter', around the **Plaza Mayor**, particularly at the weekend. The Plaza Mayor is dominated by the Baroque façade of the old **town hall** (17th century).

The **Catedral de León** which was built between the 13th and 14th centuries is the most splendid early Gothic building on Spanish soil and the purist in style. Rheims cathedral in France was the model for the church that was begun in 1255 under Alfonso X el Sabio, the Wise. Lack of money and numerous parts that collapsed delayed its completion until into the 19th century. The **glass paintings** made between the 13th and 20th century are unique in Spain and have a total surface area of about 1,900m². The light falls into the harmonious interior through 125 windows which are up to 12m high. They are at present in the process of being restored and will take some years to complete. From a 14m high platform in the inner entrance area the windows and the nave can be seen from a totally new perspective. (With guided tour, also at night, information in the cathedral or on the homepage, see below). The **choir stalls** are magnificent, for example, carved by Flemish masters from walnut and dating back to the 15th century. The curious statue of a pregnant Mother of God, **Virgen de la Esperanza** (Virgin of good hope), can be found in a side chapel of the choir gallery. The painted stone sculpture is an expression of the newly awakened realism in the 13th/14th century. (May–Sept. Mon.–Fri. 9.30–13.30 and 16.00–20.00, Sat. 9.30–12.00 and 14.00–18.00, Sun. 9.30–11.00 and 14.00–20.00. Oct.–April Mon.–

Sat. 9.30–13.30 and 16.00–19.00, Sun. 9.30–14.00, entry to the cathedral 5 € and museum 5 €; mass: Mon.–Fri. 9.00, 12.00, 13.00, 18.00, Sun./public holidays 9.00, 11.00, 12.00, 13.00, 14.00, 18.00. www.catedraldeleon.org).

A masterpiece of Romanesque architecture is the **Real Basílica de San Isidoro** (10th–12th century). The national shrine has been since 1063 the burial place of St. Isidoro, Archbishop of Sevilla in the 7th century and the most important Visigoth teacher of church doctrine. Because of the expressive **ceiling paintings** the **Panteón real**, the royal tomb, was also called the 'Sistine chapel of the Romanesque period'. The paintings, unequalled in accomplishment and condition, give a lively insight into the scenes of everyday life in the 12th century. With magnificent colours they show biblical and everyday scenes, e.g. a series of pictures of the months. There's an exhibition in the church museum of priceless articles from the treasure chamber (tesoro), the **reliquary** of St. Isidoro (11th century) and Doña Urruca's goblet made of agate (11th century). Church: daily 7.30–23.00. Museum and Panteón: Sept.–June Mon.–Sat. 10.00–13.30 and 16.00–18.30, Sun./public holidays 9.00–13.30, July/August Mon.–Sat. 9.00–20.00, Sun./public holidays 9.00–14.00; 5 €. Mass: Mon.–Sat. 7.30, 8.30, 10.30, 13.00, 18.30 and 20.00 (summer 19.30 and 21.00), Sun./public holidays 7.30–10.30 hourly, 12.30, 13.30, 19.30 and 21.00; www.sanisidorodeleon.net).

There were 17 pilgrim hostels in medieval León, the most famous was the **Monasterio (Hostal) de San Marcos** (today a Parador Nacional, high class state-run hotel). The pilgrim way goes past the over 100m long, richly adorned plateresque south façade (16th–18th century). Up to the 12th century San Marcos was a pilgrim hospice, then afterwards it became the ancestral home of the influential Order of Santiago knights. A powerful Santiago rides in his legendary guise as the slayer of Moors above the main entrance. The church of the monastery was consecrated in 1541. The adjoining cloister, the chapter houses and the sacristy today are home to the **Museo de León** in which can be seen, for example, a precious ivory statue of Christ (11th century), a Diana altar as well as Roman and Celtic archaeological finds. Opening times (the same for the San Marcos museum): July–Sept. Tue.–Sat. 10.00–14.00 and 17.00–20.00 (Oct.–June 16.00-19.00) Sun./public holidays 10.00–14.00, 1,20 € (San Marcos 60 centimos), www.museodeleon.com. The **MUSAC** is the most important museum for contemporary art in Castilla y León. Tue.–Fri. 10.00–15.00 and 17.00–20.00, Sat./Sun. 11.00–15.00 and 17.00–21.00. 5 € entry fee, Sunday afternoon free, www.musac.es.

Also worth seeing is the **Casa Botines** (around 1891), former home of two significant merchants of the town, today the headquarters of a bank. Clearly legible on the new-Gothic façade is the distinctive handwriting of the Catalan architect Antonio Gaudí (1852–1926). Gaudí had come by the commission in León through the Catalan textile magnate Eusebio Güell. The splendid **Palacio de los Guzmanes** (16th century) towers up next to it. Worth a visit is the inner courtyard richly adorned with ornaments. A few remains of the former town wall (muralla) can still be seen from the 3rd century, for example, parts of the Roman and medieval defences on San Isidoro tower.

Public holidays: the spectacular Easter processions during Semana Santa (Holy

Week). *Las Cabezadas* take place on the last Sunday in April: in the cloister of San Isidoro town councillors and clerics imitate with deep bows (*cabezadas*) a conflict of jurisdiction between secular and religious powers in the 12th century. Around the 23rd/24th June: *San Juan and San Pedro*, main town festival, numerous activities, midsummer eve bonfire and a big firework display. End of June: *Semana de la Trucha*, trout festival with cookery competitions. Around 5th Oct., *San Froilán y las Cantaderas* patron saint festival with a fair around the cathedral.

Gastronomy: *cecina* (air-dried beef and also goat meat, *cecina de chivo*) and *trucha* (trout), game like *jabalí* (wild boar), *perdices* (red-legged partridge), *codornices* (quail), *corzo* (deer), *liebre* (hare).

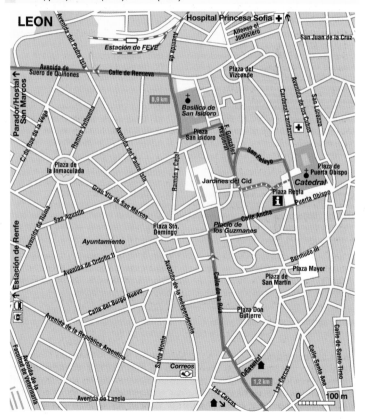

Hostels: Virgen del Camino (908m, pop. 4,500), MH, ⊕⊕⊕, 40 B/5 €. Alb. D. Antonio y Doña Cinia, c/ Camino de Villacedré, 16 (turn left at the height of the church into the small street and at the end go right, then left; the hostel is diagonally behind the red brick building). Tel: 987 302 800 and 615 217 335. Kitchen, large day room, washing machine/drier, lockers, garden, internet . 12.00–23.00, April–Oct. **Villar de Mazarife** (874m, pop. 410), **(1)** PH, ⊕⊕⊕, 55 B/7 € (5 DR 30 €). Alb. San Antonio de Padua, tel: 987 390 192. Large dormitory and two 8-bed room for groups, evening meal/breakfast, washing machine/drier, internet, massages. 11.30–23.00, all year. **(2)** PH, ⊕⊕⊕, 50 B (more if necessary)/5 €. Refugio de Jesús, tel: 987 390 697. 2 kitchens, internet, pool, garden. All day, all year. **(3)** PH, ⊕⊕⊕, 26 B/ 7 € (DR without bath 40 €, with bath 50 €). Alb. Tío Pepe. Rest., Restaurant, internet, Wi-Fi. From 7.00, open all year except mid Jan.–Feb.

Grade and route: easy. Well marked except in León. Urban area up to Virgen del Camino. Then farm tracks across plateau and about 4km on country road.

Height difference: 170m in ascent, 140m in descent.

Critical points: the path out of León waymarked with brass St. James shells in the ground, occasional yellow arrows. Look at the town map/route description carefully!

Scenery: urban area up to Virgen del Camino, then across sparsely vegetated plateau (páramo).

Local services: Virgen del Camino ⌧ €⃝ ⊡ ⊡ A ⃝@ ⌂ ✚ ⌧; Fresno del Camino

(878m, pop. 110) ⊡; Oncina de la Valdoncina (876m, pop. 20) ⊡; Chozas de Abajo (886m, pop. 80) ⊡ ⊡; Villar de Mazarife ⌧ ⊡ ⃝ @.

Remarks: (1) busses go into town from Virgen del Camino every 30 mins. so that the hostel is a good base from which to visit the sights. **(2)** The alternative from León via Villadangos del Páramo to Hospital de Órbigo (there the path joins the route described in Stage 21) is actually the original route, but less attractive since it runs predominantly next to the main road. Here is a short description: 8¾ hrs./ 33.1km; easy, well marked; paths next to N-120. You come through the following villages: Valverde de la Virgen (1 hr.) ⊡ ⌧ ⊡ €⃝ ⊟, San Miguel del Camino (¼ hr.) ⌧ ⊡ ⊟, Villadangos de Páramo (2 hrs.) ⌧ ⊡ ⊡ €⃝ A ⊟ ⊟, San Martín del Camino (1¼ hrs.) ⊡ ⊡ ⊡ ⊟ ⊟, Hospital de Órbigo (1¾ hrs.). Hostels: **Valverde de la Virgen** PH recently closed, up for sale. **Villadangos del Páramo** MH, ⊕⊕⊕, up to 70 B/3 € (poss. 4 €). Town hall tel: 987 390 003, Maite tel: 687 752 627. Kitchen, washing machine/drier, internet. 11.00–23.00, all year (open in winter after contacting Maite, no heating). **San Martín del Camino (1)** PH, ⊕⊕⊕, 60 B/5 €. Alb. Viera, tel: 987 378 565. Change of ownership planned. Kitchen, washing machine/drier. Meals, pool. 11.00–22.00, Feb.–Oct. **(2)** MH, ⊕⊕, 60 B/4–5 €. Tel: 657 102 497. Kitchen (1,50 €), internet. 11.00–22.00, all year. **(3)** PH, ⊕⊕⊕, 82 B/4–6 € (SR 20 €, DR 30 €). Alb. privado Santa Ana, tel: 680 917 423. Kitchen, washing machine/drier, internet, garden.

From the **cathedral (1)** go along c/ San Pelayo and c/ Fernando González Regueral to the **Basílica de San Isidoro** (or opposite the cathedral into c/ Sierra Pambley and right at the fork into c/ Dámaso Merino and straight on to the Basílica de San Isidoro). Past the front of the church some steps go down the old town wall. At the bottom turn right along the town wall and then turn off left into c/ de Renueva. Along this road across a large crossroads you reach the Avda. de Suero de Quiñones and the large square in front of the Parador Nacional **Hostal San Marcos (2)**. After that a bridge goes across the Río Bernesga into Avda. de Quevedo. On account of the following dangerous crossroads it's better to stay on the left hand side of the street. Carry straight on and come to a green pedestrian bridge into Avda. del Párroco Pablo Díez and to **Trobajo del Camino (3)**. At the Plaza Sira San Pedro follow the arrow on the left and then immediately right and in this way cut a section off the road route.

After about 300m cross over the road and go briefly left, then right uphill (marker stone, sign, yellow arrow; you can also continue along the big road as far as this turn-off).

Not every pair of walking boots makes it to Santiago.

From there the path is well signed through a rather thinly populated industrial park to the N-120 again. After about 2 hrs. (from the cathedral) you reach the **Santuario Virgen del Camino (4**; turn-off to the hostel is just beforehand to the left).

> *i*   The **Virgen del Camino** *(virgin of the way) is steeped in legend and is worshipped throughout the region. In 1505 she is supposed to have appeared in front of a shepherd. She promised that a chapel would be built at the spot where he threw a stone. Some years later she is said to have taken a Spaniard, who had been held captive in a wooden chest in Algeria, to the shrine together with the slave-owner, chest and chain.*

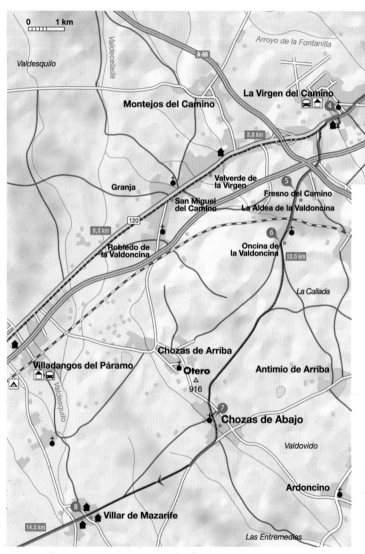

0   1 km

Valdesquilo

Valdecelada

Arroyo de la Fontanilla

A-66

La Virgen del Camino
4

Montejos del Camino

3,8 km

Valverde de
la Virgen

Granja
5

Fresno del Camino

San Miguel
del Camino

La Aldea de la Valdoncina

9,3 km

120

Oncina de
la Valdoncina
6

Robledo de
la Valdoncina

13,5 km

La Callada

Chozas de Arriba

Valdesquilo

Villadangos del Páramo

Otero

Antimio de Arriba

△
916

Chozas de Abajo
7

Valdovido

Ardoncino

8

Villar de Mazarife

14,5 km

Las Entremedias

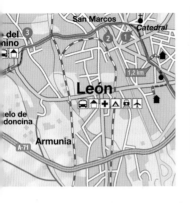

Respectful of the miracle both men devoted their lives thereafter to the virgin. The modern church building dates from the 60s and its concrete aesthetic is reminiscent of Le Corbusier. Even more surprising is the extravagantly worked Baroque altar from the 18th century with a statue of the Virgin Mary from the 16th century (in the summer 8.15–20.30, otherwise about 8.30–20.00).

At the church go left across the N-120 and then take the small road that runs downhill next to the main road. After about 100 metres frequent signs on the ground indicate the fork quite clearly. Keep left here to Villar de Mazarife.

The path leads at first across a motorway then under it and eventually arrives in **Fresno del Camino** (5; ½ hr.). Continue along a little country road over a small hill to **Oncina de Valdoncina** (6; ½ hr.). The path goes on the right, then slightly left through the village and then follow a farm track. This track ascends onto the plateau and the area of Greater León is behind you at last. Along unsurfaced farm tracks you are again walking through open landscapes. **Chozas de Abajo (7)** is reached after 1½ hrs. and along a little used country road you come to **Villar de Mazarife** (8; 1 hr.).

The hustle and bustle of the city is soon forgotten shortly after Virgen del Camino.

Hostels: Hospital de Órbigo (820m, pop. 1,000), **(1)** MH recently closed, info in the village. **(2)** RH, ◐◐◐, 80 B/5 €. Rectory tel: 987 388 444. Kitchen, prayer room, internet, nice inner courtyard, garden. 11.00–22.30, Feb.–Oct. **(3)** PH, ◐◐◐, 40 B/5 €. Alb. San Miguel, tel: 609 420 931. Kitchen, washing machine/drier, internet. 11.00–22.00. April–Oct. **(4)** PH, ◐◐◐, 26 B/9 €. Alb. Verde, Avda. Fueros de León, 76 (about 400m on the left after PH 3), tel: 689 927 926. Internet, yoga, Indian vegetarian communal meals, breakfast, garden. 11.00–23.00, May–Oct. **Villares de Órbigo** (827m, pop. 300), PH, ◐◐◐, 26 B/6 €. C/ Arnal, 21, tel: 987 132 935. Kitchen, washing machine/drier internet, Wi-Fi. Evening meal, breakfast. 11.30–22.00, closed 15th Dec.–1. Feb. **Santibáñez de Valdeiglesias** (851m, pop. 200), RH, ◐◐, 20 B/6 €. Rectory, tel: 987 377 698. Evening meal/breakfast (if run by *hospitalero*), basic hostel. About 13.00–22.00, March–Oct. **Astorga** (868m, pop. 11,600), **(1)** SH, ◐◐◐, 160 B/5 €. Alb. Siervas de María, St. James society of Astorga, in old convent, on the left right after the ascent, tel: 987 916 034. Kitchen, dining room, washing machine/drier, internet, Wi-Fi. Chiropodist in summer. Large hostel, but well organised. 11.00–23.00, all year. **(2)** PH, ◐◐◐, 100 B/8 €. Alb. San Javier, tel: 987 618 532. House dating back to the 16th century, kitchen, internet, washing machine/drier. Breakfast. All day, April–Nov.

Grade and route: easy, well marked. After Villar de Mazarife about 6km totally straight asphalt road. From Hospital de Órbigo farm tracks and paths.

Height difference: 190m both in ascent and descent.

Critical points: the path forks after Hospital de Órbigo. Continue straight ahead along the main road (*carretera*; see below). Keep on the right here (camino *señalizado*, waymarked path).

Scenery: the area is very broad and flat again up to Hospital de Órbigo, but becomes hillier and greener after that.

Local services: Villavante (836m, pop. 260)▣; Hospital de Órbigo ▨ ▨ ▲ €▨ ▨ A ✛ @ ▨ ▨ ▙; Igl. de San Juan, daily 20.00 ✛ in the town hall, c/ Álvarez Vega, 2, tel: 987 370 154; Villares de Órbigo ▨ ▲ A ▨ ▨; Santibáñez de Valdeiglesias ▨ ▨; San Justo de la Vega (851m, pop. 1,100) ▨ ▨ ▲ A ▨; Astorga ▨ ▨ ▨ ▨ €A ▨ @ ▨ i ▙. Cathedral Mon.–Sat. 10.00, Sun. 12.00, information about other masses from the tourist office ✛ c/ Alcalde Carro Verdejo, 24, tel: 987 617 810.

Remarks: here, too, the nicer alternative via Santibáñez is recommended. The alternative '*carretera*' might be the original route but, rather joylessly, it follows a footpath next to the main road.

From **Villar de Mazarife (1)** you will need strong nerves for the last time. After following a totally straight country road for about 1¼ hrs. this road joins a farm track and passes by **Villavante (2)** ¾ hr. later (possible arrows lead to the right to the bar). After half an hour cross over the motorway. After that go left and a long bend brings you round to **Puente (3)** and **Hospital de Órbigo (4)** respectively.

> ℹ️ The bridge, just under 300m long, with 20 arches built in the 10/11th century over the Río Órbigo is the longest bridge on the Way of St. James. **Puente de Órbigo** became famous for the **Passo honroso**, the courageous, if in those days al-

ready somewhat out-dated, tournament of the knight Suero de Quiñones. In the Holy Year of 1434 15 days before and after 25th July, the day of Santiago, the nobleman vowed with nine companions to fight every knight who came across the bridge. With this noble deed he wanted to free himself from the fetters around his neck that he wore every Thursday as a symbol of his unhappy love for a noble-woman. Countless knights rushed into the village since opportunities for showing courage and strength were rare in Spain which had by now become an almost peaceful country. Don Suero and his brave friends defeated 166 knights and in this way freed him from his shackles of love.

Hospital de Órbigo, on the other side of the bridge, was built around the pilgrim hospice founded in the 12th century by knights of the Order of St. John.

Public holidays: end of March: Semana de la Trucha, festival with all you want to know about the trout. The first weekend in June: medieval games (justas medievales) in memory of the Passo honroso with knights' tournaments and a medieval market.

The Camino goes right through the village. At the end of the village a sign indicates the fork in the path. Straight ahead (*carretera*) the path runs next to the N-120. Turn off right following the waymarked alternative (*señalizado*) that brings you to **Villares de Órbigo** (**5**; ¾ hr.) along a farm track. At the end of the village a beaten track goes uphill to a country road onto which you turn right. **Santibáñez de Valdeiglesias** (**6**) is already visible from the hill (¾ hr.).

At the height of the church the path bends to the right and going past the hostel, leaves the village. Farm tracks run across an undulating landscape and light oak woods alternate with cornfields. After a good 1¼ hrs. cross over a country road on the plateau. After ¼ hr. you reach the stone wayside cross of **Santo Toribio** (**7**). The silhouette of Astorga can already be seen in the distance and quite clearly the Gaudí palace and reddish cathedral.

i **Santo Toribio** was the bishop of Astorga in the 5th century. According to the legend Toribio left the town after being falsely accused. It is said that, as he cleaned his sandals on the hill, he exclaimed 'I will not take even the dust of As-torga with me!'.

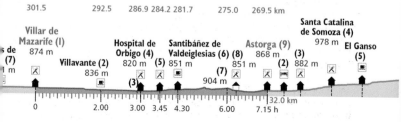

The village of **San Justo de la Vega (8)** lies below the hill (¼ hr.). At the end of the village the footpath crosses the road bridge. Arrows lead shortly afterwards to a farm track on the right below the road. This path brings you into **Astorga (9)** that is built on a hill like a fortress (1 hr., centre).

i *Originally the gold mines in the Teleno mountains and in the Médulas were controlled by the Roman military base of Asturica Augusta. In the 1st century AD Astorga developed into a well-to-do centre of administration and inter-section point. Gothic and Arab invasions up to the 9th century slowed down its development. However, from the 11th century onwards Astorga became an important pilgrim stopping-off point since both the Camino francés and the Vía de la Plata coming from Sevilla joined here. Because agriculture was not profitable on the infertile land, the carriers' trade developed into the main source of employment in the region (see page 157 Maragatería). This is how cocoa from the colonies overseas came from the Galician ports; in the 18th and 19th centuries Astorga was the centre of the Spanish chocolate industry. The **Museo del Chocolate** gives you an insight into the tastier attractions of Astorga (c/ José María Goy Tue.–Sat. 10.30–14.00 and 16.30–19.00 (Oct.–April 16.00–18.00), Sun. 11.00–14.00, 2 €). Today Astorga makes its living from the service sector and the production of mantecadas (butter biscuits) – the evidence of which is unmissable around town. The dominant building is the **Catedral de Santa María** (15th/16th century) with three attractive plateresque portals amongst other interesting things. The splendid high altar is worth a look and also the choir stalls which were carved by Juan de Colonia (both 16th century; Mon.–Sat. 9.00–10.30, Sun. 11.00–13.00). The **Palacio Episcopal** (bishop's palace, photo) next door was built from plans by Antonio Gaudí. Bishop Juan Bautista Grau Vallespinós from Catalonia commissioned the building in 1886 from his kinsman Gaudí. After Grau's death in 1893 and differences with his less progressive successor, Gaudí resigned from the management of the construction. In 1913 the building was completed under new management, but was never consecrated as a bishop's palace. Since 1963 it has housed the **Museo de los Caminos** with items on display about the history of the Way*

of St. James (including the original Cruz de Ferro). A visit to the museum offers you an opportunity to see the marvellous interior of the palace (daily 10.00–14.00 and 16.00–20.00 (Oct.–April 11.00–14.00 and 16.00–18.00), Sun. 10.00–14.00; 3 €.). Also interesting: the **Museo Romano** (near to the Plaza Mayor, daily 10.30–14.00 and 17.00–19.30 (Oct.–May 16.00–18.00), Sun. only in the morning; 2.50 €) and guided tours around the excavations (information from the tourist office). The **town hall** in the **Plaza Mayor** dates from the 17th/18th century. Two figures dressed in local costume strike the hour on the town hall clock.
Public holidays: Easter processions. 3rd week in June: Fiesta de Transhumancia, traditional herding of sheep along the Cañadas Reales (royal pastural paths) through Astorga. 22nd Aug. patron saint festival (Santa Marta), Roman style with gladiator fights, circus games and chariot races.
Gastronomy: angélicas: slabs of chocolate with whole almonds, mantecadas, hojaldrados (puff pastries) and cocido maragato (see Stage 22, Maragatería), cóngrio al ajoarriero (conger eel with garlic).

Hostels: Valdeviejas (859m, pop. 160), MH, ☕☕☕, 10 B/5 €. Alb. de Peregrinos Ecce Homo. At Ermita del Ecce Homo 130m on the right (the first turn-off beforehand makes a detour through the village), neighbourhood society, tel.; 620 960 060 (or see notice). No bunkbeds, 2 and 3-bed rooms, washing machine, drinks machine, kitchen planned. Up to about 22.00, March–Oct. **Murias de Rechivaldo** (882m, pop. 100), **(1)** PH, ☕☕☕, 40 B/8 € with own sleeping bag, 11 € with bedlinen (5 DR 45–50 €). Alb. Las Águedas, tel: 987 691 234. Also for non-pilgrims. Bar, evening meal/breakfast, use of kitchen 2 € pp. (when not used by hostel), washing machine/drier, internet, separate bathrooms, large inner courtyard. All day, in winter only registered groups. **(2)** MH, ☕☕, about 20 B+M/4 €. Tel: 987 691 150. Near private hostel on the right, small house on the main road. Large room with beds/mattresses. Washing machine. All day, someone comes to stamp passports and collect the money. Apr.–mid Oct. **(3)** PH, ☕☕, 15 B/10 € (DR 60 € mit breakfast). Alb. Casa Flor, c/ Carretera Santa Colomba, 54 (on the country road, near MH). Internet, Wi-Fi. Bar/rest. **Santa Catalina de Somoza** (978m, pop. 60), **(1)** PH, ☕☕☕, 10 B/6 € (11 DR 45 €, SR 30 €). Alb. El Caminante, tel: 987 691 098. Washing machine/drier, bar/rest. Sleeping area separated from the restaurant. All day, all year. **(2)** PH, ☕☕☕, 20 B/5 € (2 DR 35 €, SR 30 €). Hospedería San Blas, tel: 987 691 411. Washing machine/drier, internet, place for horses, groups accepted, bar/rest. 10.00–23.00, all year. **El Ganso** (1,014m, pop. 30), PH, ☕☕☕, 30 B/5 € (breakfast 3 €). Alb. Gabino, tel: 660 912 823. Just before the end of the village. Kitchen, washing machine/drier, inner courtyard, quite charming. All day (if no one there, doors open), March–Nov. **Rabanal del Camino** (1,151m, pop. 65), **(1)** PH, ☕☕☕, 34 B/5 € (tent 5 €).

Alb. La Senda, tel: 696 819 060. Kitchen, dining room, washing machine/drier, internet, garden meadow. All day, April–about mid Oct. **(2)** RH, ☕☕☕, 24 B (summer: +16 B+M)/donations. Alb. Gaucelmo, bishopric Astorga and English St. James brotherhood, tel: 987 691 901. In the village, near the church. Kitchen, garden. 14.00–22.30, April–Oct. **(3)** MH, ☕☕☕, 32 B/4 €. On the left of the village centre, square on the main road. Kitchen, washing machine/drier, internet, Wi-Fi, place for tents. Basic, but good. 11.00–22.30, April–oct. **(4)** PH, ☕☕☕, 72 B/5 € (2 DR 35 €), Alb. El Pilar, tel: 616 089 942. Next to the MH. Kitchen, washing machine, bar, restaurant, internet. From 10.00, all year. **Foncebadón** (1,433m, pop. 10), **(1)** PH, ☕☕, 30 B/7 €. In Hotel-rest. Convento de Foncebadón, tel: 658 974 818. IInternet, washing machine/drier, rest. No credit cards! All day, Feb.–Nov. **(2)** PH, ☕☕☕, 35 B/6 €. Alb. Monte Irago, tel: 695 452 950. Vegetarian food, small bio-shop, yoga, reiki, massages. Internet, washing machine/drier. All day, all year. **(3)** PH, 40 B/7 €. Alb. La Cruz de Fierro, tel: 987 691 093 and 665 258 169. New, but no details because recently still closed. **(4)** RH, ☕☕, 18 B (+M)/donations. Alb. parroquial Domus Dei, founded with help of Christophorus youth organization of Oberimsingen and Austrian Saint James brotherhood. Former church of Foncebadón. Communal cooking, breakfast. Can be very cool at night. From about 14.00, Apr.–Oct.

Grade and route: well marked. Easy up to Rabanal, then begins the ascent into the Montes de León. Partly on asphalt, but mostly farm tracks and paths.

Height difference: 590m in ascent, 50m in descent.

Critical points: none.

Scenery: the extensive region of Maragatería with its oak woods and steppe-like areas is found between Astorga and the

Montes de León. After the plains of the Meseta the landscape becomes three dimensional again from Rabanal with the ascent into the Montes de León and the beautiful views come as a lovely surprise. Gorse and heathers provide colourful tones in summer with their yellow and pink blossoms.

Local services: Valdeviejas ⊠; Murias de Rechivaldo ⬆ ⊠ @; Santa Catalina de Somoza ⊠ @; El Ganso ▣; Rabanal del Camino 🅰 ⊠ ⊠ ⬆ ⊟ @ ⬆ ⬆; Foncebadón ⊠ ⬆.

Remarks: (1) there are plenty of hostels and places to eat, but few shops and no cash machines. If necessary do some shopping in Astorga. **(2)** It can also rain in summer in the mountains and be quite cool at night.

The Camino out of **Astorga (1)** goes past the cathedral and then turns left into c/ Portería. At the end of this road turn right into c/ Sancti Spiritu and carry straight on as it becomes c/ San Pedro and c/ Camino de Santiago further on. Then continue over the old N-VI onto the country road in the direction of Santa Comba de Somoza into the Maragatería region. ½ hr. beyond Astorga the **Ermita del Ecce Homo (2)** can be found on the left , the only remains of a pilgrim hospital from the 15th century. **Valdeviejas hostel** can be found 250m on the right. Walking parallel to the country road for ½ hr. you reach **Murias de Rechivaldo (3)**.

ℹ️ *The **Maragatería** region extends westwards from Astorga as far as the Sierra del Teleno and encompasses roughly 50 villages with about 5,000 inhabitants. There is still no definitive explanation today of the origin of its inhabitants, the Maragatos, who are described as proud and strong of character. Theories range from them being descendants from Mauretanians to the Maurogothos (a mixed race of Moorish and Gothic immigrants) and to the Mauricatus (sleeveless). Or the name goes back to the Asturian King Mauregato who, in the 8th century, is said to have paid the Moors 100 virgins each year as a tribute. New theories see the origin in 'mercader' (merchant) since the Maragatos had made their living chiefly from the carrying-trade since the 16th century. Up to the 19th century the carriers transported inland from Galicia amongst other things fish, precious metals and also postal items. This came to an end with the arrival of the railway, and migration from the country into the cities, which is still happening today, left places like Foncebadón to die out. Typical of the region is the **architecture** of the massive red-coloured stone houses with their large entrance*

On the way into the Montes de León.

doors for cattle and carts, and the paved roads. The showpiece village of the region is **Castrillo de los Polvazares**. The folklore of Maragatería is well promoted as, for example, the traditional dances or the costumes of the men with their wide black harem style and black corduroy gaiters and the exquisite silver jewellery of the women. These traditions can be seen on 25th July, for example, when the Day of St. James is celebrated in Castrillo de los Polvazares, Rabanal del Camino and other places.

Cocido maragato is a famous dish and has a peculiar characteristic – the ingredients are separated and eaten in an unusual order: first there's the meat (including cecina, ham, belly pork, blood sausage, spicy sausage, chicken, sometimes pig's trotter, ear and snout) and the relleno (stuffing), a kind of dumpling made of eggs, bread, garlic, parsley, sausage and bacon. After that there's chick peas (garbanzos), potatoes, vegetables and cabbage (repollo). You are served finally with a noodle broth. There's dispute over the origins of this dish. Was it the carriers who preferred to eat the meat while it was hot and therefore before the soup? Or Napoleon's troops who, on standby day and night, liked to start the meal with the hearty courses in case, in an emergency, thay had to leave the meal early, i.e. the soup?

From Murias de Rechivaldo you come along a farm track parallel to the country road to **Santa Catalina de Somoza** (**4**; 1 hr.). With a view of the Montes de León and the Sierra del Teleno continue to **El Ganso** (**5**; 1 hr.). From here the route goes at times along the country road, but mostly along a woodland path away from it. **Rabanal del Camino (6)** is reached after a good 1¾ hrs.

i *Rabanal del Camino* was, with its numerous churches and hostels, the last stopping-off point before the wearisome crossing of the Montes de León which was also dangerous on account of the wolves and bandits. At the entrance to the village next to

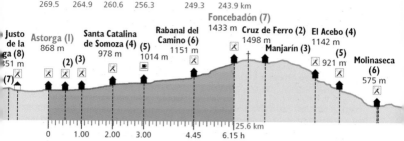

269.5   264.9   260.6   256.3   249.3   243.9 km

the cemetery can be found the **Ermita del Bendito Cristo de la Vera Cruz** (18th century). Up to the 13th century Rabanal was also a kind of outpost of the Templar Knights of Ponferrada. At the end of the 12th century they built the parish church, the Iglesia de la Asunción (Romanesque apse).

The ascent to the Puerto de Foncebadón, also once called Monte Irago, begins in earnest from Rabanal. Predominently along paths away from the country road go uphill into the semi-abandoned village of **Foncebadón** (7; 1½ hrs.).

i In the 12th century the hermit Gaucelmo founded the hostel of San Salvador del Monte Irago in **Foncebadón**. Other monks followed his example and founded a monastery. Up to the 19th century Foncebadón enjoyed special royal protection with the condition that the people there looked after pilgrims and maintained the path. The village then died out and only recently has it come to life again.

Hostels: Manjarín (1,441m, pop. 1, PH, ◐, about 35 B/donations. *Hospitalero*: Tomás, who sees himself in the tradition of the Templar Knights. The only inhabited house in the abandoned hamlet, no warm water, crude toilet, cooking facilities; basic, but very individual hostel. All day, all year. **El Acebo** (1,142m, pop. 35), **(1)** PH, ◐◐, 18 B/ 6 € (DR 22 €, 3-bed-room 33 €). Alb. Mesón, tel: 987 695 074. Bar/restaurant, internet, washing machine/drier, drinks machine. 12.00–23.00, closed 20th Dec.–10th Jan. If full, two other basic places: Alb. de la Junta Vecinal with 10 B/6 € and La Taberna de José with 7 B/6 €. **(2)** RH, ◐◐◐, 22 B/ Donations, centre. Kitchen, evening meal/ breakfast, washing machine. Prayers. 12/13.00–22.30, April–Oct. **Riego de Ambrós** (921m, pop. 45), MH, ◐◐◐, 20 B (+ M)/5 €. Neighbourhood society. If closed, tel. no. on door. Beautifully restored old building, kitchen, washing machine/drier. Inner courtyard. From around 12.30. All year. **Molinaseca** (575m, pop. 820), **(1)** PH, ◐◐◐, 56 B/7 €. Alb. Santa Marina, almost at the end of the village on the main road, tel: 987 453 077. Alfredo who runs the hostel (also responsible for the MH), has been involved with the pilgrim paths in Spain for over 20 years and recently also in Japan. He has made the pilgrimage to Santiago 12 times up to now and likes to impart his experiences to those pilgrims who are interested. A small museum is planned in the hostel. Use of the kitchen in MH, communal evening meal. Washing machine/drier, internet, very roomy, bunkbeds and normal beds. All day, March–Nov. **(2)** MH, ◐◐◐, 30 B (summer + 10 B outside)/5 €. 300m from PH, tel: 987 453 180; Kitchen, evening meal in PH. Drinks and snack machines, washing machine/drier, internet. In summer small bar. 12.00–23.00, all year. **Ponferrada** (534m, pop. 42,000), RH, ◐◐◐, 188– 270 B/donations. Refugio San Nicolás de Flüe, outside the centre, tel: 987 413 381. Kitchen, coffee machine, washing machine/ drier, internet. Prayers: 19.30, mass: Sun. 20.00. From about 13.00–22.30, all year.

Grade and route: well marked. Predominently on unsurfaced paths. Ascent to Cruz de Ferro on good paths and up a moderate incline. Paths to Manjarín, then a small pass. Some very steep and stony paths to Molinaseca.

Height difference: 250m in ascent, 1,150m in descent.

Critical points: unpleasant sections between Riego de Ambrós and Molinaseca (steep and stony). Path to hostel discreetly marked in Ponferrada.

Scenery: in clear weather you have lovely views on the high ridge after the Cruz de Ferro of the Montes de León. Yellow gorse and pink heather and cistus make a beautiful display of colour in summer. The first village of the El Bierzo region is El Acebo with slate covered stone houses. After Riego de Ambrós you will see chestnut trees for the first time that are typical of the region.

Local services: El Acebo ⊠ ⌂ ⌂ @ ▭ ▭; Riego de Ambrós ⊠ ⌂ ⌂; Molinaseca ⊠ ⌂ ⌂ 🅰 ⓘ € ▭ @; Ponferrada ⊠ € @ ▭ ▭ 🅰 ⓘ ✉ ⌂ ⌂ Basílica de la Encina Mon.–Fri. 11.00 and 20.00, Sat. 11.00 and 20.30, Sun. 10.00, 11.00, 12.30, 18.20 ✚ Paseo San Antonio 7, Hospital del Bierzo, La Dehesa, tel: 987 455 200 und Hospital de la Reina, c/ Hospital 26, tel: 987 410 059.

Remarks: (1) Snow can fall at altitude from Foncebadón onwards right into April, in which case it's best to use the road. Fog and rain can make the crossing of the Montes de León difficult even in summer. In this case you should allow more time or plan shorter stages. **(2)** Ponferrada is for many pilgrims the starting point so that the hostel can be very full in July/Aug.

Continue through the half derelict village of **Foncebadón (1)** on the ascent along dirt paths up to the **Cruz de Ferro** (**2**; ¾ hr.).

i The **Cruz de Ferro** (iron cross) on a plateau of Monte Irago is one of the simplest, but most impressive places along the Way of St. James. A long, slender oak post with the small iron cross attached to the top rises up from a large pile of stones (the original iron cross has been in the Museo de los Caminos in Astorga since 1976). The exact origins still remain a bit of a mystery. It could have originally been a Roman sign or an altar dedicated to the Roman god Merkur, the patron of travellers, and later adopted by the Christians. Or it was a boundary post of the area that King Alfonso VI left to the hermit Gaucelmo in 1103. One thing is certain; pilgrims have been laying a stone at the cross for centuries. The prayer of the Cruz de Ferro is as follows: 'Lord, may this stone, a symbol of my efforts on the pilgrimage that I lay at the foot of the cross of the Saviour, one day weigh the balance in favour of my good deeds when the deeds of my life are judged. Let it be so.' For many pilgrims the ritual also denotes the symbolic laying down of a burden. In any case, the stone should be carried with you all the way from home and not picked up just beforehand! The many other items that have been left behind at the cross have nothing in common with the original tradition and are not very pleasant to see there. The chapel dedicated to Santiago behind the cross dates back to 1982.

Now descend the pleasant path gradually downhill. You are afforded many breathtaking views of the mountains of the Sierra Teleno especially to your left. After the long deprivations of the Meseta they are a feast for the eyes. **Manjarín (3)**, for the most part derelict, comes into sight after half an hour. A house, in fairly good condition, serves as a basic hostel in this village which was first documented in 1180. After that a path continues uphill for roughly another 1¼ hrs., before, with views down into the wide valley of the Río Sil to Ponferrada, it begins to descend again. The path above the country road at first maintains height, then in the last section descends a steep and stony path to **El Acebo** (**4**; ¾ hr.).

Cruz de Ferro.

i *The county of **El Bierzo** belongs to the province of León, but is already a small prelude to Galicia with which it is closely connected historically. For a brief spell in 1822/23 El Bierzo formed an independent province belonging to Galicia. Bercianos today still feel closer to Galicia than to León. Traditional means of earning a living are still agriculture, cattle breeding and winegrowing. Thanks to large deposits of iron ore the iron industry flourished in the 18th century, but in the 19th century they could not keep pace with the more lucrative locations (Catalonia, the Basque country); many workers emigrated to America.*

The climate in the region of the valley of the Río Sil is very mild, almost Mediterranean. Many attractions of this stretch of land lie in its gastronomy. Depending on the season there's an abundance of cherries (cerezas), Spanish chestnuts (castañas), roasted, used in tarts (tarta de castaña), crème caramel (flan), with rabbit (conejo) or as a sauce with veal (ternera asada con crema de castaña), and apples (manzana), especially the reineta one (tarta de manzana reineta – apple cake). As in Navarra there are pimientos asados, roast peppers, sometimes with dried cod (bacalao), stews (guisos) or calf sweetbreads (mollejas de ternera). With its own Designation of Origin, the botillo is an oval-shaped sausage of smoked pork flavoured with garlic and peppers.

The fruity aromatic wines of the region, even if a good bottle is somewhat more expensive than, let's say, a comparable Rioja, enjoy an increasingly better reputa-

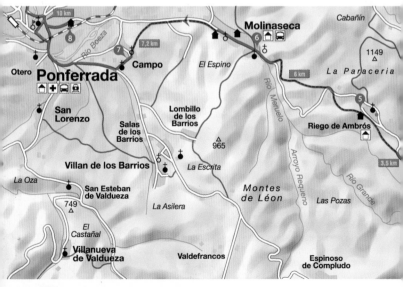

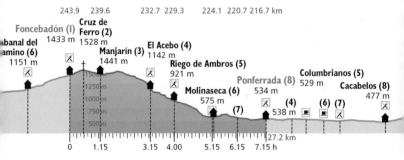

tion. Already in around 1495 the German monk and pilgrim Hermann Künig von Vach advised drinking the wine of Bierzo with caution since it 'can drive you out of your mind'. The wine harvest (vendimia) is celebrated the last weekend in August in Caca-belos and other places. Fervudo can also be tasted at this festival (warm wine with honey.

At the exit from the village of El Acebo there's a memorial to the German pilgrim, Heinrich Krause, who died after a bike accident in 1987. The path follows the country road, then turns off to the left and continues along a path to **Riego de Ambrós** (5; ¾ hr.). After Riego de Ambrós you can look forward to a very beautiful path, if at times steeply downhill. In places impressively huge chestnut trees line the path. After 1¼ hr. you reach the entrance to the village of **Molinaseca** (6). Both the hostels lie close to one another almost at the end of the village (¼ hr.).

i Before you come to **Molinaseca** the path comes past the neoclassical parish church of **Parroquia de San Nicolás de Bari** (17th century). An originally Romanesque bridge over the Río Meruelo, newly built in the 16th century, brings pilgrims into Calle Real which is lined with well preserved houses that once be-

View of the idyllically situated Molinaseca with the Iglesia de San Nicolás de Bari.

*longed to nobility. Medieval pilgrims and carriers used to carve a sliver from the wooden door of the shrine, the **Santuario de la Virgen de las Angustias**, as a good luck charm, untill they protected the door with solid iron plates. The Baroque building today dates from the 18th century. The name of the village is derived from molinos secos, drying or corn mills, and recalls a formerly important village industry. **Public holidays:** middle August Virgen de las Angustias, processions, offerings of flowers and on 17th Aug. the Fiesta del Agua, a huge water fight.*

Along the pavement beside the main road you come to the top of a small pass after just under half an hour an hour. Just afterwards turn off left to **Campo** (**7**; a good ¼ hr.). (Instead of turning off to Campo you can also follow the road a bit further on along the Carretera de Molinaseca to reach the Avda.del Castillo and the hostel. In this way you are choosing the somewhat shorter, but less attractive alternative to Ponferrada). The route via Campo goes through a suburb, then across a bridge over the Río Boeza to the **Templars' castle** of **Ponferrada** (¾ hr.). Straight ahead brings you into the centre of Ponferrada and further along the Camino. The path to the **hostel (8)** is waymarked with golden shells on the wall of the house opposite. Go right, then left through the small street and right into c/ Los Pregoneros, and then continue for another 700m. (Or before that point, after the road bridge go straight on up c/ Cruz Mirada and then right into c/ de la Loma in which the hostel is situated.)

i **Ponferrada** *is the seat of government of the county of El Bierzo and the last largish town along the pilgrim path to Santiago. Although it was inhabited over 2,000 years ago and taken over later by the Romans, Ponferrada did not begin to grow until the start of the pilgrim movement in the 11th century. Around 1082 Bishop Osmundo of Astorga ordered the building of a bridge across the Río Sil. The construction, which was reinforced with iron, lent the settlement its name: Pons fer-*

rata – bridge of iron. In actual fact it was situated in the present day district of Compostilla. From 1178 onwards, the Templar Knights, by order of the kings of León, began the expansion of the hitherto primitive fortress. After the dissolution of the Order at the beginning of the 14th century the town passed into the ownership of the Dukes of Lemos. At the end of the 15th century a battle broke out over the inheritance of the town and was stopped by the Reyes Católicos who assigned Ponferrada to the crown and named it the capital of the Bierzo region. Deposits of coal and iron ore brought jobs and affluence at the beginning of the 20th century. The building activity of the Templars at the **Castillo del Temple** was terminated in 1282. The roughly 8,000m² site has been extended and rebuilt again and again right into the 20th century. It suffered damage in 1923 when blasting operations took place in the interior space to construct a football pitch. Nevertheless it's worth a visit (mornings all year round Tue.–Sat. 11.00–14.00 (July/Aug. 10.00–14.00), afternoons 16.30 until depending on the light 18.00–20.30, 6 €). Around the year 1200 a sculpture of the Virgin Mary with child, which had been hidden from the attack by Moorish invaders, was found by the Knights Templar in an oak tree (encina). Toribio, bishop of Astorga, is said to have brought it from the Holy Land in the 5th century. According to legend, the child Jesus cried when the oak tree was going to be felled. Since 1958 the **Nuestra Señora de la Encina** has been the patron saint of the Bierzo region and is honoured in the Basilica (16th century) of the same name. The carved altar is interesting (around 1630) and the sculpture of the Virgin Mary (also called La Morenica 'the small brown lady', due to her dark colouring,) with the child Jesus (9.00–14.00 and 16.30–20.30).

The Baroque town hall (**ayuntamiento**) was built between 1692 and 1705. The former clock and bell tower **Torre del Reloj** (16th/17th century) forms the passage from the Plaza del Ayuntamiento to the medieval part of the town. In c/ del Reloj can be found the Museo del Bierzo in the prison (cárcel) built in 1565. Just nearby, the **Museo de la Radio 'Luis del Olmo'** gives an insight into the history and technology of the radio. Luis del Olmo, born in 1937 in Ponferrada, is one of the most respected (radio) journalists in Spain. Some of the last Spanish steam locomotives are on display in the **Museo del Ferrocarril** (railway museum). All three museums: mornings all year round Tue.–Sat. 11.00–14.00 (July/Aug 10.00–14.00), afternoons May–Sept. 17.00–20.30, (Oct.–Apr. 16.00–19.00), entrance ticket 2.70 €).

Outside the centre to the northeast, at the end of the Avda. Ángel Pestaña, lies the **Iglesia de Santo Tomás de las Ollas** (10th century). The Romanesque building is worth visiting with its oval chancel and the Mozarabic horseshoe arches round the apse (no fixed opening times).

Public holidays: beginning July, first full moon in summer, Noche Templaria (night of the Templars), spectacular with knights and medieval atmosphere. Beginning Sept. Fiesta de la Encina, festival in honour of the patron saints.

Gastronomy: March/April gastronomic days 'Cocina de Primavera' (spring cuisine); special dishes are served by those restaurants taking part.

Information: www.ponferrada.org, link: Turismo.

Just like a film setting: the Templars' castle of Ponferrada.

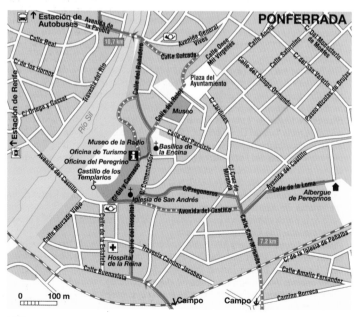

Hostels: Cacabelos (477m, pop. 4,500), MH, ✦✦✦, 70 B/5 €. Alb. municipal Santuario de la Quinta Angustia, at the exit from the village towards Villafranca, tel: 987 547 167. Quite original, hostel built around the church, 35 x 2-bed areas (no bunk beds), washing machine/drier, good sanitary facilities, internet, telephone, drinks machines. 12.00–22.30, May–Oct., otherwise ask in the town hall or at the Policía Local. **Pieros** (520m, pop. 30), ✦✦✦, 20 B/5 €. Alb. El Serbal y la Luna, c/ El Pozo, tel: 639 888 924. Meals (ovo-lacto-vegetarian), washing machine, internet, physiotherapy, 12.00–23.00, all year. **Villafranca del Bierzo** (501m, pop. 2,500), **(1)** MH, ✦✦, 58 B/6 €. Tel: 987 542 680. Kitchen, washing machine/drier, internet. Quite old beds on last visit. In summer extra mattresses in old school. 12.00–22.00, Easter–mid Nov. **(2)** PH, ✦✦✦, 84 B/5 €. Refugio Ave Fénix, tel: 987 542 655. One of the most well-known hostels on the Camino, run by Jesús Arias Jato on his own with utmost dedication, regularly extended. Bar, evening meal, breakfast, washing machine/drier, internet, plenty of showers, separate room for older pilgrims. All day until 23.00, all year. **(3)** PH, ✦✦✦, 32 B/from 8 € (3-bed-room 24 €). Alb. de la Piedra, c/ Espíritu Santo, 14 (exit from the village), tel: 987 540 260. Kitchen, washing machine/drier, Internet, Wi-Fi. 12.30–23.00, March–Nov.
Grade and route: easy, well marked.

Sometimes asphalt, sometimes farm tracks. Many linear villages between Ponferrada and Camponaraya.
Height difference: 180m in ascent, 220m in descent.
Scenery: apart from the catchment area immediately around Ponferrada the region of El Bierzo is blessed with a mild climate, very green area with cherry plantations and, especially between Cacabelos and Villafranca del Bierzo, vineyards.
Local services: Columbrianos (529m, pop. 1,400) ▣ ⬆ ☺ 🚍; Fuentes Nuevas (508m, pop. 2,700) ▣ Ⓐ ⬆; Camponaraya (495m, pop. 3,000) Ⓧ Ⓐ ☺ @ €; Cacabelos Ⓧ ⬆ ☺ @ € Ⓐ ⓘ ⬆ ⬄ ⓘ ▣ ⬙ (beach by river) 🅛 Iglesia de Santa María Mon.–Sat. 19.00, Sun. 12.00 ✚ c/ Doctor Santos Rubios, 11, tel: 987 549 262; Pieros ⬆ ⬆; Valtuille de Arriba (564m, pop. 140) ⬆ Casa Rural La Osa Mayor with special prices for pilgrims: www.osamayor. es; Villafranca del Bierzo Ⓧ ⬆ ☺ Ⓐ 🚍 ⬄ @ ⬆ ⓘ 🅛 San Nicolás Mon.–Fri. 19.00, Sun. 11.00, Colegiata de Santa María Mon.–Fri. 19.00, Sun. 12.00/19.00 ✚ c/ Díaz Ovelar s/n, tel: 987 542 510.
Remarks: many pilgrims begin the walk in Ponferrada and Villafranca is a popular end of stage destination. Hostels in both places are very full during high season, if necessary, aim to reach other villages/hostels.

From the **hostel (1)** walk back to the **Templars' castle (2)** and past it into c/ Gil y Carrasco and at the fork go right (left: bicycles). At the church square the waymarkers lead you down to the left onto/ del Rañadero. (Alternative:continue along c/ del Reloj, after the Torre del Reloj turn left into c/ Sta. Beatriz de la Silva, then go sharp left into c/ Calzada and down-

Pilgrims resting in Fuentes Nuevas.

hill to the bridge over the Río Sil.). After the bridge leave the main road to the right and continue parallel to it until to the large Avda. Huertas where you turn right. Follow this road for a long way straight ahead. At the memorial for blood donors (**Monumento a los Donantes de Sangre, 3**) go right, then carry straight on over the next roundabout and left uphill into the suburb of **Compostilla** (**4**; ¾ hr.) and a good ¼ hr. later walk through **Columbrianos** (**5**). The Iglesia de San Esteban can be found at the entrance to the village (18th century, beautiful carved Baroque altar). **Fuentes Nuevas (6)** is reached through a thinly populated area (just under ¾ hr.). After the linear village you arrive at **Camponaraya** (**7**; ½ hr.) which is just as long. At the *bodega* at the exit from

the village (¼ hr.) go up the farm track on the left of the road and cross over the A-6; then follows a lovely section through vineyards and woods. After ½ hr. you come over a country road and follow the small road into the centre of **Cacabelos** where you continue straight on to the **hostel** (**8**; a good ½ hr.).

i Up to about the 5th century **Cacabelos** was the administrative centre for the Roman gold mines of which the most productive were the Médulas about 20km away. At the beginning of the 12th century Diego Gelmírez, archbishop of Santiago, had people settle in the place and the **Iglesia de Santa María** to be built (16th century rebuild, church tower from 1904). The most amazing detail of the **Santuario de la Quinta Angustia** (18th century) near the pilgrim hostel is a figure of the child Jesus, playing cards, on the doors of the sacristy (opening times can be found in the hostel). In the 19th century the village made its living from the production of wine. At the beginning of the 20th century there was an outbreak of the Europe-wide plague of vine pests and wine production was only restarted with vines from America. High quality wines are now produced again under the Designation of Origin, D.O. El Bierzo.

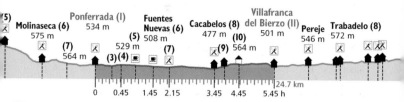

216.7 213.2 208.7 206.5   200.3 196.9 192.0 km

(5) Molinaseca (6) Ponferrada (I) Fuentes Cacabelos (8) Villafranca Pereje Trabadelo (8)
575 m   534 m Nuevas (6) 477 m del Bierzo (II) 546 m 572 m
              (5) 508 m   501 m
(7)   564 m 529 m   (9) 564 m (10)
       (3)(4)   (7)

0   0.45   1.45 2.15   3.45 4.45 5.45 h   24.7 km

Public holidays: *Easter Monday, procession in honour of the Virgen de la Quinta Angustia. End of April/beginning of May, Feria del Vino, wine festival; end of August, La Vendimia, wine-growers' festival; Sept. Batalla de Cacabelos, re-enactment of the battle of 1809.*

Gastronomy: *pulpo gallego (Galician style octopus, with coarse-grained salt, olive oil and paprika, served on wooden platters). The most authentic tasting can be done on the 9th and 26th of the month in the market in the Plaza del Vendimiador.*

The Camino leaves Cacabelos at first along the N-VI and after ½ hr. reaches the hamlet of **Pieros (9)**. About 400m after the exit from the village turn right onto the small asphalt road (arrows; sign: San Clemente. Straight on: alternative on

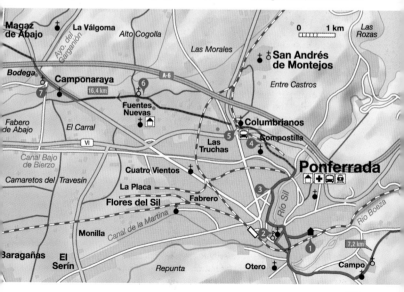

main road, 1 hr. to Villafranca). After 300m follow the soon stony farm track on the left. It brings you through vineyards into the hamlet of **Valtville de Arriba** (**10**; ½ hr.). Stay on the main path that goes round a wide bend to the left through the hamlet. Shortly after the last house at a fork in the farm track take the main path downhill (marker stone after a few steps). Through vineyards and a lovely landscape you are now heading towards **Villafranca del Bierzo** (**11**; 1 hr.).

_i_ _The medieval pilgrims named **Villafranca del Bierzo** 'small Compostela' since sick and weak people who were unable to continue their pilgrimage received the same indulgence as at the apostle's tomb on the steps of the **Puerta del Perdón** (gate of pardon) of the **Iglesia de Santiago** (12th/13th century). Like the Holy Doors of the cathedral of Santiago it only stands open during Holy Years._
The town owes its name (villa de francos) to the French Benedictine monks from Cluny monastery who settled here in the 11th century at the entrance to the narrow Valley of the Río Valcarce and took in pilgrims. They are also said to have brought viticulture into the region. During a short episode, 1822/23, Villafranca was the seat of government of the Galician province of El Bierzo and remains the 'secret' capital of the region today. In the Middle Ages there were four churches in the town, six monasteries and at least as many pilgrim hospices. The most striking church building is the former collegiate church, **Colegiata de Santa María**, (late Gothic, end of the 16th century) with enormous, slightly discordant proportions. Only the **Iglesia de San Francisco** (13th century; Gothic stucco work, 15th century) remains of the former Franciscan monastery. The convent, **Convento de la Anunciada**, is under the control of the Clarissa Order. The Baroque convent church dates from the 17th century. At 33m, one of the largest and oldest cypress trees in Europe stands behind the convent walls. The tree is said to have been planted shortly after the foundation of the convent in 1606. However you can only admire it from the outside since the convent is not open to the public. The convent of **San Nicolás el Real** was founded in the 17th century by Jesuits and in 899 passed into the ownership of the Paulian Order. The Baroque high altar is interesting, as are the cloister and a small science museum. The largest civic building is the **Castillo Palacio de Los Marqueses**, in the 16th/17th century a fortified palace of the Margrave of Villafranca. The Way of St. James goes through the town along the **Rúa del Agua**, once lined with the palaces of noblemen. (Information about visits and guided tours from the tourist office: Oficina de Turismo, Avda. Bernardo Díez Olebar).
Fiestas: _1st May, Mayos vivientes, spring festival: young people with garlands of branches and leaves process as 'living maypoles' through the town and lie down on the ground as a symbol of nature's death in winter and its regeneration in spring. At the end of June, the Fiesta de la Poesía with readings of literature in the Jardín de la Alameda (near San Nicolás el Real) with artists from the whole of Spain. On 14th September, festival of the patron saint, Santísimo Cristo de la Esperanza, including processions and parades with gigantes and cabezudos (giant figures)._

Hostels: Pereje (546m, pop. 40), MH, ⊜⊜⊜, 30 B + M/5 €. Tel: 987 540 138. Roomy, kitchen, washing machine, internet. 10.00–22.00, all year. **Trabadelo** (572m, pop. 110), **(1)** PH, ⊜⊜⊜, 20 B (bunkbeds)/6 €, 15 normal beds/8 € (+ 3 DR 44 €). Alb. Crispeta, old N-VI, tel: 987 566 529. Kitchen, rest., washing machine, drier, internet. All day, all year. **(2)** MH, ⊜⊜⊜, 38 B+M/6 €. Tel: 687 827 987. Kitchen, washing machine/drier, bar. 12.00–22.30, Mar.–Oct. **La Portela de Valcarce** (621m, pop. 35) PH, ⊜⊜, 40 B/8 € (SR/DR 25–35 €). El Peregrino, tel: 987 543 197. Washing machine/drier, internet, TV, bar, barbecue. All day, all year. **Ambasmestas** (618m, pop. 50), PH, ⊜⊜⊜, 18 B/5 €, Alb. Das Ánimas, on the left of the path, near river/barbecue site, tel: 619 048 626. Microwave, evening meal, breakfast, washing machine/drier, internet. 12.00–22.00 April–Oct. **Vega de Valcarce** (644m, pop. 250), **(1)** PH, ⊜⊜, 38 B/12 € with breakfast, with Brasilian evening meal/breakfast 25 €. Alb. N.S. Aparecida do Brasil, start of the village, tel: 987 543 054. Washing machine/drier, internet. 12.30–22.00, Easter–mid Nov. **(2)** MH, ⊜⊜, 64 B (+M)/5 €. in the village, tel. no. if necessary on door. Basic hostel, kitchen. washing machine/drier. Internet. All day, all year, with *hospitalero* in summer, if necessary in winter ask at the chemist's for key. **Ruitelán** (671m, pop. 25), PH, ⊜⊜⊜, 34 B/ 5 €, Pequeño Potala, tel: 987 561 322.Evening meal (also vegetarian), breakfast, washing machine/drier, internet, massages/shiatsu, homeopathy treatments. About 12.00–23.00 (winter from 13/14.00), all year. **Las Herrerías** (701m, pop. 50), PH, ⊜⊜⊜, 17 B/5 €. Refugio de Herrerías, tel: 654 353 940. Vegetarian meals (also possible to make coffee), washing machine, Wi-Fi in village. From about 13/14.00, Easter–Oct. **La Faba** (902m, pop. 30), SH, ⊜⊜⊜, 66 B/5 €. Run by German Ultreya society; former

rectory next to chapel of San Andrés de la Faba. Tel: 630 836 865. Test about Swabia: those people coming from Swabia can have a free night's accommodation if they can recite a song/poem by a Swabian poet. Prayers May–Aug. Mon.–Fri. 20.00, mass from June onwards alternate Sat./Sun. Kitchen, washing machine.drier. 14.00–22.00, week before Easter–Oct.

Grade and route: well marked. Path next to old N-VI. The alternative '*camino duro*' (strenuous path) between Villafranca and Trabadelo is tough. The ascent to O Cebreiro begins from Ruitelán. At times stony, at times tiring and steep forest path, very slippery in places on account of the cow pats.

Height difference: 400m in ascent.

Scenery: up to Ruitelán the path follows the green valley of the Río Valcarce through several small villages. The ascent to the Pass O Cebreiro is without doubt one of the most beautiful and emotive experiences. It goes up through a dense mixed deciduous forest and through small hamlets, like La Faba and La Laguna, where time seems to have stood still. The forest thins out with increasing height and the view opens up of the fascinating, typical Galician green mountain landscape.

Local services: Pereje ⌇⌂⌑⌸⌷@; Trabadelo ⌇⌂⌑⌸⌷@; La Portela de Valcarce ⌇⌂⌑@€; Ambasmestas ⌇ ⌂⌷@; Vega de Valcarce⌇⌷@€⌸ ⌸⌷⊠ (beach by river) @⌖ tel: 987 561 331; Ruitelán ⌑⌷⌑⌸@; Las Herrerías ⌂⌑⌷@; La Faba ⌇⌷⌑.

Remarks: (1) When planning stages, you should be aware that the '*camino duro*' alternative is very strenuous on account of its large height difference and therefore not suitable for less experienced walkers. If this is the case, consider a shorter stage. **(2)** Vega de Valcarce is the last opportunity for shopping and getting cash before Triacastela (33km).

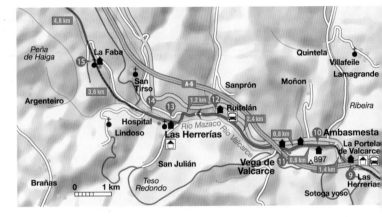

Walk the length of **Villafranca (1)** along the c/ del Agua through the centre of the old town. When this road opens out into a small square turn left and at the stone pilgrim monument cross over the Río Burbía. A few dozen metres after that, at c/ Pradela, there are yellow waymarkers giving you the choice of the easy alternative that runs parallel to the N-VI in the Valcarce valley or the '*camino duro*', the 'hard way' **(2)**.

The first alternative can be described quickly: go along a pathway next to the road via **Pereje** (1½ hrs.), to **Trabadelo (8**; 1 hr.) where both alternatives meet up again (first hostel at the start of the village, the second in the village itself).

This marvellous chestnut forest is the reward for your efforts along the 'camino duro'.

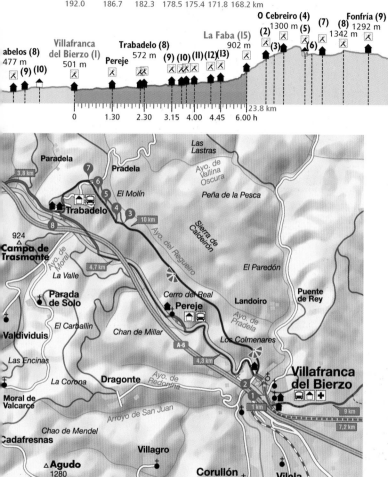

The '**camino duro**' (11km/3¼ hrs., 460m in ascent, 380m in descent to Trabadelo, height profile on p. 174) on the other hand ascends steeply uphill on the right along c/ Pradela and soon becomes a farm track. For the first

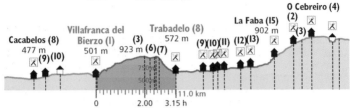

193.0   186.3 182.0 km

O Cebreiro (4)
(2)

La Faba (I5)
902 m (3)

Villafranca del   Trabadelo (8)
Bierzo (I)   (3)   572 m   (9)(I0)(II) (I2)(I3)
Cacabelos (8) 501 m 923 m (6)(7)
477 m (9)(I0)

750
500

0   2.00   3.15 h
11.0 km

quarter of an hour roughly you walk very steeply uphill, then the incline moderates. After about one hour you pass by a small pine wood then the path runs more on the level along a predominently barren high mountain path. With lovely distant views you reach the highest point at 932m **(3)**. Shortly afterwards slightly downhill you come into a wonderful forest with huge chestnut trees. After a few minutes at the T-junction **(4)** keep left along a small road (sign). A few minutes later follow the rather indistinct path **(5)** slightly left and after 200m meet a T-junction **(6)**. Go 10m to the right and left immediately afterwards. A good quarter of an hour later your path joins a small road **(7)**. A few metres to the right above your path (at the crash barrier) turns off to the left downhill. Descend this path, meet the road briefly, but take your path again to the right of it straight on. You meet the road again, go left here and then straight onto the path to the right downhill which brings you through a mixed deciduous wood to **Trabadelo** (**8**; ¾ hr.).

First walk through the village, then next to the road continue to **La Portela de Valcarce** (**9**; ¾ hr.). Shortly afterwards the route follows the turn-off on the left to Vega de Valcarce. You arrive in **Ambasmestas** (**10**; a good ¼ hr.) and the linear **Vega de Valcarce** (**11**; 10 mins. as far as PH, ¼ hr. from there to

MH), where in the Plaza Mayor, a *palloza* has been copied, an oval house with a thatched roof, once typical of the region. Half an hour an hour later you reach **Ruitelán** (**12**). From now on it's a distinctly uphill path. At the hotel of Las Herrerías turn off left downhill and reach the hamlet of **Las Herrerías** (**13**; ¼ hr.) and soon afterwards **Hospital** (**14**). Just under half an hour an hour after the hamlet the path turns off left. After a short level section the ascent begins through the dense deciduous forest. For the not very long but steep ascent to **La Faba** (**15**) you need up to ¾ hr. (Iglesia de San Andrés, 18th century.).

The autonomous region of Galicia

Galicia (pop. 2.8 million/29,574km²) is divided into 4 provinces: A Coruña, Lugo, Ourense, Pontevedra. The capital is Santiago de Compostela.

Of all the regions on the Spanish Way of St. James Galicia is the most secret. Like nowhere else in Spain, the pre-Christian mindset is so entrenched to the present day, and ancient cultures have left behind traces such as the dolmens dating back to time of megalithic culture (4000–2000 BC.) or mystic symbols engraved in stone from the Bronze Age (1800 BC).

The most deeply rooted traces were left behind by the Celts who settled here from 700 BC to the fall of the Romans around 135 BC. They provided the name (Gallaecia) and shaped the language which, due to only a weak level of romanisation, preserved its original characteristics. Gallego is a very soft melodious language with a clear connection to Portuguese that developed from Gallego.

In the 5th century the Suebian founded a kingdom that was conquered in the 6th century by the Visigoths. The Moorish invasion of the Iberian peninsula in the 8th century remained largely unsuccessful for Galicia. Not until the discovery of the apostle's tomb in the 9th century did Galicia become internationally known. A Galician kingdom existed in the 10th/11th century that was part of the kingdom of León and Castilla. From the 19th century onwards the economic depression led to a large wave of emigration, especially to South America. There are about 300,000 Galicians, eligible to vote, living abroad today.

And Galicia, predominantly making its living from agriculture and fishing, is still one of the poorest regions in Spain. Tourism hardly plays a role in this scenically extremely beautiful region. Contributory factors are the remoteness and the rainy, if also mild, climate. Galicia still has a close connection to its Celtic heritage whether it be in its music (the *gaita*, for example, Galician bagpipes), in the issue regarding witches (*meigas*), to which the Gallegos have a distinctly equivocal attitude ('I do not believe in witches,

The construction of a thatched roof for a palloza, a stone house of celtic origin.

On the ascent to O Cebreiro, view back to Castilla y Léon.

but there are some') or in their belief in the supernatural powers of stones and the sea.

Admittedly you still have to conquer the passes of O Cebreiro, San Roque and Alto do Poio, but after that Galicia rewards you for all the effort and deprivation of your long travels. The shrine and museum village of O Cebreiro and the Samos monastery are the last big cultural highpoints before the apostle's tomb. The path (in Galician, *camiño*) is now, first and foremost, a purely natural pleasure; it carries you off into a lovely idyll of cow pastures and picturesque villages, into shady oak and eucalyptus forests – an opportunity for some last reflection before arriving at your destination. The only disadvantage: from Galicia, especially in July/August, the route becomes quite noisy since many pilgrims do not start their walk until Galicia. Consequently, it can also be full and uncomfortable in the hostels where the very unpleasant rush for the best places already begins early in the morning. If at all possible try not to let yourself to be drawn into it. For Holy Year 2010 the Galician government has invested millions of euros in the Way of St. James. The network of hostels in particular has profited from this; new hostels have been created, old ones have been renovated and are still being renovated.

If you want to enjoy tranquillity and nature again at the end of your journey and still have some time left, it is recommended that you continue the path to the coast, to Finisterre and Muxía. The Camino through the mostly thinly populated and green countryside of the interior to the chiefly natural coastline with its white sandy beaches, rugged cliffs and sunsets makes the extra distance worthwhile.

Hostels: La Laguna (1,161m, pop. 25) PH, ⊕⊕⊕, 18 B/9 € (DR 38 €). Alb. La Escuela, tel: 987 684 786 and 619 479 238, Luz Divina, Isidro Santín. Washing machine/drier, internet, bar/rest. 12.30–23.00, March–Nov. **O Cebreiro** (1,300m, pop. 30), XH, ⊕⊕⊖, 106 B/5 €. Tel: 982 367 025. One of the most frequented hostels along the way, beds placed close together as in all XH. Kitchen (no utensils), washing machine/drier, extra tents in summer. 13.00–23.00, all year. **Hospital da Condesa** (1,240m, pop. 30), XH, ⊕⊕, 22 B/5 €. Tel: 660 396 810. Kitchen (no utensils), washing machine. No shop.13.00–23.00, all year. **Fonfría** (1299m), PH, ⊕⊕⊕, bis zu 80 B/8 € (DR/3-bed-room 13 €/person). Alb. A Reboleira, tel: 982 181 271 or 619 751 983. Beautiful day room, restaurant, communal meals, bar, internet, washing machine/drier, campsite, stable. 13.00–23.00, March–Nov. **Triacastela** (670m, pop. 240), **(1)** XH, ⊕⊕, 56 B/5 €. 700m before the village, on the meadow on the right of the Camino, tel: 982 548 087. Disabled facilities, washing machine/drier, quickly fills up at peak times. 13.00–23.00, all year. **(2)** PH, ⊕⊕⊕, 32 B/9 € (6 DR/40 €), Complexo Xacobeo, tel: 982 548 037/426. Roomy. Kitchen, washing machine/drier, internet, garden, issue of pilgrim passport. 11.00–23.00, all year, except Christmas to Three Kings. **(3)** PH, ⊕⊕⊕, 14 B/9 € (3 DR 40 €). A Horta de Abel, tel: 608 080 556. Kitchen, washing machine/drier, internet Wi-Fi. Beautiful stone building. All day until 23.00, April–Oct. **(4)** PH, ⊕⊕⊕, 38 B/8 €. Alb. Aitzenea, Plaza Vista Alegre (at O'Novo café/bar on the right), tel: 982

548 076. Beautiful old building, kitchen, drinks/coffee machine, washing machine, internet. 9.00–23.00, Apr.–Oct. **(5)** PH, ⊕⊕⊕, 27 B/April–Oct. 9 €, Nov.–March 8 €. Alb. Refugio del Oribio, Avda. de Castilla, 20 (on the right up the main street at Alb. Aitzenea), tel: 982 548 085. Kitchen, washing machine/drier, drinks/snack machine, internet, Wi-Fi. All day, all year. **(6)** PH, ⊕⊕⊕, 27 B/8 €. Alb. Berce do Camiño (straight on at cafébar O'Novo), tel: 982 548 127. Kitchen, washing machine, drinks machine, internet, Wi-Fi, terrace. All day, all year.

Grade and route: well marked. Ascents to O Cebreiro, San Roque and Alto do Poio moderate to difficult. Not much asphalt.

Height difference: 630m in ascent, 870m in descent.

Critical points: none.

Scenery: the ascent to O Cebreiro pass is one of the scenically most emotive stages. It's best to tackle it in the morning. There are lovely views from the pass of the surrounding mountains. In the lower areas the path emerges into the green heart of Galicia. Forests, fields and small villages now characterize the landscape to Santiago de Compostela.

Local services: La Laguna ⌧ ⊞ @; O Cebreiro ⌧ ⌂ ▱ ⛟ ⓘ ▙ 19.00; Liñares (1,223m, pop. 20) ⊞ ⌧ ⌂ ▱; Hospital da Condesa ⌧ ⊞ ▙; Alto do Poio ▣ ⌧ ⌂; Fonfría ⌧ ⊞ ⌂ @; O Biduedo (1,186 m) ⌧ ⌂; Pasantes (797m, pop. 50) ⌂; Triacastela ⌧ ⌂ ▱ € @ ▣ ▙ 19.00.

Remarks: overnight accommodation in the small villages is usually in *casas rurales* (sort of B&B).

From **La Faba (1)** continue uphill to **La Laguna** (**2**; 1 hr.). This also very remote picturesque farming village is the last in the province of León. The forest recedes and allows you an open view of the surrounding mountains – as long as the fog does not put a spanner into the works! After a good quarter of an hour a waymarker stone marks another 152.5km to Santiago. Shortly afterwards you will see a new boundary stone in **Galicia**/Province of Lugo **(3)**.

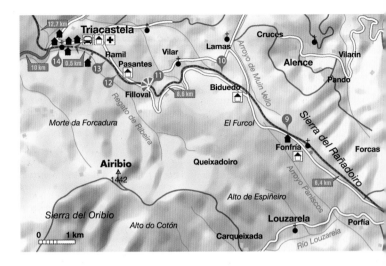

After another good half an hour you have reached the the village of **O Cebreiro (4)** which is classified as a historical monument.

> *i* *The museum village of **O Cebreiro** can be found one of the oldest pilgrim refuges along the Way of St. James. From the middle of the 9th century a small community of Benedictine monks took care of pilgrims and a monastery was founded in 1072 by order of King Alfonso VI. The shrine of **Santa María la Real**, built in the 9th century, is the oldest preserved church along the way. Here the Santo Milagro, the holy miracle, is said to have happened around 1300. The legend tells of how a devout farmer fought his way, one stormy winter night, up to the mass in O Cebreiro. The monk, who was entrusted with the liturgy and not very strong in his beliefs, thought disdainfully to himself, 'What an idiot to suffer such a storm, only*

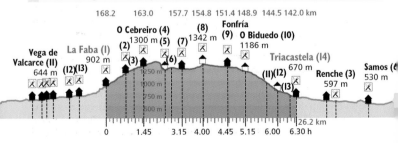

*to see a piece of bread and a bit of wine!' At the same moment the host and altar wine were transformed into real flesh and blood. Both are on display in the **Capilla del Santo Milagro** in two glass phials which, in 1486, Queen Isabella blessed on her pilgrimage to Santiago. Chalice and host are both represented in the Galician coat of arms.*

*Typical for the region are the **pallozas** which are of Celtic origin. People lived with their animals in the squat stone houses that had an oval layout and low overhanging thatched roofs. The pallozas of O Cebreiro were inhabited right up to the 1960s but today are only used for museum purposes.*

Elias Valiña (1929–1989), from 1959 the priest of O Cebreiro, was a pioneer of the modern Way of Saint James and the yellow arrow. In the middle of the 60s he wrote a thesis on the Way of Saint James and gave lectures in the whole of Europe on the importance of the Camino. In 1984 he marked the route from France to

Santiago for the first time with yellow arrows – still the signs and waymarkers for the Camino de Santiago to the present day.

Public holidays: pilgrimage on 8th/9th September in memory of Santo Milagro.

Gastronomy: quesos D.O. O Cebreiro, soft cheese made from cow's milk in the form of a chef's hat, preferably eaten with membrillo (quince jelly) or honey (miel). All over Galicia: queimada (a kind Galician flaming punch with a high percentage of alcohol), white wines (D.O. Ribeiro and Albariño), empanadas (savoury pasties).

Walk past the hostel situated at the edge of O Cebreiro village onto the gently ascending farm track on the left and keep straight on along this track (the picnic area is up on the left). You soon enter a little wood and once more negotiate a small pass after about ½ hr. (1,378m). Soon after, at the edge of the wood, the path meets a gravel path and bends to the right. **Liñares (5)** is reached round a wide bend (¼ hr.). A path next to the road leads to the top of the pass of **San Roque (6**; 1,267m; a good ¼ hr.) where a bronze statue of

Ancient chestnut tree near Ramil.

a pilgrim stands into the wind. With gentle up and down walking the hamlet of **Hospital da Condesa** (**7**; ½ hr.). After that it's another strenuous ascent to the **Alto do Poio** (**8**; 1,342m) – at first on asphalt, then on a farm track. The last quarter is a very steep pull up to the top of the pass (¾ hr. from Hospital). With this, however, the last big hurdle along the way to Santiago is overcome.

With lovely views over the Galician mountains you now come along good paths to **Fonfría** (**9**; ¾ hr.) and **O Biduedo** (**10**; ½ hr.). After that there's a noticeable incline downhill; Triacastela can soon be seen in the valley below on the right. After half an hour you arrive in **Filloval (11)** and cross over the road. Following a very lovely forest path you reach **Pasantes** (**12**; ¼ hr.) and **Ramil** (**13**; a good ¼ hr.). In the village you will find an impressively huge ancient chestnut tree. A little later on the state hostel of **Triacastela** can be found on the left of the path. The **centre (14)** is about 500m further on.

i *The name of **Triacastela** suggests three fortresses (tres castros) that reputedly once stood here. King Alfonso IX ordered settlers to come and live here in the 13th century. Besides three pilgrim hospitals there was also a pilgrim prison in Triacastela which, however, is only indicated by a sad little sign opposite O'Novo bar. The **Iglesia de Santiago** acquired its curious tower in the 18th century and the Romanesque apse dates back to the 12th century.*

In the Middle Ages it was customary to take a stone out of the limestone quarries near Triacastela and bring it to the lime kilns in Castañeda where lime was burnt for the building of Santiago cathedral.

Hostels: Casa Forte de Lusío (606m), XH, ⬤⬤⬤, 60 B/5 €. 400m on the left of the Camino, restored palace. Tel: 659 721 324. Kitchen. Nearest rest. in Renche. 13.00–22.00, all year. **Samos** (530m, pop. 200), **(1)** RH, ⬤⬤, 70 B/donations. Benedictine monastery, entrance next to the petrol station, tel: 982 546 046. Basic, hostel with Christian emphasis. 15.00–22.00, all year. **(2)** PH, ⬤⬤⬤, 8 B/9 € (2 DR 25 €). Alb. A Cova do Frade, tel: 982 546 087. Washing machine/drier. All day, all year. **(3)** PH, ⬤⬤⬤, 48 B/11 €. Alb. Val de Samos, tel: 982 638 801. Washing machine/drier, kitchen, Wi-Fi. All day, April–Oct. **San Mamede** (488m, pop. 10), PH, ⬤⬤⬤, 20 B/10 € (5 DR 38 €). Paloma y Leña, tel: 982 533 248. Evening meal (vegetarian too)/breakfast, washing machine, internet. Small but nice. All day, all year. **Sarria** (446m, pop. 8,700), **(1)** PH, ⬤⬤⬤, 15 B/9 € (DR 32/40 €). Alb. A Pedra, c/ Vigo de Sarria, 19, tel: 982 530 130. Start of village. Kitchen, washing machine/drier, internet, Wi-Fi, garden. Quite cosy. All day, March–Nov. **(2)** PH, ⬤⬤⬤, 22 B/10 €. Casa Peltre, Escalinata Mayor, 10, tel: 606 226 067. Kitchen, washing machine/drier, internet, Wi-Fi. 11.00–22.30, end March–Nov. **(3)** PH, ⬤⬤⬤, 16 B/ 10 € (low season 9 €) inclusive of bedlinen and towel. Alb. Mayor, c/ Pedreiras, 1, tel: 982 535 097. Kitchen, washing machine/drier, Wi-Fi. 11.00–23.00, April–Oct. **(4)** XH, ⬤⬤, 40 B/ 5 €. Tel: no. on the door. Kitchen (no utensils), washing machine/drier. 13.00–23.00, all year. **(5)** PH, ⬤⬤⬤, 39 B/10 € (SR 25 €). Alb. O Durmiñento, Rúa Maior, tel: 600 862 508. Roomy, meals, washing machine/drier, internet, Wi-Fi, massages (summer). 11.00–23.00, March–Nov. **(6)** PH, ⬤⬤⬤, 38 B/10 € (2 DR 45 €). Alb. Internacional, tel: 982 535 109. Possible change of ownership. Washing machine/drier, internet. 12.00–22.30, Easter–Oct. **(7)** PH, ⬤⬤⬤, 42 B/8 €. Alb. Los Blasones, Rúa Maior, tel: 982 862 508.

Almost 500 Jahre old former palace. Kitchen, Wi-Fi, washing machine/drier. Dormitory and smaller rooms, garden. 11.00–23.00, Easter–Oct. (phone beforehand in winter). **(8)** PH, ⬤⬤⬤, 40 B/9 €, Alb. Don Álvaro, tel: 982 531 592. Kitchen, washing machine/drier, internet. Drinks round the hearth in the evening, garden, massages. All day, all year. **(9)** PH, ⬤⬤⬤, 22 B/July–Aug. 10 €, otherwise 9 €, DR 20 €. Alb. Dos Oito Marabedís, Rúa Conde de Lemos, 23, after Los Blasones 2nd street on left, tel: 618 748 777. 2 kitchens, washing machine/drier, internet. 12.00–23.00, May–Oct. **(10)** RH, ⬤⬤⬤, 104 B/10 €. Monasterio de la Magdalena (in the monastery), tel: 982 533 568 (reservations too). Large hostel, ideal for groups. Kitchen, washing machine/drier, internet. Pilgrims pass. 13.30–24.00, all year. **(11)** PH, ⬤⬤⬤, 28 B/10 € (DR 35 €). Alb. San Lázaro, c/ San Lázaro, 7, tel: 982 530 626. Washing machine/drier, microwave, internet. All day, Apr.–Oct. **Vilei** (521m, pop. 40), PH, ⬤⬤⬤, 24 B (extension planned)/9 € (DR 40 €, 3-bed-room 50 €, 4-bed-room 15 €/ pp). Pensión-alb. Casa Barbadelo, tel: 659 160 498. Washing machine/drier, bar/rest. Internet. All day, mid March–Oct. 600m further on: **Barbadelo** (570m, pop. 10), **(1)** PH, ⬤⬤⬤, 8 B/10 €. Alb. O Pombal (350m on left after Vilei), tel: 686 718 732. Washing machine/drier, kitchen. 13.00–23.00, April–Oct. Following the Camino to the right: **(2)** XH, ⬤⬤, 18 B/5 €. Tel: 982 530 412. Kitchen, 13.00–23.00, all year. **(3)** PH, ⬤⬤⬤, 26 B/ 10 € (2 DR 30 €). A Casa de Carmen, tel: 982 532 294. Place for tents (free), meals. Washing machine, drier, internet. From 13.00, April–Nov.

Grade and route: well marked, easy. In places next to the LU-634 to Samos, otherwise forest paths. From Samos the long, but more lovely alternative to Perros/Calvor on small country roads is recommended and then to Sarria.

Entrance to the monastery hostel in Samos.

Height difference: 410m in ascent, 520m in descent.

Critical points: none.

Scenery: dense deciduous forests make this a beautiful section to Sarria, in spite of the nearness to the road, and the path goes in places through very small hamlets. From Sarria to Portomarín enjoy the idyllic landscape with streams, forests, meadows and pretty villages.

Local services: Renche (597m, pop. 30) ⊠; Samos ⊠⌂⊠✉€@⌂⊠ℹ⊠⊡ see info box; Aguiada (497m, pop. 36) ▣⌂; Sarria ⊠⌂⊠✉€@⌂⊠ℹ⊠⊟⊡ ⚓ Igl. de Santa Marina pilgrim mass daily at 19.30 ✚ c/ Calvo Sotelo, 136, tel: 982 254 634; Vilei/Barbadelo ⌂⊠.

Remarks: (1) The alternative via Samos is quite nice, in spite of the section next to the road. **(2)** It's worth making an overnight stop in Samos especially on account of the Gregorian songs during the masses and prayers in the monastery church. **(3)** Many pilgrims begin their journey in Sarria to walk the last 100km that are necessary in order to receive the Compostela. Therefore, from Sarria at the latest, especially July/August, you can anticipate large crowds of 'short distance walkers' in the hostels – not always welcomed by those who have aleady been on the road for weeks.

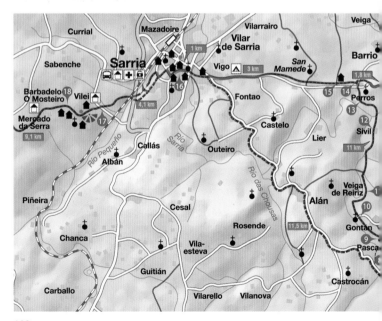

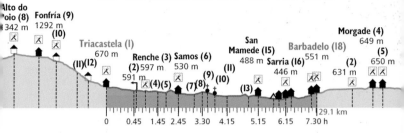

At the end of the village of **Triacastela (1)** walk left in the direction of Samos and then parallel to the country road (LU-634) as far as **San Cristovo do Real (2**; ¾ hr; Albergue Casa Forte de Luisó just afterwards on the left, on the far side of the LU-634). At the start of this village leave the road to the right and continue along a forest path as it ascends and descends beside the Río Oribio. At an old mill cross over the stream to the left, go straight after

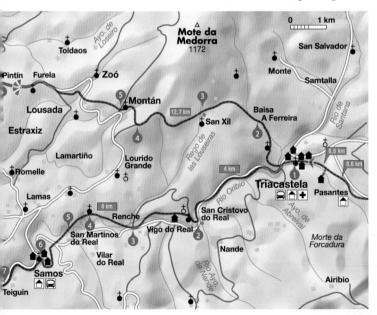

to the right and then uphill to **Renche** (3; ½ hr.). After the village you need to go downhill again, cross the stream and continue along the undulating path to **Freituxe** (4; just under ½ hr.) and to **San Martiño do Real** (5; just under ¼ hr.). The path continues to ascend and then leads left, above the road, down to **Samos** (6; ½ hr.).

*The Monasterio de San Julián y Santa Basilisa, or also called simply **Monasterio de Samos** (see photo below), was founded around the 5th/6th century and is one of the oldest monasteries in the western world. The rules of the Order of St. Benedict have been in effect since the 10/11th century. At the end of the 8th century the later King Alfonso II was brought up in Samos. The apostle's tomb was found during his reign and he became one of the first sponsors of the pilgrim way. The monastery experienced its heyday in the 16th century. During the war against Napoleon (beginning 19th century) the monastery served as a military hospital. In the course of the dissolution of the monasteries by Minister Mendizábal (middle 19th century) the monks lost the abbey, but returned in 1880. There's a small community of monks living there again today. It's well worth a visit to the monastery (with guided tour, in Spanish) where you can see the Romanesque portal to the old church (12th century), the small Gothic cloister (16th century, also called Claustro de las Nereidas, cloister of the water spirits), the largest cloister in Spain with a lateral length of 56 x 56m (Claustro grande, 17th century) as well as the monastery church from the 18th century. With a bit of luck, during your visit, you will be able to hear the church organ with its 3,850 pipes. The library comprising more than 30,000 (historic) volumes is not open to the public. That and large parts of the monastery had to be rebuilt in 1951 after a devastating fire when a distillery tank containing pure alcohol blew up.*

The wall paintings on the first floor of the large cloister with scenes from the life of St. Benedict, were completed after the reconstruction in 1957.

Guided tours: Mon.–Sat. 10.00–12.30 and 16.30–18.30, Sun./public holidays 12.45–13.30 and 16.30–18.30 or according to notice.

Mass: summer daily 20.00, winter 18.30. Sung prayers: 8.30 Lauds, 19.30 Vespers. www.abadiadesamos.com.

The **Capilla del Salvador** (Mozarabic architectural style, 9th or 10th century) is also worth seeing and is situated outside the village. Because of the more than 25m high cypress tree next to it, reputedly over 1,000 years old, it is also called the Capilla del Ciprés.

The alternative from Samos to Sarria takes an idyllic route away from the road.

If you choose the road alternative from Samos (LU-633) you will come via **Foxos** (¼ hr.), **Teiguín** (**7**; ¼ hr.) and **Ayan** (1¼ hrs.) to **Sarria** (**16**; 1 hr.). For the nicer alternative follow the yellow arrows shortly after Teiguín (7) to the right up onto the little road in the direction of Pascais (8; ¼ hr.). At the small hamlet about 10 mins. after Pascais (A Rectoral) go left and immediately right **(9)**. About 20 mins. later at a small chapel **(10)** turn right into the little street and then take the path immediately on the left of it. This leads you back to the little country road and further to **Veiga de Reiriz** (**11**; ½ hr.) and the farmstead of **Sivil** (**12**; a good ¼ hr.). Keep left there and continue along the little road to reach **Perros (13)** and **Aguiada/Calvor** (**14**; just under ½ hr.) where you turn left onto the Camino and Stage 27b. The **Xunta hostel (6)** lies about 500m to the right.

Along a path next to the road you arrive at the hostel of **San Mamede** (**15**; ¼ hr.) and continue straight ahead where you turn left onto the Camino and Stage 27b. into the outskirts of **Sarria** (¾ hr.). From there you come through the not very attractive modern part of town (supermarkets and banks on the main road) up into the **historical centre** (**16**; ¼ hr.).

Fog – a frequent companion in Galicia.

The Monasterio de la Magdalena in the early morning.

[i] **Sarria** *in pre-Roman times existed as a fortress of the Iberian line of Seurros. King Alfonso IX founded the town (like Triacastela too) in the 13th century and died here on his pilgrimage to Santiago in the year 1230. The most beautiful road in the old town is the **Rúa Maior** which runs like so many urban pilgrim paths right through the centre and is lined with grand houses from the 18th century. Today's county court (juzgados) was, up to 1839, the pilgrim hospital of San Antón. The **Templo del Salvador** (13th century, Gothic, beautiful side portal) stands next to it. Only the fortress tower is still preserved from the medieval castle. At the entrance to the town can be found the **Monasterio de la Magdalena**, established as a hostel in the 13th century by two Italian pilgrims.*

__Gastronomy:__ a cattle and food market is held on the 6th, 20th and 27th of the month near to the old fortress tower where you can also buy fresh pulpo gallego (Galician style octopus).

Walk through the old town of Sarria along the Rúa Maior and then come along a very beautiful forest path into the hamlet of **Vilei (17)** and 600m further on to **Barbadelo/O Mosteiro (18**; 1 hr). The Iglesia de Santiago was part of a monastery that came under the jurisdiction of the abbey of Samos in the 11th century.

Hostels: Calvor (534m, pop. 90), XH, ◖◗, 22 B/5 €. Tel: 982 531 266. Kitchen (no utensils), washing machine/drier, telephone. In a remote location. 13.00–23.00, all year. For hostels from Calvor onwards see Stage 27a.

Grade and route: well marked, easy in spite of constant up-and-down. Small asphalt roads and unsurfaced roads.

Height difference: 300m in ascent, 410m in descent.

Critical points: none.

Scenery: more countrified, characterised by small villages, meadows and forests with knotty oaks. Something typical for Galicia are the *pasadoiros* – large stone slabs laid in a row to enable you to cross streams; *corredoiras* – narrow paths that are closed in on both sides; and *hórreos* – long stone granaries on stilts.

Local services: San Xil (780m, pop. 20) ✉; Sarria see Stage 27a.

Remarks: few local services, think about food and water.

The path via San Xil leaves **Triacastela (1)** to the right. It goes at first along a little asphalt road through a dense forest uphill to the hamlet of **A Ferreira (2**; ½ hr.).

A wooded path brings you to **San Xil (3**; ½ hr.) and after that it descends an asphalt road. After ½ hr. a **yellow arrow (4)** indicates a wooded path to the right into a dense forest through which you come to the little country road again after a short while. At the small chapel keep to the right and after a few minutes you reach **Montán (5**; ¾ hr. from San Xil). After walking through several small villages you come to the **Calvor hostel (6**; 1¼ hrs.) which is on the route, but outside the village . A good ¼ hr. later Stage 27a joins from the left at **Aguiada (14)**.

The path next to the road leads to the hostel of **San Mamede (15**; ¼ hr.) and straight on to **Sarria (16**; 1 hr.). A very beautiful path through the wood brings you into the hamlet of **Vilei (17)** and into the nearby **Barbadelo (18**; 1 hr.). For the route description see also p. 186, Stage 27a.

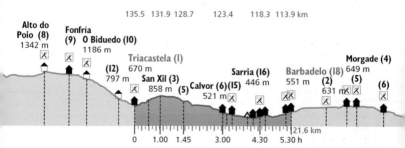

135.5 131.9 128.7   123.4   118.3 113.9 km

Alto do Poio (8) 1342 m
Fonfría (9) O Biduedo (10) 1186 m
Triacastela (1) 670 m
(12) 797 m
San Xil (3) 858 m
(5)
Calvor (6)(15) 521 m
Sarria (16) 446 m
Barbadelo (18) 649 m 551 m (2) (5) 631 m
Morgade (4) 649 m
(6)

0   1.00 1.45   3.00   4.30 5.30 h   21.6 km

Hostels: Morgade (649m, pop. 5), PH, ◉◉◉, 6 B/10 € (5 DR 28 and 35 €). Alb. Casa Morgade, tel: 982 531 250. Washing machine/drier, internet. 11.00–23.00, Easter–Nov. **Ferreiros** (650m, pop. 20) **(1)** XH, ◉◉, 22 B/5 €. Tel: 982 157 496. Kitchen (no utensils), washing machine/drier. 13.00–23.00, all year. **(2)** PH, ◉◉◉, 16 B/10 € (DR 35 €). Alb. Casa Cruceiro de Ferreiros, tel: 982 541 240. Garden, rest./bar, Wi-Fi, washing machine, drier. 11.00–22.30, March–Nov. **Mercadoiro** (536m, pop. 10), PH, ◉◉◉, 32 B/10 € (2 DR 40 €). Alb. de Peregrinos de Mercadoiro, tel: 982 545 359 (possible to reserve by phone). Washing machine, Wi-Fi. Meals. All day, March–mid Nov. **Portomarín** (389m, pop. 1,800), **(1)** PH, ◉◉◈, 30 B/10 €. Alb. O Mirador, tel: 982 545 323. After the bridge steps straight ahead, then left. 4/6-bed rooms (curtains as doors). Washing machine/drier, internet, bar/rest., viewing terrace. 9.00–23.30, all year. Below it: **(2)** PH, ◉◉◈, 120 B/10 €. Alb. Ferramenteiro, tel: 982 545 362. Kitchen, washing machine/drier, internet, café. All day, April–mid Oct. **(3)** PH, ◉◉◉, 16 B/10 € (4 DR 25 €). Alb. Manuel, Rúa do Miño, 1. Tel: 982 545 385. Kitchen, washing machine, drier. Basic but good. All day, April–about Oct. **(4)** XH, ◉◉, 100 B/5 €. Tel: 982 545 143. Past the church going east, then left. Kitchen (no utensils), washing machine/drier. Beds placed close together. 13.00–23.00, all year. **(5)** PH, ◉◉, 14 B/10 € (DR 40 €, SR 28 €). Alb. El Caminante. Centre, up left from Casa de Concello, then left. Washing machine/drier,Wi-Fi, rest.11.30–23.00, April–Oct. **(6)** PH, ◉◉◉, 14 B/10 € (SR 20 €/DR 30 €). Alb. Porto Santiago, c/ Diputación, 8, tel: 618 826 515. Kitchen, internet, washing machine/drier. All day, all year. **(7)** PH, ◉◉◉, 14 B/10 € (+DR). Alb. Ultreia, c/ Diputación, 9, tel: 982 545 067. Kitchen, washing machine/drier. Internet, Wi-Fi. All day, all year. **Gonzar** (551m, pop. 40) **(1)** XH, ◉◈, 28 B/5 €. Tel: 982 157 840. Directly on the street. Kitchen (no utensils). 13.00–23.00, all year. **(2)** PH, ◉◉◉, 26 B/10 € (4 DR 35 €). Casa García, tel: 982 157 842. Centre. Washing machine/drier, rest. All day, March–Nov. **Hospital da Cruz** (Alto da Cruz) (672m, pop. 15), **(1)** XH, ◉◉, 22 B/5 €. Tel: 982 452 232. Directly on the road. Kitchen (no utensils), washing machine. 13.00–23.00, all year. **(2)** Alternative (1.4km/20min.): **Ventas de Narón** (705m, pop. 15), **(1)** PH, ◉◉◉, 18 B/10 € (2 DR 30 €). Alb. Casa Molar, tel: 696 794 507. Bar/rest., washing machine, drier. 11.00–23.00, all year. **(2)** PH, ◉◉, 22 B/10 € (4 DR 30–35 €). O Cruceiro, tel: 658 064 917. Washing machine/drier, rest. 12.00–23.00, all year.

Grade and route: well marked, easy to moderate and long. Country roads, farm tracks and forest paths.

Height difference: 540m in ascent, 400m in descent.

Critical points: none.

Scenery: Galicia can be seen from its most attractive side on the way to Portomarín. Far away from the main roads continue past lush cow pastures through numerous hamlets and forests. The path after that runs at times parallel to the C-535.

Local services: Rente (593m, pop. 15) ⌂; Mercado da Serra (630m, pop. 25) ▣ ✗ ⌂; Peruscallo (631m, pop. 37) ✗; Morgade ⌂ ⌂ ▣ ✗; Ferreiros ▣ ✗; Couto/Rozas ⌂; Portomarín ✗ ⌂ ▣ € @ ▣ A ▣ ✗ ☎ Mon.–Fri. 20.30, Sat. 20.00, Sun. 12.30 ✚ c/ Lugo s/n, tel: 982 545 113. Gonzar ✗; Castromaior (602m, pop. 30) ▣ ⌂; Hospital da Cruz ✗; Ventas de Narón ✗ ⌂.

Low tide on the Río Miño at Portomarín.

After **Barbadelo (1)** the Camino continues through small picturesque settlements like Rente, Mercado da Serra, A Pena and **Peruscallo (2;** 1¼ hrs.). Just after A Brea you will come to **km. stone 100** on the right of the path **(3;** ¾ hr.), but in fact it's about another 105km. Soon after you pass **Morgade (4)** and ¼ hr. later **Ferreiros (5)**. Continue through many hamlets and with lovely views of the sparsely vegetated plain to reach **Mercadoiro (6;** 1 hr.). Through Moutras and A Parrocha you arrive in **Vilachá (7;** ¾ hr.). You can already see Portomarín on the other side of Río Miño, but first you need to go down to the river and then cross the bridge over the reservoir. Ascend the steep steps after the bridge straight ahead, at the top go diagonally right and at the well turn left.

Portomarín church was relocated stone by stone to make way for the reservoir.

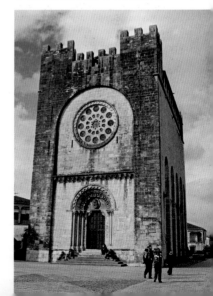

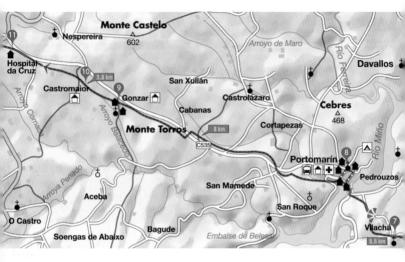

After the small park area turn right into the old town of **Portomarín** (**8**; ¾ hr. from Vilachá).

i **Portomarín** *today is a product of the 1960s. At that time the Río Miño was dammed up to create the* **Embalse de Belesar**. *The old village, once one of the most flourishing and one of the richest places in Galicia, disappeared below the water. The churches of San Pedro and San Nicolás were transported in their entirety, stone by stone, and rebuilt in the new town. The fortress-like* **Iglesia de San Nicolás** *(end of 12th century, see photo page 189) is the work of a student of the master Mateo, cre-*

A typical horréo, a Galician granary.

ator of the Pórtico de la Gloria, in the cathedral of Santiago. The influence of the master Mateo can be seen most clearly in the figurative style of the main portal.

Gastronomy: *Portomarín is famous for Orujo, a high-proof distillate from pressed grape skins, similar to Grappa. The milder alternative (but just as high-volume) is Orujo de hierbas, a herbal schnaps which people like to take to help their digestion. On Easter Sunday there's a festival in celebration of the Orujo.*

Leave Portomarín by descending the main road. At the exit from the village go across a bridge and then for a good half an hour walk uphill through a forest. Cross over the C-535 to the right at the brick works. Continue along a path on the right next to the C-535 to a poultry farm where the road is crossed again, this

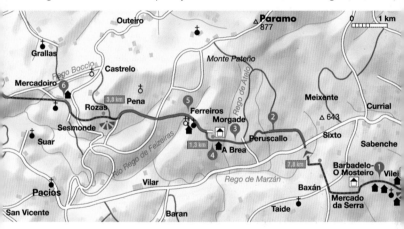

time to the left. You reach **Gonzar (9)** along beside the road (2 hrs. from Portomarín). Away from the road again you walk to **Castromaior** (10; a good ¼ hr.) and after a long ascent arrive in **Hospital da Cruz** (11; not quite ½ hr).

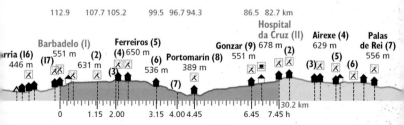

Hostels: Ventas de Narón (see Stage 28). **Ligonde** (621m, pop. 65), **(1)** RH, ☕☕▵, 20 B/donations. Albergue Fuente del Peregrino. Looked after by protestant volunteers. Evening meal, breakfast, grace, small, but fine. Beds rather close together. All day, June–Sept. **(2)** MH (poss. closed), ☕☕☕, 20 B/8 €. Former school, kitchen, washing machine/drier, internet. 13.00–23.00, April–Oct. **Airexe** (629m, pop. 20), XH, ☕☕, 18 B/5 €. Tel: 982 153 483. Kitch-

2012. Washing machine/drier. 13.00–23.00, all year. **(3)** PH, ☕☕☕, 42 B/10 €. Buen Camino, tel: 639 882 229. Kitchen, washing machine/drier, internet, rest. Roomy. All day, Easter–Oct. **(4)** PH, ☕☕☕, 100 B/10 €. Alb. Mesón de Benito, Rúa da Paz s/n, tel: 636 834 065. Washing machine/drier, microwave, rest., internet, Wi-Fi. Ideal for groups. All day, all year. **San Xulián do Camiño** (470m, pop. 45), PH, ☕☕☕, 18 B/ 10 or 12 € depending on season. O Abriga-

en, (possibly some crockery), washing machine/drier, 13.00–23.00, all year. **Portos/ Lestedo** (582m, pop. 3), PH, ☕☕▵, 10 B/ 10 €. Casa A Calzada, tel: 982 183 744. Rest. All day, all year. **Palas de Rei** (556m, pop. 870), 1km before centre: **(1)** XH, ☕☕, 112 B/5 €. Pabellón de Peregrinos, Os Chacotes, tel: 607 481 536. Kitchen (no utensils). Washing machine/drier. 13.00–23.00, all year. **(2)** XH, ☕☕, 50 B (+M)/5 €. Tel: 982 374 126. Renovations planned for

doiro, tel: 676 596 975. Cosy old building, bar/rest., washing machine/drier. From 12.00, Easter–Oct. **Pontecampaña** (420m, pop. 10), PH, ☕☕☕, 18 B/ 10 €. Alb. Turístico Casa Domingo, tel: 982 163 226. Also for non-pilgrims, bar/rest., garden. Washing machine /drier, communal meals. 12/13.00–23.00, May–Oct. **Mato/Casanova** (487m, pop. 1), XH, ☕☕, 20 B/5 €. Tel: 982 173 483. Kitch¬en (no utensils), washing machine/ drier. 13.00–23.00, all year. **Mélide** (457m,

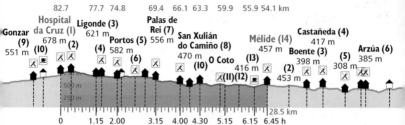

82.7   77.7 74.8   69.4 66.1 63.3   59.9 55.9 54.1 km

Hospital Ligonde (3)   Palas de
da Cruz (I) 621 m   Rei (7)
Gonzar 678 m (2) Portos (5) 556 m San Xulián   Mélide (14) Castañeda (4)
(9) (10)   (4) 582 m   do Camiño (8)   457 m 417 m   Arzúa (6)
551 m   (6)   470 m   O Coto   Boente (3) (5) 385 m
                              (10) 416 m (13) 398 m 308 m
                                    O Coto (11)(12) 453 m (2)
                                    416 m

0   1.15 2.00   3.15 4.00 4.30   5.15   6.15 6.45 h
                                    28.5 km

pop. 4,700), follow the Camino almost to the end of the village: **(1)** PH, ☺☺⌂, 30 B/12 €. Alb. O Apalpador. Rúa San Antón, 23 (next door to XH), tel: 679 837 969. Kitchen, washing machine/drier, internet. 12–23.30, May–Oct., otherwise contact by phone. **(2)** XH, ☺☺, 170 B/5 €. Tel: 981 507 275. Kitchen (no utensils). Washing machine/drier. 13.00–23.00, all year.

Grade and route: well marked, easy. Mainly small country roads up to Palas de Rei, after that a constant up-and-down along unsurfaced farm tracks and forest paths.

Height difference: 380m in ascent, 600m in descent.

Critical points: none.

Scenery: the forests thin out a bit and you find yourself walking across plateaus without any shade and it can therefore be very hot in summer. However, a quick succession of many small settlements make the route interesting.

Local services: Ventas de Narón ⚔ ☖; Ligonde ☖; Airexe ⚔ ☖; Portos ⚔ ☖; Lestedo ☖ ☖; A Brea ⚔; O Rosario (621m, pop. 25) ℹ; Palas de Rei ⚔ ☖ € @ ☐ A ✉ ☐ ☐ daily 20.00, Sun. 12.30 and 20.00 ✚ Avd. de Lugo, tel: 982 374 132; San Xulián de Camiño ☐ ⚔; O Coto (475m, pop. 3) ⚔ ☖; Furelos (416m, pop. 150) ☐; Mélide ⚔ ☖ € @ ☐ ℹ ☐ ☐ A ✚ c/ Doctor Fleming, 2, tel: 981 506 176.

Remarks: numerous hostels within short distances allow flexible planning of stages.

193

From **Hospital da Cruz (1)** walk across a road bridge and continnue to **Ventas de Narón** (**2**; a good ¼ hr.). Then follow little interconnecting roads between the villages. The view soon opens out of the Sierra de Ligonde on the right. Then you reach **Ligonde** (**3**; not quite 1 hr.) and **Airexe** (**4**; ¼ hr.; possible shortcut along a path just after the MH in Ligonde).

i *In the little wood just before Ligonde there's a very beautiful stone wayside cross on the left of the path (**cruceiro**, 17th century). As is customary in Galicia, the cross shows two people (here: Christ on the cross and the Virgin Mary).*

The walk is unvaried as it passes through small settlements like **Portos** (**5**; ½ hr.), Lestedo, **A Brea (6)** and Rosario to **Palas de Rei** (**7**; 1¼ hrs.). The name of the village dates back to a king's palace that disappeared a long time ago. Leave Palas de Rei by following the N-547. The Camino then goes round a bend to the right around the village of Carballal. After ¾ hr. you come to **San Xulián do Camiño** (**8**; Romanesque church, restored in the 18th century) and shortly afterwards, **Pontecampaña** (**9**; ¼ hr.).
Continue now across hilly terrain to **Mato /Casanova** (**10**; a good ¼ hr.). At O Coto you enter the province of A Coruña and arrive in **Leboreiro** (**11**; a good ¾ hr.). Shortly afterwards you pass the **Da Madalena industrial zone** (**12**; ½ hr.). Walking parallel to the road brings you via **Furelos** (**13**; ½ hr.) to **Mélide** (**14**; ¼ hr.; the hostels are reached by going right at the large crossroads and immediately left almost to the end of the village (just under ¼ hr.).

i **Mélide**, *(in Galician, Melid) is the geographical centre of Galicia. The Camino Primitivo from Oviedo, the oldest Way of St. James, joins the Camino Francés here. Like Triacastela and Sarría, people also settled in Mélide in the 13th century by the order of Alfonso IX. The **Capilla de San Roque**, on the Avda. de Lugo, dates from this time. The allegedly oldest wayside cross in Galicia stands next to it (14th century, Gothic). The old town rather lacks the charm of other villages along the way. The **Iglesia de Sancti Spiritus** is still preserved (former Franciscan convent, 14th century), with the graves of the nobility. The **Iglesia de Santa María de Mélide** (Romanesque, 12th century) stands outside the town.*
Gastronomy: *the pulpeiras of Mélide have the reputation of being the best pulpo (octopus) that is prepared in Spain. Melindres are a sweet speciality, a kind of honey biscuits. Every 15th and last Sunday of the month there's a large market. In June/July several gastronomic fairs take place with Galician specialities.*

Hostels: Boente (430m, pop. 30), PH, ◖◗◖, 28 B/10 €. Alb. Os Albergues, tel: 981 501 853. Washing machine, drier, internet. Rest. 12.00–22.00, April–Oct. **Castañeda** (417m, pop. 160) PH, ◖◗◖, 4 B/10 € (1 DR 30–35 €). Alb. Santiago, tel: 981 501 711. Washing machine/drier, internet, rest. All day, April–Sept. **Ribadiso da Baixo** (308m, pop. 10), **(1)** XH, ◖◗◖, 70 B/5 €. Tel: 981 501 185. Gets full very quickly due to popularity. Places for tents. Kitchen, washing machine/drier. 13.00–23.00, all year. **(2)** PH, ◖◗◖, 66 B/9–10 €. Alb. Los Caminantes I, tel: 647 020 600. Kitchen, internet, Wi-Fi, washing machine/drier. 12.00–22.30, Easter–Oct. **Arzúa** (385m, pop. 2,600), 1km before the centre: **(1)** PH, ◖◗◖, 48 B/10 €). Alb. Don Quijote, Avda. Lugo, 130, tel: 981 500 139. Internet, washing machine/drier. All day, all year. **(2)** PH, ◖◗◖, 84 B/9–10 €. Alb. Turístico Santiago Apóstol, tel: 981 508 132. Kitchen, washing machine/drier, internet, rest. All day, all year. **(3)** PH, ◖◗◖, 39 B/10 €. Alb. Ultreia, Avda. Lugo, 126, tel: 981 500 471. Washing machine/drier, kitchen, internet. All day, all year. In the centre: **(4)** XH, ◖◗◖, 46 B/5 €. Tel: 981 500 455. Beautiful old building, kitchen (no utensils), washing machine/drier. 13.00–23.00, all year. **(5)** PH, ◖◗◖, 60 B/10 €. Alb. Vía Láctea, tel: 981 500 581. Kitchen, washing machine/drier, internet, Wi-Fi. Dormitories separated by walls open at the top. All day, all year. **(6)** PH, ◖◗◖, 20 B/ 12 €. Alb. Da Fonte, tel: 659 999 496. On the Camino, almost at end of village. Beautifully furnished old town house. Kitchen, washing machine/drier, internet. If no-one there see tel. no. on door. April–Oct. **(7)** PH, ◖◗◖, 26 B/10 €. Los Caminantes II, c/ Santiago, 14 (right before PH 6 to the main road and then left), tel: 647 020 600. Washing machine/drier, internet, Wi-Fi. 12.00–23.00, Easter–Oct. **Salceda** (365m, pop. 165), just under 300m on the left of the Camino: PH, ◖◗◖, 12 B/7, 9 or

12 € depending on season (SR 25–35 €/DR 40–50 €). Pousada Salceda, on N-547, km 75, tel: 981 502 767. Washing machine/drier, Wi-Fi. Lovely country hotel location with garden. All day, all year. **Santa Irene** (372m, pop. 15), **(1)** PH, ◖◗◖, 15 B/13 €. Alb. Santa Irene, about 300m before XH, tel: 981 511 000. Evening meal/breakfast for staying guests, washing machine/drier, terrace. 12.00–22.00, Easter–Oct. **(2)** XH, ◖◗◖, 36 B/5 €, tel: 981 511 330. Recently renovated, situated directly on road, kitchen. 13.00–23.00, all year. **Pedrouzo (Arca do Pino)** (285m, pop. 570), after A Rúa, 500m on the left up the N-547 (Camino: straight on; from the centre directly to the Camino: at Rúa or Casa do Concello (town hall) yellow arrows), **(1)** PH, ◖◗◖, 14 B/10 € (5 DR 35/ 40 €). Alb. O Burgo, at petrol station at village entrance, tel: 630 404 138. Washing machine/drier, internet. Reception 12.00–20.30, April–Oct. **(2)** XH, ◖◗◖, 120 B/5 €. Tel: 660 396 826. Kitchen, washing machine/drier, internet. 13.00–23.00, all year. **(3)** PH, ◖◗◖, 56 B/10 €. Alb. Porta de Santiago, 300m further on from XH. Tel: 981 511 103. Washing machine/drier, internet. 12.00–23.00, all year, best to

Oncoming trafic on the pilgrim path.

phone ahead in winter. **(4)** PH, ⊕⊕⊕, 52 B/10 € (SR 30 €). Alb. Edreira, Rúa da Fonte, 19. Tel: 981 511 365. Microwave, washing machine/drier, internet. 12.00–23.00, March–Oct. (otherwise by reservation). **(5)** PH, ⊕⊕⊕, 36 B/10 €. Alb. Otero, c/ Forcarei, 2 (after PH 3 first strett on right and then left), tel: 671 663 374. Washing machine/drier, microwave, internet. Roomy. 10.00–23.00, April–Oct./Nov.

Grade and route: well marked, easy in spite of hilly terrain. Mainly forest paths.

Height difference: 520m in ascent, 680m in descent.

Critical points: none.

Scenery: the path still goes through the almost endless chain of hamlets and settlements. The climate becomes noticeably milder; here and there palms, cacti and banana bushes enhance the vegetation. The paths go through fragrant forests of eucalyptus more and more often.

Local services: Boente ⓧ ⌂; Castañeda ⓧ ⌂; Ribadiso da Baixo ⓧ; Arzúa ⓧ ⌂ ⊠ @ ⊠ € Ⓐ ⓘ ⌂ ✚ c/ Fernández de Riba, tel: 981 500 450; A Peroxa (394m, pop. 9) ⌂; Calle (366m, pop. 20) ▣ ⌂; Boavista (388m, pop. 29) ▣; Salceda ⓧ Ⓐ @; O Xen (410m) ▣; Brea (390m, pop. 92) ▣ ⌂; O Empalme (414m) ⌂ ⓧ; A Rúa (261m, pop. 53) ⓧ ⌂; Pedrouzo/Arca do Pino ⓧ ⌂ Ⓐ € ⊠ ⊟ @ ✚ opposite hostel, tel: 981 511 196.

Remarks: there are many hostels as well along this route to allow flexible planning of the stages.

The constant up-and-down continues after **Mélide (1)**, now more and more frequently through sweet-smelling eucalyptus woods. A forest path brings you via **Raído (2**; ¾ hr.) and **Boente (3**; ½ hr.; church with pretty figure of St. James). From there descend into the valley of the Río Boente and uphill again to **Castañeda (4**; ¾ hr.). The medieval pilgrims used to bring the limestone from Triacastela to the limekilns here to make their contribution to the building of the cathedral of Santiago. Today there's nothing left to be seen of the lime factories.

The route goes steeply up and then downhil into the hamlet of **Ribadiso da Baixo (5**; ¾ hr.). The Xunta hostel, in an idyllic location beside the stream, is one of the most popular on the Camino. You walk along the old country road to eventually reach **Arzúa (6**; ¾ hr.). Three hostels lie at the start of the village, the others are about 1km away in the centre.

Beautiful views enhance the Camino to Pedrouzo.

ℹ️ The most interesting monument of **Arzúa** is the Gothic **Capilla de la Madalena** (14th century). The town is known above all for **Queixo**: a round, roughly 0.5–3.5kg cheese with its D.O. Arzúa-Ulloa mark of origin. It is made from cow's milk,

has a soft consistency and a mild flavour. Also typical throughout Galicia is the cone-shaped Tetilla (which means little breast; see page 203 for its origins), another very mild cheese made from cow's milk. The cheese fair (festa do queixo) is held in Arzúa on the first Sunday in March when up to 100,000 cheeses are sold.

54.2 51.2 48.7 46.4 43.4 40.6   34.7 32.9 29.9 27.1 24.3 21.0 km

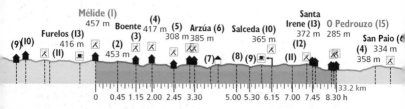

Mélide (I)
457 m   Boente 417 m (5)   Arzúa (6)   Salceda (10)
          (4)   308 m 385 m   365 m
Furelos (13)   (3)
416 m   (2)
        453 m

Santa
Irene (13) O Pedrouzo (15)
372 m 285 m
                    San Paio (6
(4) 334 m
358 m

(9)(10)   (II)   (2)   (7)   (8) (9)   (II)
                                                                  (12)

0   0.45 1.15 2.00 2.45 3.30   5.00 5.30 6.15 7.00 7.45 8.30 h

33.2 km

Eucalyptus forest before A Rúa.

You now continue along small roads and unsurfaced paths across a hilly, very beautiful agricultural landscape and pass by many hamlets and villages like **Pregontoño** (**7**; a good ½ hr.), **A Calzada** (**8**; 1 hr.), **Outeiro** (**9**; ½ hr.) and **Salceda** (**10**; ¾ hr.; hostel south of the N-547). Cross over the N-547 several times, then finally a short distance after **Brea** (**11**; ¾ hr.) go left and walk parallel to the road on a gentle incline up to **O Empalme** (**12**; ½ hr.). There go right across the N-547 again, after the restaurant right to the wood and then left. Shortly afterwards your route goes under the road to the chapel and private hostel of **Santa Irene** (**13**; ¼ hr.).

If you want to carry straight on or go directly to the Xunta hostel 5 mins. away, follow the farm track straight on without walking under the road. From the Xunta hostel go downhill through the wood to **A Rúa** (**14**; a good ¼ hr.) and along a little asphalt road to the N-547. The Camino runs straight ahead without touching Pedrouzo. The village centre and hostels of **Pedrouzo/Arca do Pino** (**15**) lie roughly 500m away up the N-547 on the left (20 mins. from A Rúa).

Hostels: Monte do Gozo (371m) XH, ◐◐, holiday complex with youth hostel, hotels, campsite, 400 B/5 €. Tel: 660 396 827. 8-bed rooms in cabins, laundry, bar/rest., shop, Wi-Fi. The huge complex is not the most tranquil end to the walk. 13.00–23.00, all year. **Santiago de Compostela** (257m, pop. 94,000) **(1)** XH, ◐◐◐, 80 B/1st night 10 €, 2nd and 3rd night: 7 €. Residencia de Peregrinos San Lázaro, Rúa San Lázaro s/n, tel: 981 571 488. Just after the large bridge, behind Museo Pedagógico (right hand side of the road), 2km before centre. Kitchen, washing machine/drier. Reception 9.00–21.00, all year. **(2)** PH, ◐◐◐, 40 B/10 € (July/Aug. 12 €). Alb. Santo Santiago, Rúa do Valiño, 3, tel: 657 402 403. Washing machine/drier, internet. Several nights possible. All day, all year. **(3)** PH, ◐◐◐, 80 B/ 10 €. Alb. Acuario, Rúa do Valiño, sign on the Camino to the left downhill, tel: 981 575 438. Kitchen, washing machine/drier, internet. Possible to leave sack and stay for more than one night. 9.00–24.00, March–Nov. **(4)** SH, ◐◐◐, 110 B/6 €. Alb. de Peregrinos Jaime García Rodríguez, Fundación Ad Sanctum Iacobum Peregrinatio (managed by the pilgrim office, info there too), Rúa de Moscóva s/n (near PH 3). Tel: 981 587 324. Washing machine/drier, internet. 11.30–24.00, all year. **(5)** PH, ◐◐◐, 18 B/ 15 € (1 DR 42 €). O Fogar de Teodomiro, Pl. de la Algalia de Arriba, 3, tel: 981 582 920. Reserve online: www.pousadateodomiro.com. Centrally situated. Kitchen, washing machine/drier. Wi-Fi. 10.00–23.00, all year. **(6)** PH, ◐◐◐, 34 B/June–Sept. 16–18 €, otherwise 14–16 €. Alb. Mundoalbergue, c/ San Clemente, 26, tel: 981 58 86 25 and 696 44 87 37. Kitchen, washing machine, drier, Wi-Fi, garden. All year. **(7)** RH, ◐◐◐, 177 B/ Easter, June–15 Sept, 7–12 Oct.: 12 € (rest of the time 10 €, SR 17 € and 15 €). Seminario Menor, Avda. Quiroga Palacios, 2A, tel: 881 031 768. Internet, laundry service. 13.30–23.00, mid March–Oct. **(8)** Alternative with moderate prices: Seminario Mayor, c/ San Martín Pinario, near cathedral, July–Sept., basic rooms in the monastery, single room 23 € (incl. breakfast); tel: 981 583 009. Further information on well-priced hotels and B&Bs from the tourist office.

Grade and route: easy, well marked. Partly along forest paths, partly country roads.

Height difference: 330m in ascent, 360m in descent.

Critical points: none.

Scenery: characterised by eucalyptus forests as far as city area of Santiago.

Local services: San Paio (334m, pop. 50) 🍴; Lavacolla (292m, pop. 170) 🍴 🏠 📮; San Marcos (368m, pop. 830) 🛏 🍴 ☑ 📮; Monte do Gozo 🏠 🍴 🛏 @ € 🅰; Santiago de Compostela all services, 🛏 cathedral 12.00 pilgrim mass, 🛏 Rúa do Hórreo (luggage lockers in pilgrim office, but not in station, see below), tel: 981 591 859, Renfe: tel: 902 240 202, www.renfe.es ✈ Lavacolla. Tel: 981 547 501 🚌 Rodríguez de Vigurí, tel: 981 542 416 ✉ main post office (*Oficina Principal de Correos*) Rúa do Franco, 4 (near cathedral).

Remarks: the pilgrim certificate, the *Compostela*, is available from the pilgrim office in Santiago de Compostela. There is also a left-luggage office. Oficina de Peregrinos, Rúa do Vilar, 1, tel: 981 562 419, Palm Sunday–Oct. Daily 9.00–21.00, Nov.–Palm Sunday Mon.–Sat. 10.00–20.00, Sun. 10.00–14.00 and 16.00–20.00, closed 25th Dec. and 1st Jan. In which case the Compostela is issued in the Sacristy of the cathedral.

www.peregrinossantiago.es.

From the centre of **Pedrouzo (1)** it's best to walk to the town hall (*Casa do Concello*) and follow the yellow arrows through the Rúa do Concello in a few

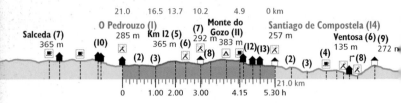

minutes as far as the Camino. You reach **San Antón** (**2**; ½ hr. from the cross-roads with the Camino/N-547, shorter from the centre) and **Amenal** (**3**; ½ hr.). After that a forest path goes steeply uphill. Once again the Camino shows its quiet country side before entering the catchment area of Santiago. The path leaves the forest on a hill and turns off right to circle round the **airport runway** (**4**) that lies on the historic pilgrim route.

At the big roundabout keep left and after just under 1 hr. you reach the **12km waymarker** (**5**) to the cathedral; in fact about 14km to the cathedral. Then you pass the hamlet of **San Paio** (**6**). Walk over a hill and arrive in **Lavacolla** (**7**; just under 1 hr.)

*ℹ️ Medieval pilgrims used to wash themselves thoroughly in the small stream of **La-vacolla** (in Galicain, labacolla) so that they would arrive clean and sweet-smelling at the apostle's tomb. Although probably based on a misunderstanding this ritual was good practice for hygienic reasons. The French monk, Aymeric Picaud, author of the medieval pilgrim guide Codex Calixtinus, must have falsely interpreted the meaning of Lavacolla. Instead of correctly 'full of scree' (in Galician, rego dos coi-*

os) he understood 'lava colea', which means something like 'wash your genitalia'!

After Lavacolla the path ascends to **Villamaior** (8; a good ¼ hr.), then goes across the sparsely vegetated plateau, past the transmitter masts of **TV Galicia** and **TV España** (9), into the catchment area of Santiago. After 1¼ hr. **San Marcos** (10) is reached and shortly afterwards finally **Monte do Gozo** (10; a good hour). (Sign for the hostel in the Monte do Gozo complex near the chapel on the right, or continue straight on along the Camino).

Monument on Monte do Gozo.

ℹ️ Millions of sighs of contentment have been uttered by people on **Monte do Gozo** in the course of the thousand year history of the pilgrims – countless moments of the highest pleasure (in Spanish, gozo) at the first sight of the towers of Santiago cathedral. However, you need a bit of luck with the unpredictable Galician weather and even then, the view may not come up to expectations because the town has since grown massively in size. The view is better further south, below the substan-

tial monument, a memorial to the Pope's visit in 1993. In the Middle Ages the first pilgrim in the group to catch sight of the cathedral was called the pilgrim king. Many of the surnames that are widespread in Europe like King, Rey (Spanish), Roy or Leroi (French) are attributed to this. Today Monte do Gozo is, in effect, synonymous with a gigantic holiday complex before the gates of Santiago.

From **Monte do Gozo** and the route goes slightly downhill (second entrance to the hostel on the left) and crosses the Santiago ring road, the motorway and the railway track. After the roundabout you keep on the left hand side of the Avda. do Camiño Francés. Past the Palacio de Congresos (on the right hand side of the road, the Museo Pedagógico and behind that the **Residencia de Peregrinos San Lázaro, 12**) you come into **Rúa do Valiño** (13; Alb. Santo Santiago on the right, left down the steps to the private hostel of Acuario, on the ground floor of the large apartment block).

The Camino goes straight through Rúa das Fontiñas, the Fonte dos Concheiros, crosses Avda. de Lugo, comes through Rúa dos Concheiros into Rúa de San Pedro and arrives via the Porta do Camiño into the old town (to the right through Rúa de Entremuros to the PH O Fogar de Teodomiro). Now it goes through Rúa Casas Reais, Rúa das Ánimas, across the Praza de Cervantes into Rúa da Acibechería and continues across the Praza da Inmaculada onto the Praza do Obradoiro to the **Cathedral** of **Santiago de Compostela** (14; 1¼ hr.).

[i] **Santiago de Compostela**, *the destination of the Way of St. James, is, next to Rome and Jerusalem, the third large place of pilgrimage and one of the most significant destinations for pilgrims in Christendom. Created by and for the cult of St. James, the town is today an architectural and cultural synthesis of artistic styles – but in no way an open-air museum, far more a very vital and modern university town. The old town appears as if built from one huge mass of bright-coloured Galician granite. Along the **Rúa dos Concheiros**, its name derived from the St. James shell sellers (concheiros) who used to sell the St. James shells here, and the **Rúa de San Pedro** pilgrims arrived at the entrance to the historical old town, the **Porta do Camiño**, until 1835 the location of one of the seven town gates. Past the **Igrexia de Santa María do Camiño** (18th century) you reach the **Praza de Cervantes**, with a statue of the Spanish writer Miguel de Cervantes. Continue along **Rúa da Acibechería** (azabache, in English, jet, shiny black semi-precious stone, a typical souvenir from Santiago). The street opens out onto the Praza da Inmaculada which is closed off on the right by the huge building of the Benedictine monastery of **San Martín Pinario** (founded shortly after the discovery of the apostle's tomb in the 9th century, today's building 16th–18th century). To the left stands the north façade of the cathedral, next to it the archbishop's palace Pazo de Xelmírez (12th/13th century). Bishop Diego Xelmírez (in Spanish Gelmírez, 1099–1140 Bishop of Santiago de Compostela) was the most important religious-political figure in the early years of the St. James cult.*

Beyond this the **Praza do Obradoiro** opens up in front of the cathedral. It is dominated by the monumental Baroque west façade of the Catedral de Santiago de Compostela. Behind the façade lies the **Pórtico de la Gloria** carved between 1166 and 1188 by the inspired genius of Maestro Mateo. The central elements of the rich decoration with figures is the middle pillar with the statue of St. James, with Christ the Redeemer above and surrounded by the four evangelists. The base of the column shows signs of wear from millions of pilgrims' hands. Touching the column has since been forbidden. On the left of the middle pillar stand the prophets of Jeremia, Jesaja, Moses and Daniel on a column, the latter with an enchanted smile on his face. According to many he was delighted with the bare-bosomed that had been carved by the hand of an expert on the opposite side. The church leaders ordered to be flattened the breasts that were causing unseemly speculations. The farmers, so it is said, made a protest of their own: they made a cheese in the shape of the Corpus delicti and called it Tetilla (little breast).

The kneeling figure facing the altar is said to be master Mateo who, allegedly, was destined never to be allowed to see his work. He's also called Santo dos Croques, the saint of the clout on the head, since you can receive a share of his genius by touching his head three times with your forehead (access is no longer allowed). The **Botafumeiro**, the silver-plated censer weighing roughly 60kg (100kg full) and 160cm high, is only used in certain circumstances, otherwise it is kept in the library. It was once used to make more bearable the strong body odour of pilgrims. Today it is a popular spectacle when, hanging from the 35m long rope, it is swung through the transept. It has twice overshot and ended up outside the church.

The 97m long church interior is dominated by the lavishly carved **altar** with the gold, silver and jewel encrusted **St. James**. Not until the steps behind the altar are climbed and the apostle embraced, is the pilgrim journey at an end. The alleged bones of the Saint lie supposedly in the crypt below the altar. Cathedral: 7.00–21.00, museum: June–Sept. Mon.–Sat. 10.00–14.00 and 16.00–20.00, Sun./public holidays 10.00–14.00, Oct.–May only until 13.30 and 18.30, 5 € . One hour guided tours in Spanish/English across the roofs of the cathedral, daily 10.00–14.00 and 16.00–20.00 (on the hour) after booking: tel: 981 552 985, fax: 981 554 403, email: cubiertascatedral@catedraldesantiago.es. 10 €; pilgrims with compostela, people over 65, students and groups: 8 €.

Smiling Daniel.

To the left of the cathedral stands the **Hospital de los Reyes Católicos**. The pilgrim hostel founded in 1489 by King Fernando and Queen Isabella is today a Parador Nacional (state-run luxury hotel) and reputedly the oldest hotel in the world only with. There is still the tradition of inviting the first ten pilgrims to breakfast (9.00), lunch (12.00) and evening meal (19.00). For this you have to arrive at the allotted times at the garage door on the left below the main entrance and present the original or a copy of the compostela (up to 3 days after issue). The square is closed off to the west by the **Pazo de Raxoi** (1777), town hall and seat of parliament for the autonomous administration, to the south by the **Colegio de San Jerónimo** (17th century), once a school for children of destitute parents, today an institute for Galician studies. South of the cathedral lie the **Praza de Platerías** in front of the similarly named, oldest preserved portal of the cathedral and the **Praza de Quintana** ontowhich the **Porta Santa** (17th century, adorned with sculptures from the 12th century) opens out during Holy Years.

Museums: Museo das Peregrinaciones, history of the Pilgrim Way, Rúa de San Miguel, Tue.–Fri. 10.00–20.00, Sat. 10.30–13.30 and 17.00–20.00, Sun. 10.30–13.30, 2.40 € (Sat. 17.00–20.00 and Sun. free). **Museo do Pobo Galego**, museum of Galician folklore, San Domingo de Bonaval, Tue.–Sat. 10.00–14.00 and 16.00–20.00, Sun./public holidays 11.00–14.00, 3 €. **Centro Galego de Arte Contemporáneo**, museum for contemporary art, c/ Valle Inclán, Tue.–Sun. 11.00–20.00, free. In January 2011 in front of the city gates the inauguration took place of the most recent city project, the **Cidade da Cultura de Galicia** cultural centre designed by the American architect Peter Eisenman, (www.cidadedacultura.org).

Botafumeiro: the incense burner should be available to see: 6th Jan., Easter Sunday, Ascension Day, 23rd May, Whitsun, 15th Aug. (Feast of the Assumption), 1st Nov. (All Saints), 8th Dec. (Feast of the Immaculate Conception), 25th. und 30th Dec.

The south portal of the cathedral.

Public holidays: Around Ascension Day (Fiestas de la Ascensión), processions, cattle market and Pulpo a la Feira. 2nd half of July. Santiago Apóstol, big celebration in honour of St. James, amongst other things, spectacular firework display above the cathedral.

Gastronomy: Spanish pilgrims often enjoy a mariscada (fish and seafood platter) and finish off with a sweet dessert, a tarta de Santiago (almond cake).

Information: Of. de Turismo, Rúa do Vilar, 63, tel: 981 555 129. Mon.–Fri. 9.00–19.00, Sat./Sun. 9.00–14.00 and 16.00–19.00; Easter, summer daily 9.00–21.00. www.santiagoturismo.com.

SANTIAGO DE COMPOSTELA

1 Four hostels before the centre
2 Residencia de Peregrinos San
  Lázaro
3 Private hostel O Fogar de
  Teodomiro
4 Galician folklore museum
5 Museum for contemporary art
6 Puerta del Camino
7 Pilgrim museum
8 San Martín de Pinario monastery
9 San Paio de Antealtares

10 Cathedral/Praza do Obradoiro
11 Hostal de los Reyes Católicos
   (Parador Nacional)
12 Galician parliament/town hall
13 Colegio de San Jerónimo
14 Pilgrim office
15 Tourist information
16 Central post office
17 Police
18 Seminario Menor
19 Hospital

The way to Finisterre and Muxía

More and more pilgrims are continuing their walk to Finisterre (in Galician, Fisterra, from the Latin, Finis Terrae), to the end of the earth as people believed in ancient times. The headland that projects into the sea like a finger was already for Celts, Phoenicians and also Romans a mystic place where they celebrated Sun. and fertility rites. The discovery of the apostle's tomb awoke a new fascination for the 'end of the earth' and this received a Christian justification with legends about St. James located in Finisterre and Muxía. The sunsets alone over the Atlantic make the the three day stages worthwhile to the coast roughly 90km away.

Galicia's northwest region is called Costa da Morte, death coast. Countless ships have sunk in imponderable waters. The sinking of the Prestige oil tanker in 2002 caused the last and worst catastrophe. About 70,000 tons of crude oil spilled into the sea and contaminated the seabed and tens of thousands of sea birds perished. For the Galician coast, which lives mainly from fishing and the shellfish industry, it was not only an ecological disaster, but also an economic one. Although it will never be forgotten there is now a sense of normality creeping back. Every day in the Finisterre Lonja (fish market) you can watch the sale of fish by auction. In 2007 Cape Finisterre was included in the list of European Heritage due to its unique location and history.

You can go no further – at the end of the Camino, at last, at the 'end of the earth'.

Hostels: Castelo (96m, pop. 190) PH, ◐◐◐, 6 B/15–16 € (with breakfastt). Casa Rural Riamonte, Castelo-Ames, tel: 981 890 356 and 629 740 742. Kitchen, Wi-Fi, garden. Hostel open Easter–Oct. B&B all year. Before Negreira, roughly 700m on the left of the Camino: **Logrosa** (163m, pop. 60), PH, ◐◐◐, 20 B/17 € (+ SR, DR and 4-bed rm.). Tourist hostel. Tel: 981 885 820 or 646 142 554. Washing machine/drier, internet, evening meal. Reservation necessary. 13.00–21.00, April–Nov. **Negreira** (167m, pop. 3,500) **(1)** PH, ◐◐◐, 50 B/12 € + 30 B/15 € with room key. Alb. San José, Rúa de Castelao, 20 (signs before village, 500m to the right, 400m from hostel to centre), tel: 881 976 934. Kitchen, washing machine/drier, internet, 12.30–22.30, all year, best to phone ahead in winter. **(2)** PH, ◐◐◐, 40 B/10 €. Alb. Lua, Avda. de Santiago, 22 (centre), tel: 629 926 802. Washing machine/drier, internet, microwave. 12.00–22.30, March–Oct. **(3)** XH, ◐◐◐, 22 B/5 €. about 1km outside, follow the Camino out of Negreira uphill, then look for a sign to the hostel 250m away. Kitchen (equipped). Place for tents. All day, all year.

Grade and route: hilly terrain (forest paths, farm tracks), quite exhausting for a while.

Height difference: 430m in ascent, 530m in descent.

Critical points: none; newly waymarked, yellow arrows (some also in the opposite direction, to Santiago).

Scenery: very attractive with many eucalyptus and oak forests and small villages.

Local services: Ventosa (135m, pop. 70) ☒; Aguapesada (60m, pop. 135) ☒; Trasmonte (215m, pop. 70) ☗; Ponte Maceira (153m, pop. 65) ☒; Negreira ☒ ⌂ ☐ @ € Ⓐ ⌨ ✉ ⓘ ✚ c/ Castelao s/n, tel: 981 881 808.

Remarks: Xunta hostel in Negreira is a good quarter of an hour away from the centre, so it's best to buy food in Negreira beforehand, also for the next few days if necessary, as there's only a small shop in Olveiroa before reaching Cée. Accommodation in the small villages along the way is generally in *casas rural* (B&B style).

The path to Finisterre begins in the **Praza do Obradoiro (1)**. Past the Hostal Reyes Católicos go some steps down to Rúa das Hortas. Follow this street to a right hand bend towards the crossroads Campo das Hortas. Diagonally

View from Sarela do Baixo of Santiago de Compostela.

left over the crossroads you will find the start of the Campo do Cruceiro do Gaio which turns off left while the Camino continues straight ahead along Rúa da Poza do Bar. For the correct route follow the sign for the Hotel San Lorenzo. At the end of the road you come to the Carballeira de San Lourenzo, a small green park with oak trees. Take the footpath on the right through the park (waymarker) and then go slightly downhill and cross over a small bridge in the bottom of the valley and turn left, past some derelict houses. Shortly afterwards at a fork there's a sign for Finisterre. The Camino winds its way through a little wood, then ascends to join a little asphalt road along which you come to **Sarela do Baixo** (**2**; a good ½ hr.). There is a lovely view back of Santiago cathedral.

The path goes on the right through the wood to **Carballal** (**3**; ¾ hr.). Walk through scattered settlements and a little wood to reach **Quintáns** (**4**; ¾ hr.), then uphill along a forest path to the hill called **Alto do Vento** (**5**; a good ½ hr.). Shortly afterwards to the right you pass **Ventosa (6)** and the right hand turn-off **(7)** to the Castelo hostel. Walking along beside the road you arrive in **Augapesada** (**8**; a good ½ hr.). At the exit from the village the route ascends a sometimes very steep woodland path to the **Alto do Mar de Ovellas** (**9**; 1 hr.). Carballo is passed shortly after that. Now walk along the country road to **Transmonte** (**10**; ¼ hr.) and **Ponte Maceira** (**11**; ½ hr.).

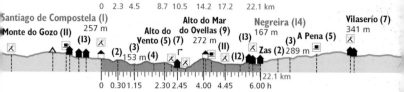

0   2.3 4.5   8.7 10.5   14.2 17.2   22.1 km

Santiago de Compostela (I)   Alto do Mar   Negreira (14)   Vilaserío (7)
                                              do Ovellas (9)   167 m   341 m
Monte do Gozo (II)   257 m   Alto do   272 m   A Pena (5)
                     (13)   Vento (5) (7)   (13)   (3)
                         (2) (3) (4)   (II)   Zas (2) 289 m
                         153 m   (12)

0   0.30 1.15   2.30 2.45   4.00 4.45   6.00 h

22.1 km

ℹ️ *The Gothic bridge at* **Ponte Maceira** *was built in the 14th century and restored in the 18th century. It spans the* **Río Tambre** *with an elegant sweep up to a point in the apex. From the bridge (see photo on the left) there's a lovely view over the river and of several restored mills as well as a beautiful medieval manor (pazo) in the middle of some park lands. The* **Capilla de San Brais** *at the foot of the bridge dates back to the 18th century.*

After the bridge turn left. Walk for a short stretch along a lovely riverside path and then on a country road to **Barca** (**12**; a good ½ hr.) and through the suburb of **A Chancela** past the turn-off left to **Logrosa** (**13**; after 200m turn off right to the San José hostel) to **Negreira** (½ hr.). The Camino goes right through the length of the town (past Hostal Lua) and then, gently uphill, you head for the Gadis supermarket (last shopping opportunity before the hostel). At the supermarket go right and shortly afterwards left, away from the main road. You pass an old manor that was restored in the 17th and 18th century.

Exit Negreira through an archway and then go diagonally left uphill. The Camino continues to the right at a junction. The **Xunta hostel (14)** lies straight ahead 250m along the road (a good quarter of an hour/1km from the centre).

Hostels: Vilaserío (341m, pop. 70), **(1)** PH, ⊕⊕⊕, 30 B/12 €. Alb. turístico O Rueiro (also for non-pilgrims), tel: 981 893 561. Laundry, Wi-Fi, bar/rest. From 12.00, probably all year. **(2)** MH, ⌂, exit from the village, rather like emergency accommodation, mattresses. Showers. Donations. **Santa Mariña** (331m, pop. 60), PH, ⊕⊕⊕, 10 B/10 €. Alb. Antelo, tel: 981 852 897. Washing machine/drier, Wi-Fi. Rest. 12.00–23.00, all year. **Ponte Olveira** (268m, pop. 30) PH, ⊕⊕⊕, 10 B/10 € (15 places in tents, free). Alb. O Refuxio da Ponte, tel: 981 741 706. Washing machine/drier. Internet, rest. All day, all year. **Olveiroa** (281m, pop. 130), **(1)** PH, ⊕⊕⊕, 48 B/12 € (DR

Grade and route: well marked. Long, but easy stage. Much of it is along country roads, otherwise farm tracks and forest paths. Only shade at the start.
Height difference: 500m in ascent, 400m in descent.
Critical points: none.
Scenery: scenically quite delightful stage. The Camino runs across the hilly hinterland and the high plains of the Xallas region. Widely scattered settlements and hamlets with only a few inhabitants determine the character of this agricultural region.
Local services: A Pena (345m, pop. 180) ▣; Vilaserío ✕; Santa Mariña ✕ @; Ponte Olveira ✕ @; Olveiroa ▣ ⌂ ⊟ ✕ @.

from 30 €, SR 25 €. Alb. Hórreo, tel: 981 741 673, 617 026 005. Internet, washing machine, kitchen, small shop. All day, all year. **(2)** XH, ⊕⊕⊕, 34 B/5 €. Tel: 658 045 242; Kitchen (equipped). 16.00–23.00, all year.

Remarks: there are few opportunities to stop for something to eat on this long stretch so take enough water and food with you. Since there is little shade, the walk can be very exhausting in warm weather.

From the **Xunta hostel (1)** go a short way back downhill and take the first path to the left to the church. At the cemetery turn right into a small hamlet. Walk straight through the hamlet and leave it again in between the stone pillar and the huge chestnut tree. The forest path soon meets the country road along which you come to **Zas (2)**. Go right there across the road and then continue along a forest path to the hamlet of **Camiño Real (3**; a good hour). You reach **Rapote (4)** up a gentle incline and **A Pena (5**; 1 hr.) and shortly afterwards, keeping slightly left, **Portocamiño (6)**. Here continue right up along the country road and soon after the sign for the wind park (*Parque eólico de Corzán*) take the path on the right. This brings you uphill and again

Sunrise just after Negreira.

to the country road. Turn right here and as far as the path turning off left downhill to **Vilaserío**. Turning right will bring you to the bar and **private hostel** (**7**; 1¼ hr.). After the bar take the road to the left downhill and walk – past the municipal hostel (500m from the PH) – to **Cornado** (**8**; ½ hr.). At the well

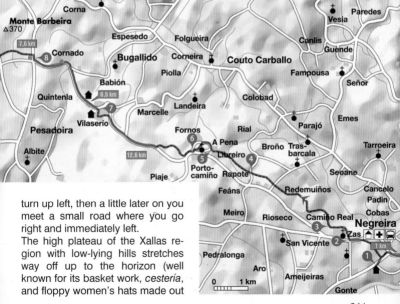

turn up left, then a little later on you meet a small road where you go right and immediately left.

The high plateau of the Xallas region with low-lying hills stretches way off up to the horizon (well known for its basket work, *cestería*, and floppy women's hats made out

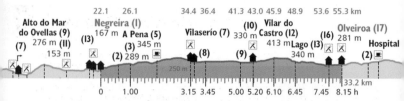

	22.1	26.1		34.4 36.4	41.3 43.0 45.9 48.9	53.6 55.3 km

Alto do Mar
do Ovellas (9)
(7)   276 m (II)
153 m

Negreira (I)
167 m A Pena (5)
(13)   (3) 345 m
       (2) 289 m

Vilaserío (7)

(8)

(10) Vilar do
330 m Castro (12)
       413 m Lago (13)
(9)   340 m

Olveiroa (17)
         281 m
(16)   Hospital
          (2)

250 m

33.2 km

0   1.00   3.15 3.45   5.00 5.20 6.10 6.45   7.45 8.15 h

of straw, *sombreros de paja*). You reach **Maroñas (9**; 1¼ hrs.) along agricultural paths and **Santa Mariña** (¼ hr.) At the T-junction there turn left, go along the road past the **hostel (10)** and then turn right and walk on to **Bon Xesús (11**; ¾ hr.).

The highest mountain of the region rises up on the left of the path, Monte Aro (556m). Continue now along a small asphalt road, gently ascending, to **Vilar do Castro (12)**. Follow the road there to the right out of the hamlet. At the little road just afterwards go up to the left and you come over a small pass (½ hr. from Bon Xesús). From the top of the hill you have a lovely view of the Fervenza reservoir. **Lago (13**; a good ¾ hr.) is situated down the hill (two alternatives at the junction before the village: the direct path carries straight on, left goes through the hamlet). Stay on the main road and then keep left along the small country road. This road leads via **Albeiroas (14**; not quite ¼ hr.) and Corzón, which you keep on the right, to **Mallón (15)**. In Mallón turn right onto the country road. Via **Ponte Olveiroa (16**; ¾ hr.; hostel on the right, at the left hand bend in the road) you come over a small hill to **Olveiroa** (½ hr.). To find the **Xunta hostel (17)** follow the sign which takes you left away from the road into the village. There in the centre follow the sign into the small narrow street to the right.

The path runs repeatedly through shady forests.

Hostels: Camiños Chans (30m, pop. 400) PH, ◐◐◐, 24 B/12 € (10 € low season). Alb. O Bordón, tel: 981 746 574 and 655 903 932. Washing machine/drier, kitchen, Wi-Fi. 12.00–23.30 (in winter until 22.00), all year. **Cée** (3m, pop. 3,600), **(1)** PH, ◐◐, 42 B/10 €. Alb. A Casa da Fonte, Rúa de Arriba, 36, tel: 699 242 711. Washing machine/drier, internet. Large dormitory. Reception 12.00–21.00, March–Nov. **(2)** MH, ◐, 12 B/free. Instead of following the Camino to the left at the start of the town, stay on the main road until it turns off left downhill, then go straight on into Rúa de Buenaventura, 16; school building on the right with Protección Civil (looks after the hostel), tel: 981 747 411. Just a hostel to sleep in. All day, all year. **(3)** PH, ◐◐◐, 30 B/10 €. Alb. O Camiño das Estrelas, Avda. Finisterre, 78 (signs), tel: 981 747 575. Washing machine/drier, internet. 13.00–23.00, all year. **Corcubión** (10m, hostel at 114m, pop. 1,560) SH, ◐◐◐, 20 B/donations. 1.5km from the centre of Corcubión at the Alto de San Roque, looked after by Galician society of the Way of St. James, tel: 679 460 942. Communal meals. From about 17.00–22.00, all year. **Finisterre/Fisterra** (17m, pop. 3,000), **(1)** XH, ◐◐, 36 B/5 €. Tel: 981 740 781. Centre of town near bus stop. Kitchen, washing machine/drier. Opening times vary, from about 16.00–24.00, all year. **(2)** PH, ◐◐◐, 18 B/10 €. Alb. do Sol (Hogar de Miguel), c/ Atalaya, 7 (near school), tel: 617 568 648. Kitchen, communal meals, pilgrim atmosphere. All day, all year. **(3)** PH, ◐◐◐, 20 B/12 €. Alb. Finistellae, c/ Manuel Lago Pais, 7, tel: 661 493 505. Kitchen, washing machine/drier, internet. All day, Easter–Oct., only by reservation after that. **(4)** PH, ◐◐◐, 30 B/10 €. Alb. da Paz, behind the harbour, near Playa de Ribeira/Castillo (castle), tel: 981 740 332. Washing machine/drier, internet. All day, all year. **(5)** PH, ◐◐◐, 16 B/April–Sept. 15 €,

otherwise 12 €. Alb. O Encontro, c/ El Campo s/n, tel: 696 503 363. Kitchen, washing machine, drier, internet. All day, all year.

Grade and route: easy to moderate, well marked. Predominantly forest paths and tracks up to Corcubión. Corcubión to Finisterre at times along the road.

Height difference: 450m in ascent, 720m in descent.

Critical points: none.

Scenery: a long, but very attractive stage on the way to the Atlantic. Just after Olveiroa the vegetation is reminiscent of heathland. The coast looms closer and closer from Hospital onwards. The only blot on the landscape is the iron works after Hospital. Bare areas still show the affects of the forest fires in 2006. From Cée the path follows the Ría (estuary) de Corcubión that penetrates a long way inland, climbs over a small mountain ridge and then affords views of small bays with turquoise blue water and white sandy beaches until finally, the elongated Praia de Langosteira is reached across which you arrive directly into Finisterre.

Local services: Hospital (343m, pop. 50) ▨ am Weg; Camiños Chans ⌂ ▨ 🖃; Cée ▨ ✗ 🗉 € @ ⓘ Ⓐ ⊠ ╋ Hospital Comarcal, tel: 981 706 010; Corcubión ✗ 🗉 Ⓐ @ 🚌 € ⊠ ╋ Avda. Viña s/n, tel: 981 225 906; Estorde (9m, pop. 150) ✗ 🚌 ⌂; Sardiñeiro (9m, pop. 520) ✗ 🗉 🚌 € ⌂; Finisterre 🚌 ✗ 🗉 € Ⓐ ⊠ @ 🚌 🖃 parish church in the town Mon.–Sat. (except Tue.) 20.00, Sun. 10.00 and 19.00 (Apr.–Sept.), 20.00 (Oct.–March), Iglesia de Santa María das Areas (on the way to the lighthouse) Sun./public holidays 12.00 ╋ Cala Figueira s/n, tel: 981 712 264.

Remarks: after Hospital there's a fork in the Camino: one alternative goes to Finisterre, the other to Muxía. The alternative to Finisterre is described next, the destination of most pilgrims, and the path from Finisterre to Muxía in the last stage.

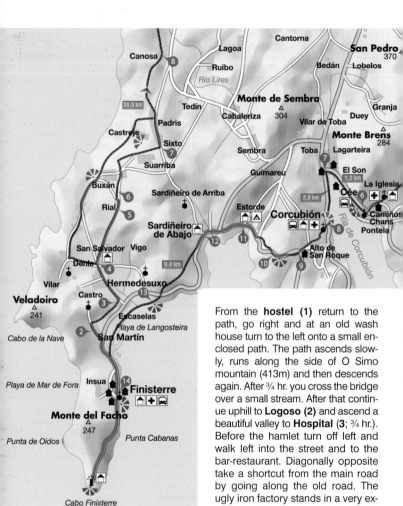

From the **hostel (1)** return to the path, go right and at an old wash house turn to the left onto a small enclosed path. The path ascends slowly, runs along the side of O Simo mountain (413m) and then descends again. After ¾ hr. you cross the bridge over a small stream. After that continue uphill to **Logoso (2)** and ascend a beautiful valley to **Hospital (3**; ¾ hr.). Before the hamlet turn off left and walk left into the street and to the bar-restaurant. Diagonally opposite take a shortcut from the main road by going along the old road. The ugly iron factory stands in a very exposed position on the hill. Shortly afterwards at the roundabout a double waymarker stone indicates the dividing of the routes to Finisterre and Muxía. For the first time you can see the sea in the distance. Follow the road for about 400m to the left and then turn right onto the lovely forest path

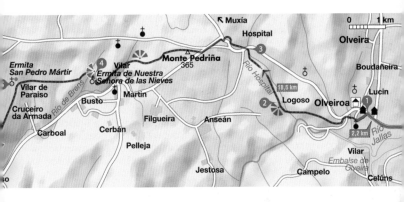

across a heath-like plateau. After a good 1¼ hrs. you arrive at the remotely situated **Ermita de Nuestra Señora de las Nieves (4)**.

> *ℹ* *The **Ermita de Nuestra Señora de las Nieves** dates back to the 18th century. The water from the spring by the chapel is supposed to be good for nursing mothers and female animals. On 8th September the Ermita is the destination for a fiesta-like pilgrimage.*

After the chapel the path goes uphill. The coast appears much clearer on the horizon and the headland of Finisterre can be seen on the right. After a good ¾ hr. you reach the **Ermita de San Pedro Martír (5)**. The spring at the medieval chapel is said to be good for rheumatism, aching feet and warts. Walk past the Ermita and in a good quarter of an hour you come to the sign for the *Cruceiro da Armada* (wayside cross a short way off the path) . From the 283m high hill you are afforded a breathtaking view of the coast in good weather, the Ría de Corcubión and Cap Finisterre. What a sight for the medieval pilgrims who had never seen the sea before! Shortly afterwards you come downhill to reach

At last, the Atlantic!

55.3 58.9 60.3			66.4	69.9	74.3	77.9	81.1 84.2 87.2 km

(10) Ponte Olveira (16) Olveiroa (1) 281 m Hospital (3) (2) 343 m Lago (13) 302 m Ermita de San Pedro Mártir (5) (4) 298 m 268 m (6) (8) (9) 114 m (12) Finisterre (14) 17 m San Salvador (13)

0   1.00 1.30   2.45   3.30   4.30   5.30 6.15 7.00   7.45 h

31.9 km

Camiños Chans (6; just under ¾ hr.). The descent ends at a T-junction: the hostel can be found about 50m to the left, but the Camino goes right for just under 100m to the main road and there to the right almost at sea level following the road to **Cée** (7; ¼ hr., large market on Sundays). From Cée follow the path along the coastline to **Corcubión** (8; a good ¼ hr.).

> ℹ️ The little harbour town of **Corcubión** has been a listed site since 1985. The houses are typical of the area with their white enclosed balconies (galerías) and stone pedestals. The **Iglesia de San Marcos** was built around 1430 in the so-called coastal Gothic style (gótico-marinero). The church tower dates back to the 19th century when it replaced the old one which collapsed in a storm. During the oil disaster of 2002 residents and volunteers helped to build a barrier thereby averting contamination in the bay of Corcubión and Cée.
>
> **Public holidays:** 16th July Romería del Carmen, a ceremonial procession in honour of St. Carmen, patron saint of seafarers. End of July Fiesta medieval, a medieval festival. 1st Saturday in August, Fiesta de la almeja, clam festival with the tasting of Albariño and Ribeiro white wines.

The Playa de Langosteira is without doubt one of the most beautiful beaches on the coast of Spain.

View from Finisterre harbour.

Along the promenade next to the main road you come to a small crossroads with a green traffic island. A waymarker leads you straight on into the town and then diagonally left up to the church. At a block of flats a tile with a St. James shell indicates some steps to the right. Through a narrow little street you come to a park. Go straight across. Then through the very narrow enclosed path you reach a forest path and going uphill you arrive in **Vilar**. Walk to the right and shortly afterwards cross over the C-552.

Corcubión hostel (9; ½ hr.) lies near **Alto de San Roque**. Stay on this side of the road briefly, then cross over the road to **Amarela (10**; ¼ hr.). Follow the C-552 for a short way and then turn onto a small forest path. A short time later the white sandy bay of Estorde comes into view. From **Estorde (11)** follow the road into the elongated village of **Sardiñeiro (12**; a good ½ hr.). At the same height as the zebra stripes follow the sign for the Praia do Rostro to the right and turn immediately left into the narrow little street. At the small supermarket continue up right away from the road onto a forest path. Sometime later you cross over the C-552 for one last time; along a lovely coastal path you come to the 2km long sandy beach of **Playa de Langosteira (13**; a good ¾ hr.; Galician *Praia*). Walk to the end of the beach and then left into the centre of **Finisterre (14**; ¾ hr.). The small coastal road leads from the town centre to the **faro** (lighthouse; just under an hour.).

217

Santo Cristo de Finisterre is honoured in the Iglesia de Santa María das Areas.

ℹ️ *The Celts used, to follow the path of the Sun. to* **Finisterre** *(Galician* **Fisterra**). *On the summit of Monte del Facho (242m), above the lighthouse, they used to celebrate the Sun. and fertility rites. The Phoenician Sun. temple Ara Solis is also said to have stood there. For the Romans the so-called Promontorium Nerium was the Finis Terrae, the end of the earth, the Mare Tenebrosum, the sea of darkness began, as they called the Atlantic.*

The integration of pagan and Christian customs began with ith the discovery of the apostle's tomb. In those days the highly respected **Santo Cristo de Finisterre** *(14th century) was the western representation of Christ. The wooden sculpture is said to have been thrown or to have fallen overboard during a storm and then left stranded in Finisterre. It is kept in the Iglesia de* **Santa María das Areas** *which is located on the path to the lighthouse. Parts of the apse, the east portal and some of the pillar capitals of the first Romanesque building have been preserved from the 12th century. Gothic and Baroque elements were added over the centuries (1st July–15th Sept. 10.00–14.30 and 16.00–20.00). A pilgrim hospital once stood in the place of today's cemetery. Finisterre itself is a small fishing town where there's not much going on, except in August and weekends in the summer. A tradition that still exists today and handed down through medieval pilgrim reports concerns the burning of the clothes you wore on the pilgrimage, at least some of them, at the lighthouse. The ritual demands that you bathe in the sea, burn your clothes and sit and watch the sunset, so that you awake on the next day,* a new person. However, be careful not to go straight into the sea below the light-house. Much safer is the wonderful **Playa de Langosteira**. The sandy bay is almost 2km long and with a bit of luck you will discover some real St. James shells. The 17m high lighthouse **(faro)** was built in 1853. Its beams reach a distance of about 57km. 70 percent of freighters from around the world is controlled from Cape Finisterre. Webcam: www.costameiga.com/turismo/webcam.htm.

The **Fisterrana**, the written proof of having arrived at the 'end of the earth' on foot, by bike or on horseback, can be received in the hostel by pilgrims who come to Finisterre already possessing the Compostela.

Gastronomy: fish, octopus and mussels depending on the season. Daily, except on the days when the fishermen cannot go out due to the weather, you can watch the public auction of the day's catch in the **Lonja** (fish market/auction hall) at the harbour from 16.30 to about 19/20.00. In the auction hall there you will also find a small exhibition of fishing nets and and information boards about life at sea. Entrance: 1 €.

Public holidays: Holy Week, Semana del Cristo, processions and passion plays with numerous amateur performers; festival of national importance. 1st Sunday in August Fiesta del Longueirón, (similar to navaja, razor clam). In August (no fixed date) Fiesta del Pulpo, octopus festival. www.concellofisterra.com.

Finisterre lighthouse with only the sea beyond.

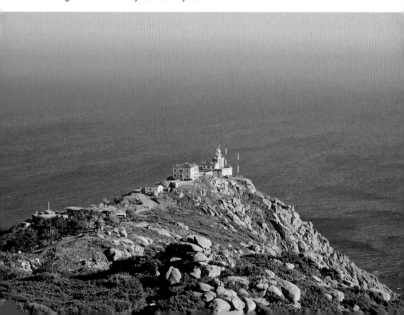

Herberge: Muxía (10m, pop. 1,600) **(1)** MH, ●●●, 32 B/5 €. Near *polideportivo* (sports centre). As far as the square by the school, turn right there and go straight on past the bar. At the T-junction turn left and immediately right up the mountain. Tourist information, tel: 981 742 563. Roomy, starkly modern, kitchen (poorly equipped), day room. Opening time: 16.00–22.00, all year. **(2)** PH, ●●●, 36 B/12 € (Pilgrims) (2 DR 40 €). Alb.-hostel Bela Muxía, Rúa Encarnación, 30, near tourist office, tel: 687 798 222. Kitchen, washing machine, drier, coffee, drinks and snacks machine, Wi-Fi. All day, all year.

Grade and route: well marked, easy. Predominantly forest paths and farm tracks.

Height difference: 450m in ascent and descent.

Critical points: after Hermedesuxo de Baixo two equally long alternatives: one near the coast, the other a bit further inland.

Scenery: a pleasant section with, typical for Galicia's coast, the combination of woods and green pastures and views of white sandy beaches.

Local services: San Salvador (39m, pop. 35) ⌂; Lires (41m, pop. 165) ⌂ ▣; Muxía ✗ ⌂ ⌂ 🚌 € ℹ 🅰 ✉ @ ✚ Rúa Saúde s/n, tel: 981 742 066.

Remarks: (1) the first part of the route can be found on the map that goes with Stage 34. **(2)** A good day's walking; if you start early enough you can leave your luggage in Finisterre and take the bus back from Muxía (several departures from Muxía, in the afternoon e.g. Mon.-Fri. 16.00, change in Cée. Up-to-date info re departure times to Finisterre available from the tourist office, see (3), or on a notice at Bar Noche y Día (near harbour). **(3)** Pilgrims can obtain the pilgrim certificate '*Muxiana*' on presentation of the *credencial* (Mon.–Fri. 10.00–14.00 and 16.00–20.00, Sat./Sun./public holiday 11.00–13.00 and 15.00–17.00, tel: 981 742 563).

Leave **Finisterre (1)** on the C-552 in the direction of Santiago de Compostela. Just before the bus stop stop/Hotel Arenal a waymarker stone indicates the suburb of **San Martiño de Duio** up to the left (**2**; ½ hr.).

ℹ *The lost town of Dugium is said to have stood at **San Martiño de Duio**, the location of the legend concerning the entombment of St. James. After the boat with his body had landed in Padrón, Queen Lupa sent the two disciples to Dugium to obtain permission from the Roman legate for the burial of the body. However the disciples were locked up and given the death penalty. Angels helped the two of them make their escape and Dugium disappeared into the sea as a punishment.*

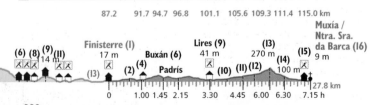

Walking parallel to the coast you come through the new residential area of San Martiño to reach **Escaselas (3)**, then you continue left along the small country road to **Hermedesuxo de Baixo (4**; ½ hr.). The coastal alternative goes straight ahead along the road via **Denle** to **Padris** (a good 1½ hrs.). The second alternative turns off right shortly after Hermedesuxo to **San Salvador** (shell signpost). An ascending forest path leads to **Rial (5)** and soon afterwards to **Buxán (6**; ¾ hr.). Keep right there at the end of the village and then carry straight on to the stop sign near to the bus stop stop of **O Sixto (7**; the arrow just beforehand points left to the coast). At the stop sign go left uphill in a few minutes to **Padris** (a good ½ hr. from Buxán).

Soon after Padris the coastal alternative from below left meets your path. From Padris a lovely woodland path runs uphill. At the highest point the wood comes to an end and you follow the signpost diagonally right downhill (not the arrow straight ahead) to **Canosa (8**; just under ¾ hr.). Go right there and then left around the hamlet. After 300m you need to keep a look out for the rather unclear path forest path which continues straight ahead. Walk down this path to a bridge where you go left and immediately right and then parallel to the road to **Lires (9**; a good ¾ hr.).

Shortly after Lires cross the stream on a broad new bridge; on the left you can still see the stepping stones which you used to have to cross

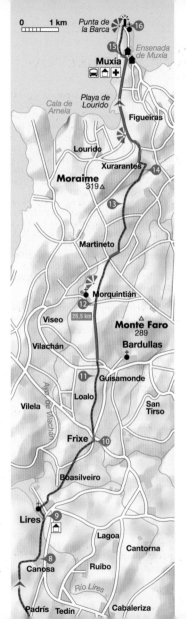

The shrine of the Virxe da Barca on the headland before Muxía.

through the cold stream water. After that continue uphill through a small, but dense deciduous wood and then again downhill to **Frixe** (**10**; ½ hr.) and along a sometimes boggy path to **Guisamonde** (**11**; just under ¾ hr.). Via a small country road you come to the small hamlet of **Morquintián** (**12**; ½ hr.). At both of the following turn-offs keep to the right and for quite a stretch follow the ascending road past some derelict houses. At the next T-junction crossroads keep right uphill (ignore the old signposts to the left and immediately right which lead you astray) and shortly afterwards turn left onto the first forest path. This path leads up to the highest point of this stage (**13**; 270m; ¾ hr.).

Then descend through a eucalyptus wood to **Xurantes** (**14**; ½ hr.). Follow the road, and at the next opportunity turn off right and keep going in the direction of the sea. Walk along the rocky coastline to **Muxía** (**15**; a good ½ hr.). Follow the promenade into Rúa da Atalaia and then a footpath to the **Santuario de la Virxe da Barca** (**16**; a good ¼ hr.). The sunsets there are in no way inferior to those from Cape Finisterre! A path runs uphill and slightly left at the large granite sculpture to a lovely viewpoint of the coast and Muxía.

[i] *The virgin in the stone ship, the **Virxe da Barca**, was the reason for **Muxía** becoming a popular destination for St. James pilgrims. In few places is the common presence of Celtic and Christian belief as tangible as here. According to legend the virgin appeared to James in a stone ship when his courage failed him during the missionary journey in the northwest of the Iberian peninsula. The plain stone*

church (18th century) on the headland of Muxia is dedicated to her. The **Piedras Santas**, large, strangely shaped stones on the reef, are considered to be the remains of the Virgin Mary's ship. In the Celtic tradition they are said to have magic powers. The most prominent of these stones is the kidney-shaped A **Pedra dos Cadrís** that – accroding to Christian interpretation – symbolises the sail of the ship. Those who climb through it nine times are said to be cured of kidney disease and rheumatism.

There area only a few stone houses left from the once smart little fishing village of Muxía with its approximately 1,000 inhabitants. After the discovery of extensive fishing grounds in the 60s the village grew in size without any foresight of town planning. A lovely example of the coastal-Gothic style (gótico-marinero) that developed in the coastal villages is the one-nave **Iglesia de Santa María** (14th century) standing up above the centre of the town.

Muxía is the only town in Galicia in which congrio, conger eel, is still air-dried. The racks can be seen near to the promenade. During the oil disaster after the Prestige went down in 2002 this promenade sadly came to fame since it was here that the oil was first discovered as it was washed ashore.

Gastronomy: fish, seafood and especially percebes (barnacles).

Public holidays: Good Friday Fiesta del Congrio, gastronomic festival. End of July Processión de la Virgen del Carmen, marine processions in honour of the patron saint of seafarers. Saturday to Monday before the 2nd Sunday in Sept. (except when this falls on the 8th, then on the 15th Sept.) Romería de la Barca, the largest and most important pilgrimage in Galicia, three day celebration with processions, festival and a big firework display.

Information: www.concellomuxia.com.

Sandy beach just before Muxía, an ideal place to relax after all your exertions.

Index

Some vocabulary in case of an emergency

This short list of phrases concentrates mainly on medical vocabulary that can be used if needed in an emergency. Situation-related expressions are mentioned in the text.

agua potable	drinking water	médico	doctor
agua no potable	not drinking water	¿Dónde hay un médico?	Where can I find a doctor?
ampolla	blister	Necesito un médico.	I need a doctor.
desinfectante	antiseptic for wounds		
calambre	muscle cram	peligro	danger
deshidratación	dehydration due to insufficient intake of water	peligroso	dangerous
		pie	foot
		pierna	leg
diarrea	diarrohea	tapón para el oído	earplugs
dolor de cabeza	headache		
esquince	sprain	tendinitis	inflammation of the tendon
esparadrapo	roll of sticky tape		
farmácia	chemist	tirita	plaster(s)
¿Dónde hay una farmácia?	Where is a chemist?	tobillo	ankle
		torcerse el pie	twist one's ankle
fuente	well/spring	vendas	bandages
insolación	sunburn	zapatero	cobbler

Pronunciation

»c« before »e« and »i« is pronounced like »th«, »c« before »a«, »o« and »u« is pronounced like »k«; »z« is pronounced like »th«; »ch« is pronounced like in chemist; »j« is pronounced like the »h« in »home« except that it is »raspier«; »LL« (for example »tobillo«) like »y« in yes; »ñ« is pronounced like the »ny« in the word »canyon«.

Front cover: the final destination, the cathedral in Santiago de Compostela.

Frontispiece (page 1): One of the most famous chapels on the Camino: Santa María de Eunate just before Puente la Reina.

P. 28/29: St. James shell and the yellow arrow, two real companions like here on the way to Los Arco (Stage 6).

All 128 photos by Cordula Rabe.

Cartography:
47 mall walking maps to a scale of 1:100,000 and 6 town plans:
www.rolle-kartografie.de
2 overview maps to a scale of 1:3,700,000 and 1:5,600,000
© Freytag & Berndt, Vienna

Translated by Gill Round

3rd completely revised edition 2013
© Bergverlag Rother GmbH, Munich

ISBN 978-3-7633-4835-0

We look forward to any suggestions for improvements to this walking guide!
BERGVERLAG ROTHER · Munich
D-82041 Oberhaching · Keltenring 17 · Tel. +49 89 608669-0
Internet www.rother.de · **E-Mail** leserzuschrift@rother.de